WICCA SPELLS & WICCA MOON MAGIC

2-IN-1

GUIDE TO MASTERING & CASTING SPELLS WITH CANDLES AND CRYSTALS. LEARN ABOUT MOON MAGIC. YOUR BOOK OF WICCA RITUALS AND WITCHCRAFT

ILLES ARIN

ILLES ARIN

THIS BOOK INCLUDES

BOOK 1:

WICCA SPELLS
A DEFINITIVE GUIDE TO MASTERING WICCAN SPELLS

BOOK 2:

WICCA MOON MAGIC
LEARN THE POWER OF THE MOON AND THE MYSTERIOUS LUNAR ENERGIES.

© Copyright 2020 - All rights reserved.

The content contained within this book may not be reproduced, duplicated or transmitted without direct written permission from the author or the publisher.

Under no circumstances will any blame or legal responsibility be held against the publisher, or author, for any damages, reparation, or monetary loss due to the information contained within this book. Either directly or indirectly.

Legal Notice: This book is copyright protected. This book is only for personal use. You cannot amend, distribute, sell, use, quote or paraphrase any part, or the content within this book, without the consent of the author or publisher.

Disclaimer Notice: Please note the information contained within this document is for educational and entertainment purposes only. All effort has been executed to present accurate, up to date, and reliable, complete information. No warranties of any kind are declared or implied. Readers acknowledge that the author is not engaging in the rendering of legal, financial, medical or professional advice. The content within this book has been derived from various sources. Please consult a licensed professional before attempting any techniques outlined in this book.

By reading this document, the reader agrees that under no circumstances is the author responsible for any losses, direct or indirect, which are incurred as a result of the use of information contained within this document, including, but not limited to, — errors, omissions, or inaccuracies.

WICCA SPELLS

A DEFINITIVE GUIDE TO MASTERING WICCAN SPELLS

ILLES ARIN

Table of Contents

INTRODUCTION 14

CHAPTER 1: WHAT IS WICCA? 18
    THE PRINCIPLES OF WICCA 18
    WICCA TODAY 20
    THE GOD AND THE GODDESS 24
        The Triple Goddess 25
            The Maiden 25
            The Mother 27
            The Crone 28
        The God 29
            The Oak King 29
            The Holly King 30
            Lugh 32
            The Green Man 33
            The Sun God 34

CHAPTER 2: INTRODUCTION TO WICCA SPELLS 36
    STEPS TO WRITING YOUR OWN SPELLS 40
        Determine Your Goal, Intention, or Magical Purpose 40
        Determine What You Will Need to Achieve Your Intention 41
        Determine the Timing 42
        Decide on Your Words and Incantations 42
        Organize the Spell into a Workable Format 43
        Use Your Spells 44
    THINGS TO CONSIDER WHEN CASTING A SPELL 44
        Safety 44
        Harm None. 45
    GROUNDING AND CENTERING FOR SPELL CASTING 45
    HOW TO CAST A CIRCLE AND THE REASON BEHIND IT 47

CHAPTER 3: BASIC STEPS FOR ANY SPELL 50
    EDUCATE YOURSELF 50
    PICK EXACTLY WHAT YOU WOULD LIKE 51
    GATHER YOUR TOOLS 51
    GROUND AND CENTER 51
    ESTABLISH YOUR SPELL COMPONENTS 52

WRITE YOUR SPELL!	52
WORK THE SPELL	53
ASSESS	53
CHAPTER 4: WICCAN RITUALS	**54**
PREPARATION OF OBJECTS AND RITUAL AREA	56
PERSONAL PREPARATION	56
CREATION OF THE HOLY SPACE	56
WELCOME TO ELEMENTS AND GODS	57
ALIGNING A SABBATH, ESBAT OR PURPOSE RITUAL	58
THE BANQUET	58
FINISH THE RITUAL	59
THE EFFICACY OF RITUAL	59
Steps to effective invocatory ritual:	*60*
CHAPTER 5: WICCAN SPELL CASTING WITH CANDLES	**62**
HOW TO WORK WITH CANDLES IN YOUR SPELLS	62
CANDLE MAGIC	63
CANDLE COLORS	65
Black	*66*
Blue	*66*
Brown	*67*
Green	*67*
Gold	*67*
Orange	*67*
Pink	*68*
Silver	*68*
Red	*68*
Violet	*69*
White	*69*
Yellow	*69*
CHOOSING THE RIGHT CANDLES TO USE	70
Types of Candles	*72*
USING YOUR CANDLE IN RITUAL	74
THE SECRETS OF CLEANSING AND CONSECRATION	75
How to Cleanse a Candle?	*76*
Cotton and Alcohol	77
Purified with Sage	77
Sea Salt	77
Moonlight Cleanse	78
How to Consecrate the Candle?	*78*

Anointing and Dressing the Candle *79*
    Coat the Candle with Magical Herbs 80
    Carving and Engraving 80
    Spray with Holy Water 81
COLOR MAGIC IN CANDLES 81
   Magical Properties of Color *82*
   Reading the Candle Flame: Divine Communication *84*
   The Intent Behind the Days of the Week *86*
PRACTICING SAFETY WITH CANDLE MAGIC 88

CHAPTER 6: WICCAN SPELL CASTING WITH CRYSTALS 90

WHAT ARE CRYSTALS? 90
   Amorphous Crystals *91*
COMMON CRYSTALS 91
   Crystal Magic *94*
THE POWER OF CRYSTALS 95
THE ENERGY OF CRYSTALS 98
   Hold a Crystal Between the Palms of Your Hands During Meditation *99*
   Create a Special Place for Your Crystals *100*
   Place Crystals Around Your Home *100*
   Place a Crystal Directly on Your Body *101*
   Carry Crystals with You *101*
   Make Sure You Are Open to the Experience *101*
   Focus on the Crystal You Are Most Attracted To *102*
CHARGING CRYSTALS 102
   Magical Tools *103*
   Incantations *103*
   Steps in Charging *103*
CRYSTALS IN WICCA PRACTICE 105
CRYSTALS IN CHAKRA CLEANSING, HEALING, AND BALANCING 107
CRYSTALS FOR LIFE ENHANCEMENT AND ASSISTANCE 112
THE BEST CRYSTALS FOR MAGIC 112
   Amethyst *112*
   Quartz *113*
   Jet *114*
   Obsidian *115*
   Lapis Lazuli *116*
   Labradorite *117*
   Selenite *118*
HOW CRYSTAL ENERGY WORKS 119

GETTING TO KNOW YOUR CRYSTALS	119
MEANING OF CRYSTALS IN SPELL WORK AND MAGIC	124
CLEANSING YOUR CRYSTAL	125
Air Cleansing	*126*
Earth Cleansing	*127*
Fire Cleansing	*127*
Water Cleansing	*127*
Singing Bowl Cleansing	*128*
Personal Energy Cleansing	*128*
CONNECTING TO YOUR CRYSTALS	129
PROGRAMMING YOUR CRYSTAL	129

CHAPTER 7: CRYSTAL AND CANDLE SPELLS 132

GROWING LUCK SPELL	132
HEALING PHYSICALLY SPELL	133
RELATIONSHIP HEALING CANDLE SPELL	135
GOOD LUCK CANDLE SPELL	137
FLAMING FINANCES	137
BURNING AWAY ALL NEGATIVES	138
GENERAL LUCK SPELL	139
LOVE CANDLE SPELL	140
PROTECTION CANDLE SPELL	141
BASIC MONEY SPELL	141
CLEARING OUT SPIRITS CANDLE SPELL	142
PROSPERITY CANDLE SPELL	143
ATTRACT NEW LOVE SPELL	143
WICCAN WHITE CANDLE BLESSING SPELL	144
CLEANSING/PURIFICATION CANDLE SPELL	145
GARDEN BLESSING	146
SIMPLE HOME PROTECTION SPELL	147
SORE THROAT SPELL	148
BANISHING BAD THOUGHTS SPELL	149
A CRYSTAL LOVE SPELL	150
ENERGIZING SPRING SPELL	151
COLD HARD CASH SPELL	152
CHARMING KITCHEN BLESSING	153
MONEY CHARM SPELL	154
CHARM FOR ATTRACTING QUALITY RELATIONSHIPS	155
REPAY A DEBT	156
SLEEPING PEACEFUL	157

FAST RESULTS SPELL	158
BANISHING A GHOST SPELL	159
MAGIC MOTIVATION MORNING POTION	159
CREATIVITY AND FOCUS SPELL	161
POTION FOR DREAMS	164
FIX A FRIENDSHIP SPELL	165
BETTER SLEEP SPELL	166
INNER POWER CANDLE SPELL	167
SPELL TO NOURISH THE HEART	168
SPELL FOR PERSONAL SUCCESS AND ACHIEVEMENT	169
GREEN CANDLE MONEY SPELL	170
BUSINESS SUCCESS SPELL	171
STOMACH RELIEF SPELL	172
BLESS SOME ONES HEALTH	173
ARGUMENT CLEARING SPELL	173
GENERAL HAPPINESS SPELL	174
MARRIAGE AND RELATIONSHIP HEALING SPELL	175
WICCAN ANTI-HARASSMENT CANDLE SPELL	178
WICCAN WHITE CANDLE BLESSING SPELL	179
CANDLE SPELL TO GET A JOB	180
CINNAMON MONEY MAGNET CHARM	181
YOUTH PRESERVATION SPELL	182
RED BEAUTY SPELL	183
A SIMPLE SPELL FOR ABUNDANCE	184
A TREASURE CHEST	185
WICCAN ANTI-HARASSMENT CANDLE SPELL	187
A CONFIDENCE CANDLE SPELL	188
DOUBLE MONEY SPELL	189
BRINGING LOVE BACK SPELL	189
HEADACHE RELIEF SPELL	190
BEAUTY CHARM SPELL	191
CALLING IN THE CASH	192
PYRITE FOR PROSPERITY CHANGE JAR	193
DESIRE SPELL	194
PURIFIED LUCK SPELL	195
QUICK GOOD LUCK SPELL	196
UTILIZE THIS SPELL FOR BANISHING STRESS AND STRESS	197
CONCLUSION	**200**

Introduction

Many of us have likely considered using spells for love, wealth, revenge or defense at some point in our lives. It is also probably a certain fact that some of us have looked through different books and other tools so that we can find some spells for ourselves.

Spell casting comes in many ways, as diverse as the many traditions and religions that use spell casting. Notwithstanding the movies, spell casting is also much more complicated than just spinning a wand and murmuring a couple of fantastic words.

A spell is any kind of experience that includes the intention to manifest something into your physical life experience. A spell is a direct line of communication between you and the cosmos to achieve a goal. A spell is your voice and action asking for what you want to occur and giving energy to the outcomes through creative expression.

Spells come in a variety of shapes, sizes, formats, colors, aromas, and they occur at different dates, times, moons, seasons, and so on. There are limitless possibilities when working with magic and manifestation, and that is really all it is: a way to show yourself and the energy of all life, who you are, and what you want.

A spell can be anything that you want it to be and is ultimately a creative process, to give you insight and support in where you want practice. Once you get the hang of using a few simple spells from this book, you will gain the confidence to start creating and utilizing your spells. With any spell, you will always work with specific intentions and find the best methods that will work for you along the way.

Spells are a way for you to gain an energetic connection to the reality you are working to create and set into motion. For a lot of Wiccans who practice magic, spells are the gateway to link with spirits and the great Divine. You can easily transport yourself into another realm when you are in a circle cast for protection, imbuing the space with your precise intentions and magic ritual. It is a sacred dance that calls upon the energies of all that is around you to hear your call for something relevant to your life.

A spell works as an opening and affirmation of what energy you want to promote, enhance, and delegate to the earthly plane of reality. It is energy that you hone and connect to so that it can be powerfully, elegantly, and eloquently delivered into the energy of everything around you.

Wiccan spells are a creative life force waiting for you to breathe them into existence. Your spells will hold the key to aligning with your own powerful, personal magic and will help you work more closely with the Wiccan beliefs of harmony, balance, and nature. To work with a spell and cast it into the energy of all things is to work with the Divine power of all life. A spell is a tool of connection to your practice, to yourself, to the God and Goddess, or whatever life-force energies you may worship and devote your energy to.

This journey has everything to do with practicing safe and effective magic and will give you all of the guidance you need to take your trip to the next level.

This book will offer you some necessary introductory information about Wiccan spells, as well as some guidelines to help you practice safely and effectively within your own practice. Because the energy you are working with is so powerful, it is crucial that you are prepared to handle the results of what you are working on manifesting into your reality.

It will be an excellent resource for you for a variety of spells to include in your own Book to help you get going with your casting and craft. You will find an assortment of spells for love, prosperity, health, and luck.

If you are new to the use of Wicca and magic spells, candles and tarot cards then I want to share some tips on how to use them as tools and devices for the ritual arts. This is an all-encompassing book of illusions for Wiccans, witches, and practitioners with a candlestick, mirror, healing, and defensive spells for beginners. Let us begin.

CHAPTER 1:

What is Wicca?

Wicca is a relatively new, contemporary religious movement with roots in ancient pagan beliefs and cultures that pre-date Christianity. Although there are some associated principles, Wicca has no central authority. At the core of Wicca is a deep reverence and worship of nature and the natural cycles of the seasons. It is an incredibly adaptable religion that continues to grow and evolve according to the needs of people who follow the Wiccan path.

The Principles of Wicca

These are the basic traditional principles of Wicca. They may not apply to every single Wiccan practitioner. That is the beautiful thing about Wicca – you do not have to conform to anyone, rigid belief system.

- **Nature worship.** Wiccans regard nature with respect and acknowledge the spiritual (and scientific) connection of all life on earth. Nature, in this sense, could be defined as 'the collective phenomena of the physical world, including the earth's landscapes, plant communities, animals and bodies of water'. Human creations are generally not considered part of nature. However, humans and everything associated with them is a part of nature itself. This is the idea behind nature worship – respecting and acknowledging the natural state of the world and the raw power of life and death. Most Wiccans believe that everything in nature is equal – humans, plants, animals... even rocks, mountains and oceans all hold significance and spiritual essence.

- **Magic and witchcraft.** Magic can be defined as the natural or supernatural forces that surround us as part of the energy of the earth or the universe. Scott Cunningham, a renowned writer of Wiccan topics, defined magic as "the projection of natural energies to produce needed effects". A Wiccan may be attuned with magic, or practice shaping and directing magic for beneficial purposes. Magic is not a super-power used to control others, but an energy source that can be used to encourage certain outcomes, inspire change or aid in spiritual contentment or clarity. Some Wiccan practitioners may perform magic on a daily basis for various activities. Others may simply acknowledge the existence of magical forces that work in mysterious and extraordinary ways.

- **Magical tools.** Broomsticks, caldrons and wands are all tools commonly associated with witches and magic. While Wiccans are not flying around on broomsticks, brewing eye of newts in caldrons, or blasting thunderbolts out of their wands, all of these tools have unique, symbolic purposes useful in magical practices. Other common magical tools include herbs, stones, plants, twigs, crystals, seashells, recycled animal parts, candles, tarot cards, incense, talismans and much more.

- **The Goddess and the God.** Wicca is based on a duo-theistic worldview with the belief in a Goddess and a God. While the Goddess is usually focused on the most in Wiccan beliefs, both figures are considered equal. Read the next section for more information about Wiccan deities.

- **The Wiccan Rede.** "And it harm none, do what ye will". In other words, "If it harms none, do what you will". This is a moral statement of Wicca that is accepted by many, but there can be multiple interpretations of the Rede. Some believe it means that you can do what you want as long as you absolutely do not harm other life forms. Others interpret it as advice: do your best not to harm others, feel free to make choices but be ready to take responsibility for your actions. A selected number of Wiccans do not follow the Rede at all, but may follow another pagan inspirational text or mantra.

- **Reincarnation.** while not all Wiccans believe in any particular type of afterlife, many believe reincarnation. Reincarnation may occur when a person passes, and is reborn into another form, such as a human or an animal. They may take pieces of their old self with them, but live new lives and fill their soul with many lives and experiences until they are ready to achieve a higher being. At this point, the soul may choose to become one with the forces of nature, or they may occupy a place called the Summerland. This is a place where spirits come to rejoin one another, rest and reflect. The soul might make the decision to continue the process of reincarnation.

- **Free will.** There are no over-ruling texts or threatening doctrines in the Wiccan religion that demand living a certain way. Wiccans have the freedom to think and act as they please, as long as they are mindful of the Wiccan Rede and willing to take responsibility for their mistakes.

Wicca Today

When Wicca came out of the mist and went around the world, countless people began to identify with this religious manifestation and why it was the only one until that moment that had a female central deity as the creator. This was in the mid-1950s and extended into the early 1970-80s.

From its inception in 1951, the Wicca has acquired new expectations and has undergone significant transformations: being hugged by the feminist and environmental movements; earning a new face which is much more matrifocal and Goddess-oriented than at the beginning of its history; and relegating God to a secondary position.

It is understandable since the sacred male was revered for thousands of years, while the Goddess was mutilated and forgotten. It was in 1970 that the feminist movement embraced Wicca as their religion. They found in the Goddess a strong figure, capable of causing deep changes in the thinking of society and its way of looking at the world. Many Feminist traditions emerged from this and contributed a substantial creative, quality material that would forever change Wicca!

Women who fought for gender equality rights found in this religion a safe haven to feel strong, alive, and active. It was in Wicca that they found a religion that can redeem their dignity, both social and religious. From the search for a new religion, a thought group where women were not were excluded rose in the US through the efforts of countless women engaged in feminist causes, a Wicca with a new identity more focused on the Goddess figure. From this growing movement came several traditions of this religion, from the branches where the Goddess and God are less visible and the Goddess exercises supremacy and preponderance.

Along with Wicca's growth and outreach in the mid-1980s, came the 'Rabeira' and several other pagan movements. Druidism, Kemetism, Hellenism, Asatrú and other countless world Neo-pagan movements have only begun to be visible, thanks to the efforts of Wiccans seeking to revive an Earth-centered religion, in the Sacred Feminine, in the search for connection with the flag of the struggle for freedom in strongly monotheistic countries. This shows that each one can revere the Divine in his own way, rescuing almost forgotten rituals in the time.

As Wicca brought in its structure (from Celtic, Nordic, Greek, Sumerians and whatever seemed correct, as these cultures connected with the heirs of the Goddess Religion over time), many groups separated, seeking the spiritual and cultural identity of the Gods, with which they felt more connected. Thus, arose the reconstructionist movement, who try to reconstruct the worship of the ancient Gods exactly as it was in the past. Many people who had started belonging to these movements then began to criticize Wicca's flexibility, saying opposing things: that she was not the true heiress of the European Religion, which was not Celtic; and that Wicca was Gardner's invention, etc.

Even with contrary opinions, Wicca continued its climb and was experiencing a revolution within its own environment. Along with this, congresses, meetings, and seminars began to be held to discuss the practices of this religion in the US. Because of the many attacks on Wicca, one council, with the most renowned Wiccans of the time, was created to write the *13 Principles of witchcraft*, which was published in the form of public notice.

Wicca has been gaining strength and visibility worldwide as an official religion. In the United States and several other countries, officers of the beloved forces have the right to chaplaincy, which has been largely and unrestrictedly granted to Wiccan priests.

The first principle says, "Like American witches, we do not feel threatened by debates about the history of art, the origins of various terms, the legitimacy of various aspects of different traditions. We are concerned about our present and our future."

Along with this new identity that Wicca was beginning to assume, the Goddess as the center of worship of this religion was increasingly emphasized. She became invoked in the rites as 'the Goddess of the Ten Thousand Names' (just like Isis, who was all Goddesses in one).The statement that all Goddesses are the same Goddess is definitely accepted among the Wiccans, and widely used in various segments of paganism.

Wicca, hence, becomes a religion that recognizes the Goddess as the Creator, the main deity and even though some Wiccans consider themselves polytheists (some consider themselves monotheistic, panentheistic or henotheistic). Our religion reveres the one and only Goddess who manifests in different forms, names, and attributes.

If in the mid-1950s, Wicca was considered much more a magical system rather than a religion, then today, the reality is completely different. Many Wiccan groups organized to legitimize it as a true religion, making it accepted, recognized and respected in different segments of society. Wicca's highest visibility is still in the United States and Europe, where it is considered a chaplaincy religion in the army and marriages recognized by the State.

In various countries, Wicca has been growing substantially. We see each day more and more literary works proposed to clarify its religious and philosophical aspects and we are constantly facing with people decorating our sacred symbols, like the Pentagram or the Triluna, in the subway, bus, bank queue or streets.

Today, there are a lot more people practicing the art of witchcraft alone, than in groups, which are called covens. She transformed from a secret religion into a modern alternative religiosity, strongly centered on the figure of the Goddess Mother. Conscientious, environmental and social groups of different ethnicities have incorporated much of their culture into Wicca, making it more flexible, and therefore eclectic. The saying "All Goddesses are the Goddess," has become a Wiccan axiom in the last decade. Hence, Hindu, Native American, African, Hawaiian, Chinese, and many other goddesses of these cultures were assimilated by Wicca, and came to be recognized as different faces of the Goddess.

Most of today's religions of mankind are based on figures and male Divine principles, with Gods and Priests rather than Goddesses and Priestesses. For millennia, women's values have been put into many cultures, in which women are subdued and occupy a lower position than men, whether at the social or spiritual level.

Wicca seeks to reclaim the Sacred Feminine and the role of women in religion, and priestesses of the Great Mother. It seeks the complementary balance between man and woman, symbolized through the Goddess and God, who complement each other. Wicca gives the Goddess a leading role in both practices either in their myths, so it is the main deity worshiped and invoked in the sacred rites.

The God and the Goddess

In Wicca, two major deities are worshipped, generally—the God and the Goddess. They are considered two halves of one entire being, a representation of the duality of the universe, the Masculine and the Feminine. Throughout the world, there are many names for gods and goddesses, focusing on whichever aspects they have domain over.

Not every Wiccan or pagan worships both God and Goddess, and it is their right to do as they wish about it. Some worship the Goddess exclusively, others, the god. Some devote their attention to one particular deity, depending on their background or upbringing, cultural experiences, or merely just a calling upon their intuition by that deity. Others worship many deities. It is up to you to take your time, listen to yourself, and decide who and how you will worship, if indeed you choose to worship at all. Such is the liberty that Wicca provides.

The Triple Goddess

The Goddess herself is thought to be comprised of three main aspects, the maiden, mother, and crone. This is syncretized with the fact that the Divine feminine mirrors humanity's ability to create life, and as such, life is often marked by certain milestones: childhood, coming-of-age, motherhood, reaching maturity, and the wisdom of age.

Regardless of the aspects of fertility, childbirth, and procreation, the Triple Goddess and her three forms have meaning and messages for everyone, young or old, regardless of gender.

A popular symbol for Wiccans and often used in jewelry is the symbol for the Triple Goddess: a full moon bracketed by a waning and waxing crescent.

The Maiden

The Maiden is symbolized by the time of the new moon and waxing moon. She represents the power of youth, as well as beauty, hope, the power of faith and belief, and the ability to see the bright side of things. She is the brave hunter as portrayed by Artemis, the beautiful nymph of Aphrodite, the lover of life and excitement as seen in Oshun. The Maiden does not merely represent sexual virginity—that is more of a human construct than anything else. Instead, the Maiden represents the individual, free to walk the world in search of knowledge, adventure, and experience.

Some maiden goddesses are: Artemis and Oshun, Parvati, Rhiannon, Diana, Brigid, Kore, Freya, Nimue, and Persephone. The colors of the maiden are white, pink, and pale blue.

The Maiden is curious, daring, and will often seek you out if there is something you are ignoring that needs your attention such as an opportunity or a decision that will bring positive results. Whenever you need a helpmate in your endeavors, you can call upon the Maiden to work by your side. She is full of enthusiasm and unstoppable energy.

The Maiden answers only to herself. She is a protector of men, women, and children alike. The Maiden may also appear to you when you need a shield maiden; when the forces of the world are simply overwhelming, and you feel you have no one to turn to.

The Maiden is also good at getting us to recognize when we forget to take a moment to stop and enjoy life's simple pleasures. She wants us to run barefoot on the grass, gaze at the flowing river, dance in the moonlight, wake up with the dawn.

The Maiden is also the protector of animals. While she represents the hunter, she does not abide by senseless killing. Instead, she is more of a woodsman and an expert of nature. Flowers sacred to her are any white flowers, and the owl and bear are also sacred to the Maiden.

The Sabbaths of Imbolc and Ostara are sacred to the Maiden. At Yule, all three aspects of the Goddess are celebrated.

The Mother

The Mother aspect of the go Goddess is the most commonly worshipped aspect. Here we see the Goddess as giver and sustainer of life, providing us with abundance, nourishment, motherly healing, and empathy, as well as stern guidance when we need it. Some mother goddesses are sweet, patient and kind, others are also loving but firmer, directing us to the proper path to ensure our utmost happiness.

In this aspect, the Goddess becomes the well-spring of life and the provider. She is at her highest physical power, represented by the height of summer and the laden fruit trees, and tall, waving crops of grains. The Mother brings balance and a sense of satisfaction to us—life is abundant, we are worthy of happiness, and all is well.

The color red is associated with the Mother Goddess as it obviously conveys the blood of the menstrual cycle and of the womb. She gives us her lifeblood that we may carry on our own bloodlines. Blue is another color associated with the Mother Goddess, as with Yemaya, a beloved goddess of the ocean worshipped in Nigeria, the Americas, and the Caribbean. Animals beloved to the Mother are pregnant animals, the dove, and deer.

While the Maiden is more of an inspirer, cohort, and adventure companion, the Mother Goddess is here to guide us in life and often help us make difficult decisions. Just like a mother, she wants what is best for us, and seeks to show us the way in moments of miraculous, loving kindness. When we feel like we cannot go any further, the Mother Goddess will draw near, allows us to cry against her mantle of stars, and soothe our pains and hurts while inspiring us to draw more strength and soldier on.

She will work with you to avoid the pitfalls of addiction and excess. You will see clearly within her light what changes you need to make in your life to bring happiness, harmony, and peace to your days, as well as your nights.

The Mother Goddess is most powerful during the full moon. Perform magic for abundance, self-love, healing, and personal strength when calling to the Mother Goddess. Ask for her help with marriage, childbirth and fertility, life partners, caring for your animals and garden, making important life decisions, and help with awakening your natural spirituality.

The Sabbaths of Beltane, Litha, and Lammas are sacred to the Mother Goddess.

Some mother goddesses are: Bast, Ceres, Corn Mother, Frigg, Hathor, Isis, Macha, and Venus.

The Crone

The Crone is often overlooked by practitioners of witchcraft and Wicca, but she is the one we should be listening to the most when it comes to magic. The Crone represents the wise woman, the shamanic healer, and the witch. She has lived a full life and has plenty of information to share, to help us get a grip on situations, and gain the advantages that wisdom provides. She is a survivor and knows both love and pain. She is a healer of the most expert degree. She has knowledge of every herb, flower, tree, and animal on Earth, and can help you gain that knowledge as well. The Crone is a sorceress, and brings us the gift of the magical arts.

The Crone is the aspect that has been the most caricatured throughout the history of pagan faiths. She has been called Evil Witch, Old Hag, and the Dark Goddess. The Crone stands at the crossroads between the living and the dead. She understands that death is nothing to be afraid of, and is only a beginning, and not an end. She lifts the veil for us and invites us to have a look, giving us courage as we hold her thin, wizened hand. With the Crone by our side, we can look at life in a completely different way, slow down a little, and deeply understand things we may have once taken for granted.

The Crone's color is black, representing the fact that black absorbs the full spectrum of the rainbow. Her darkness is both creative as well as destructive—creative in that from nothing comes something, from the womb comes life, from the darkness of space is born new stars—and destructive in that in time, all things must end, so that they may be reborn, recycled, repurposed and born again.

The God

The Wiccan god is the counterpart to the Goddess, representing virility and the masculine aspects of the universe. He, too, goes through stages of life, born as an infant at Yule, running free as a youth through Imbolc and Ostara until he meets his life mate, the Goddess, at Beltane. The god can perform many roles in our lives: he can be a teacher and master to our apprentice, he can be a loving, doting father, he can be a keeper of mysteries that guides us towards deeper enlightenment, he can be a drinking partner. The god's roles as father, brother, hunter, scribe, blacksmith, captain, guide, shepherd, master at arms, devotee of peace, and myriad. He exists in all of us and seeks to unlock our greatest potential.

The Oak King

The Oak King—the counterpart to the Holly King—originated in ancient British tribes. Instead of thinking as the Oak and Holly Kings as two separate entities, they are in fact two aspects of the same god, the shadow and the light, the sun and the darkness, the summer and the winter. The Oak King represents abundance. He ensures the harvest and the hunt will be successful and is the extrovert who loves celebrations and communities coming together to partake of his endless food and drink. He is the farmer with dirt beneath his fingernails; he is the hunter taking what he needs to provide for his village. The Oak King is a force of directed energy. He is like the arrow sent from the archer's bow.

The Oak King represents expansion and growth. His abundance comes from hard work, the force of will and of personality, of taking the initiative and going for one's goals. He is forthright and honest, open and direct. There is no guile about him. Like the sun, he shines brightly, showing his intentions for all the world to see. Brash and bold, the Oak King is not afraid of adversity.

Gods representing the Oak King include: Pan, Janus, Jupiter, and Frey.

The Holly King

The Holly King represents the darker, or waning half of the year; the Holly King is born in Midsummer, and grows to maturity to finally fade at Yule, when the Oak King is reborn. The Holly King reaches maturity around Samhain and presides over the ceremonies of the dead. He is a somber, wise version of the God, unafraid of the dark and the mysteries that lie therein.

The Holly King represents many things, including the natural cycles of death and decay. He is the harvest and the dying of the Summer, the rich colors of Autumn and the crackling of a warm fire, the long, cold sleep of Winter, and the widening of the veil that separates the spirit world from the material world. His knowledge is ancient and secret; like the Moon, he leads those who are unafraid of midnight processions and twilight offerings.

If there was nothing but expansion, the world would be overrun. The version of the God that the Holly King represents brings balance to life. The dying plants provide nutrients for the Earth, and drop their seeds into the cooling soil so that when the Wheel of the Year brings Spring back into our lives, new crops, flowers, and seedlings will sprout up, enlivening us with hope and inner promise. The Holly King makes no apology for who He is: he is necessary and unrelenting.

The Oak King and the Holly King are both considered to be sacrificial gods, representing the ebb and flow of nature over the course of the Wheel of the Year.

The Holly King's key words are withdrawal, decay, release, rest

The Holly King's colors are black, silver, crimson, and brown.

The Holly King's legends include Santa Claus, King Arthur's opponent Mordred, the Green Knight, the Corn King, and Bran.

Food and drink to be offered to the Holly King include spiced cider or wine, dark ale, mead, cranberry juice and dark grape juice, roasted meats and dishes made from gourds.

Gods representing the Holly King include Anubis, Thoth, Father Winter, Loki, Ogun, and Saturn.

Lugh

Lugh is a heroic aspect of the God who the Celts worshipped. His name is invoked in the alternate name for Lammas—Lughnasadh. His ceremonial death marks the beginning of the official harvest, and also the 'dying of the light', as his name means 'shining one.' He represents in this aspect the Sun, and the coming of Winter.

Lugh can be helpful when invoked to overcome obstacles, as he is a warrior god of incredible prowess and sense of honor. His symbols include the spear and the sword, or any weapon that affords its bearer a long reach. The raven, wolf, horse, and wren are sacred to him, and wrens will often sing upon a branch in a winter garden when someone in the home requires extra courage. Offerings to Lugh may include whiskey, wheat bread, blackberries, golden coins, and dark wine.

The Green Man

The Green Man is the aspect of the god most concerned with flora and fauna of the Earth. He roams the woodlands, fields, rainforests, camps, savannahs and the tundra alike, to watch over every plant and animal the goddess gives birth to. He is the archer and the guide, presiding over animal husbandry, woodcraft, and homesteading. He is the lumberjack and the stealthy ranger, the bold archer and the sly tracker. He is represented by both the wolf and the fox.

The Green Man is most active in summer when the world is full, and life is teaming. He comes to us when we need rejuvenation, or when we need to get in touch with the natural world. The god Cernunnos accurately represents the Green Man, as does Herne.

The Sun God

The Sun god is one of the more important aspects in Wiccan mythology. He brings life to the Earth—without the sun, life would be impossible, and simply not exist. Even the tiniest, blind albino creature living in a subterranean cave that never sees light depends on the sun for its existence, because the plankton and microbes that drift through the underground waterways begin in the oceans, enlivened by the sun.

The Wheel of the Year celebrates the return of the Sun God each year from his journeys. Some sun gods are Ra, Ogun, and Apollo.

CHAPTER 2:

Introduction to Wicca Spells

What is a spell, anyway? In your practice or study of Wicca so far, you may have discovered that there are not always spells involved and that you do not have to cast them in order to practice the Wiccan religion. Even if you are not Wiccan or are just wondering about Wicca, you may be curious and looking for answers about spells, what they do, and how to use them in your personal spiritual practice.

They are considered magic, or magick, as you may sometimes see it spelled. Some say that if you practice magic, then you are a spell caster and, therefore, a Witch. Labels are common but not always needed or necessary to enjoy a magical life. Truthfully, every culture has practiced some form of witchcraft or magic, and as it has developed with our species, we have developed with it.

Spells are an essential part of what magic involves. When you are talking to someone about how you want to improve your life or trying to think positive thoughts about your career shift, you are essentially casting a spell. So, what is a spell then?

A spell is any kind of experience that includes the intention to manifest something into your physical life experience. A spell is a direct line of communication between you and the cosmos to achieve a goal. A spell is your voice and action asking for what you want to occur and giving energy to the outcomes through creative expression.

Spells come in a variety of shapes, sizes, formats, colors, aromas, and they occur at different dates, times, moons, seasons, and so on. There are limitless possibilities when working with magic and manifestation, and that is really all it is: a way to show yourself and the energy of all life, who you are, and what you want.

A spell can be anything that you want it to be, and is ultimately a creative process to give you insight and support in where you practice. Once you get the hang of using a few simple spells from this book, you will gain the confidence to start creating and utilizing your spells. With any spell, you will always work with specific intentions and find the best methods that will work for you along the way.

What you may be thinking, at this point, is how does a spell work? As you have read, a spell is a tool of manifestation. It is a powerful way to take the time to set a focused goal or intention through the use of specific ingredients, timing, and clarity of thought.

Spells are a way for you to gain an energetic connection to the reality you are working to create and set into motion. For a lot of Wiccans who practice magic, spells are the gateway to link with spirits and the great Divine. You can easily transport yourself into another realm when you are in a circle cast for protection, imbuing the space with your precise intentions and magic ritual. It is a sacred dance that calls upon the energies of all that is around you to hear your call for something relevant to your life.

A spell works as an opening and affirmation of what energy you want to promote, enhance, and delegate to the earthly plane of reality. It is energy that you hone and connect to so that it can be powerfully, elegantly, and eloquently delivered into the energy of everything around you. It is a ripple effect made possible by the stones you cast into the waters of life. It is not just as simple as an affirmation that you repeat to yourself over and over, although words are heavily used in casting spells. So much of asking for what you want from the universe includes a special time, space, ritual, ingredients, and connection to your deities and honoring of the elements, at least from the Wiccan point of view.

All spells share some common qualities, steps, and ingredients, and they will always have an impact of some kind. The best way to practice casting Wiccan spells is to use your knowledge of nature, the elements, the directions, and the cycles of life. These aspects might be what sets a Wiccan spell apart from other practices. If you are engaging in the moon cycles, seasonal celebrations, the balance of light and dark, and all of the life that exists in our cosmos, you will be in a format practiced by many Wiccans today.

There are several ways to treat a spell, and as you may already know from practicing Wicca, or learning about its beliefs and philosophies, there is a statement of power that has an impact on the right kind of energy to use when casting any magic, spell, ritual, or otherwise. The Wiccan Rede is a commonly known element of the craft, and states that you should "harm none" in your work.

What this means is that if you are casting a spell and you are using your power and energy, along with the strength of all creation, to perform a spell of ill will on another person, you are not accessing it in the right way, according to Wiccan teachings. Spells are not used to hurt others, and what you do will come back to you threefold. Coming into an agreement with your magic that you will do no harm means that you are willing to work with magic and spells only to improve or benefit your life and the overall energy of other things, not the other way around.

The best way to enjoy Wiccan spellcasting is to embrace the elements and use all of the fun and exciting tools that help you empower your spells. You will have so much fun acquiring what you will need, and as you build your altar and collect your tools, you will get delightful ideas about how to create your unique spells.

Some people want to know if there is a wrong way to cast a spell, and the answer to that is no if you are harming no one. Spells are a creative experience, and many Wiccans and witches find beautiful harmony and balance through aligning with their intuitions to craft the right spell for them and their practices. You can always branch out from what you have already learned from the other spells you have seen and practiced.

Several of the spells that are listed in this book are great methods to get you started, so you can understand how so many spells are crafted. The main thing about spells is understanding the energy you are working with and how to set your intentions clearly, but more on that in the next chapter.

Wiccan spells are a creative life force waiting for you to breathe them into existence. Your spells will hold the key to aligning with your own powerful, personal magic and will help you work more closely with the Wiccan beliefs of harmony, balance, and nature. Wiccan spells will introduce you to working with some or all of the following manifestation practices:

- Candle magic
- Herbal magic and remedy
- Honoring Gods, Goddesses, and Deities
- Moon cycle power
- Crystal magic
- Elemental magic
- Creative visualization

- Altar space and consecrated or charged tools for your work
- Sun cycles
- Seasonal celebrations
- Harvest
- Empowerment, wealth, prosperity, protection, love, abundance, good luck, and good health
- Spiritual awakening and communication with the Divine and more!

Wiccan spells are a gateway to trusting your intuition, calling upon the universal energies and celebrating nature and the Goddess and God. It is performing a ritual of manifestation using all that is around you and choosing the path that is right for you through your relationship with Wicca.

All of the spells in this book are guidelines and ideas to get you started and help you understand more about Wiccan Spells and how to use them. In the next chapter, you will get a deeper understanding about how to cast spells safely and effectively, guidelines for casting a circle and preparing for a spell, and basic concepts and steps to what a successful spell looks like.

Steps to Writing Your Own Spells

Determine Your Goal, Intention, or Magical Purpose

Quite possibly the most important step in designing your spell, the goal or purpose is what will help you structure everything about your spell. What are you wanting to accomplish? Are you looking for love? Are you trying to draw more financial abundance or prosperity into your life? Are you wanting to honor a specific deity?

There are a lot of possibilities and they all require a specific intention. Be clear. Be direct. Keep it simple. Know what it is you are trying to magically manifest in a very honest and direct format so you can build and create your spell around that goal.

Determine What You Will Need to Achieve Your Intention

Spells need tools and ingredients, although some might need only a candle or a crystal. Whatever you are going to need, you will need to decide your list of ingredients for your recipe. Some of the ingredients will come from the following list and all of them should be goal-specific according to your intention for the spell:

- Colorful candles
- Incense
- Herbs
- Objects from Nature
- Crystals and/or stones
- Altar Tools
- Bowls, containers, mixing spoons (all consecrated for rituals)
- Special garments
- Indoor or Outdoor set up/ altar (spell specific)

You may find even more items that you will need than what is listed here, and you can always add things to every spell that you create based on what kind of Wicca you are practicing and what kind of spell you are casting.

Determine the Timing

Every spell has a different energy that needs to guide it. Your spell may need to fall on a specific date, or even at a specific time of day. You may need the full sun, shining down on your spell, or you may need the darkness and energy of a New Moon.

Every spell has a time to make it work, and that time could also be anytime. Some spells will be open to work whenever you are needing them to be performed and the results may be different for you, depending on your approach.

Many Wiccans will cast their spells in accordance with what moon, or seasonal cycle they are in, in order to help the power of the spell feel enhanced or to generate a greater manifestation possibility.

Whatever time you decide to work your spell is important to the nature of your original goal. Choose the timing based on your intentions. If you are trying to grow your money and security, you may want to cast your spell on a New Moon and watch your money grow as the Full Moon grows, too. You may need the energy of the dawn hours to bring a powerful focused day and work experience into fruition, as a fresh start from the morning sunlight.

All of your spells can be written in the *Book of Shadows* you are building, and it is helpful to give yourself feedback on the most powerful times to perform each spell. You may need to play around with the timing for each spell, if you are repeating them, so that you can hone in on the timing that manifests the greatest return for you.

Decide on Your Words and Incantations

As you learned from the Step-by-Step Guide for Rituals in the last chapter, your words are important. They carry the meaning of your goal into the energy of the universe to help make it manifest, so you want to make sure that you are clear in your wording and meaning.

Writing your spell is a big part of the process and should always be done beforehand and not after you have cast your circle. If you want your spell to work, you need to find the right words for your goal. The world of magic is not sinister, but it can have a sense of humor as to how you receive your rewards and gifts from your spell work. 'Be careful what you wish for' is a popular saying, and in spell casting, that couldn't be truer.

Make sure you know what you are asking for before you set your intentions. It will likely come back to you.

Organize the Spell into a Workable Format

Once you have determined all of the elements from Steps 1-4, you are now ready to construct the spell. They are the puzzle pieces and now you have to put the puzzle together. This part can be the most fun as it is the design phase of your spell.

Here is where you get to be the architect and determine what happens first, next and last. You will decide when to light the ritual candles you have chosen, and what words you will say alongside the sacred act of lighting them. You will decide exactly what method you will take to incorporate your herbs (burning, drinking as tea, displaying at the altar, wrapping for drying purposes, etc.).

You will decide when to speak the words of manifestation in conjunction with each sacred and magical act.

Building the spell is part of the work you will incorporate into your *Book of Shadows*. It acts as a journal of your writing spells and your progress with them, so do not be afraid if you have to scribble things out and change some elements and factors. It is an ever-evolving work of art, just like every spell you create and every piece of magic you perform.

Use Your Spells

After you have created your spell, the best part is using it. You will want to make time and space and collect all of your ingredients to have fun with your work of magic art. Using your spells is the pay off and the reward and your goals and intentions are set into motion every time you use them.

Do not hesitate to borrow these spells and change them to your liking.

Things to Consider when Casting a Spell

Enjoying your spell work is easy, especially when you are taking the right precautions. Even when you are not using any potentially dangerous tools or implements, it is still a good practice to go into your work with a mindset of feeling prepared, protected, and safe.

Having a standard protocol for your witchcraft and spell work will help you remain respectful of yourself and all the energies that you choose to incorporate into your process.

Safety

Consider how often you will be using these tools and how much energy they will accumulate over time. Cleansing and purifying your tools is an easy and effective way for you to keep your tools in a higher state of vibration and clarity for use in spell work.

Sometimes, the energy of something can feel 'off,' and you may not be sure why that is. This can happen with your tools for Wiccan spell work, and a weird tool can cause you to fumble and could even cause some injury.

Safe handling of candles, matches, fire, blades, and smudging sticks is always highly recommended. Make sure you have the right dishes and containers to keep your candles standing upright and your smudge stick away from anything it could set fire.

You may also want to make sure your altar and ritual space is well-ventilated while you use smoke for purification.

Practicing proper tool safety is a must, even when it means clearing and purifying the energy of your tools and implements regularly, to prevent them from collecting unwanted energies, that could mar your spells and incantations or make them difficult.

Harm None.

This is a potent tool to help you stay safe from causing damage to yourself and others while you cast. The Threefold Law states that anything you do can return to you three times, meaning your energetic impact through rituals and spells will return to you three times over.

That is incredibly powerful energy to return to you, and if you are casting to bring more wealth and abundance into your life, that would be a good thing. However, if you are casting a spell to make someone fall out of love with another person to fall in love with you, that is harmful to not only one, but two people. It will come back to you at some point by the power of three, according to Wiccan beliefs.

Grounding and Centering for Spell casting

Success with spell casting is not just about safety and what tools you might use; it is also about how you prepare your mind, body, and spirit. The idea behind grounding and centering is that you ask yourself to unite with your authentic energy and power to call upon the work you want to do accurately.

Calming the mind, focusing on your intentions, and getting aligned for your magical purpose are a massive part of how to successfully cast. If your mind is wandering and thinking about what you are going to need from the grocery store, then you will not be focused on your power for manifestation. A lot of people will sometimes consider the centering process as something very akin to meditation.

In general, meditation is an all-encompassing term that essentially asks you to clear your mind and stay focused on the moment you are in. Meditation is another way to describe the centering process to help you ready your energy to make magic.

Grounding is another term to help you understand the quality of vibration—or energy—that allows you to stay within the power of Earth and her abundant fuel for magic. To ground yourself is to connect to the floor of everything, everywhere.

You ground into the floor of your body and mind, and you also ground into the energy of whatever deities you are supporting.

Grounding helps us to siphon any excess energy into the ground and then pull the available power endlessly from the Earth through us. It is a way to help the direction of your energy flow so that you feel supported, balanced, and prepared for whatever spell or ritual you are about to perform. In many ways, the grounding and centering process is what directs your intuition, instinct, and power into what you are working on. It is a focus of energy on all levels.

Not everyone will ground and center before casting, and if you were to compare results of spells from someone who does and someone who does not, you might be surprised to find that there is more return for those who are practicing their grounded-ness before and after casting a spell.

For many who practice Wicca, the grounding process can occur with the casting of the circle, as this activity has very stabilizing, opening, and centering qualities. Before any spell, if you want to have greater success with manifestation, it is crucial to prepare your energy to work with it according to your wishes and goals.

Some people will use a circle of protection while others might use a specific meditation, incantation, or poem. You can also use crystals and stones that are specifically for the purpose of grounding and using incense and smudging can have a very centering and grounding impact.

You will need to determine the right method for you, and if you want to have success with your spells, consider a grounding and centering ritual before you get started to make sure your energy is in right alignment with your spell's purpose.

How to Cast a Circle and the Reason Behind it

Casting a Circle is one of the most common aspects of practicing with Wiccan spells and all kinds of pagan ritual and witchcraft.

First, let us talk about why you want to cast a circle before you start a spell. Then, you can see exactly how it is done.

A circle in Wicca and witchcraft serves multiple purposes. It is specific energy to help you feel safe and protected, while it calls upon the elements, directions, and spirit to help you in your work.

Traditionally, the circle is your gateway to magic and will always keep you in alignment with the energy of nature. Here, within the circle, you will find the support you need to accomplish your goals from all directions of the universe.

You should always cast a kind of circle, even if it completely simple, like spinning in a circle to acknowledge energy around you that will shield you from outside forces. A circle is an energetic bubble that holds your power and your magic inside.

It can be a way to keep you spiritually safe, only inviting in the energies you want to work with.

Many will use a candle, an object from nature, or an altar tool to mark each direction with one of the four primary elements. The fifth element, spirit or ether, is what is above you. In Wicca, it can pertain to the God/Goddess energy you call upon to worship in your work.

The purpose of your circle is to protect you and also to empower you while you cast. It is a connection to the Divine and promotes the gateway and opening for manifestation while it holds you in the balance of all life.

CHAPTER 3:

Basic Steps for Any Spell

The Majority of us Magickal spells are worked together with by Individuals, Rituals regularly, and lots of us, or spells, are pleased to utilize a formulation that somebody else has established and to pull a spell-book out. It is a very simple strategy: clean and neat, assemble materials' list browse through and execute every step. Voila: a charm! Is it as straightforward as putting together a new bookshelf? Well, yes--it could be, and a piece of Magick is the thing. But I am here to convince you Craft of spell work, as you construct yourself, from the bottom up, you infuse it with your tastes, your deliberateness, your fantasies, your ideas, and your energies. This charm will not only be something that you read from the pages of somebody else --it resonates through your heart and will carry your signature. It'll be complete and more powerful than any charm could be, which makes you an essential part of the Magick from begins to finish. We use Magick as a method of altering the truth as soon as we practice spell-craft. We do it by working with as a number of the corresponding truths as potential -- date, time, location, elemental correspondences, the aid of deities, etc.--in hopes that we're able to shift reality in 1 direction or another and change the results. Nowhere is that more performed than in rituals, spells, and spells, as we make it and place our character our own.

Educate Yourself

Step one in almost any working would be to prepare one's self. This company of changing reality, after all, is not straightforward. The resources of spell writing are easy and economical: begin with pen or pencil scratch paper, a couple of index cards, along with a stack of your Magickal books. You may construct a little altar of substances created to inspire your creative forces in your workspace or only group. An amethyst crystal can encourage insights and intuition. A candle scented with honeysuckle or lilac will inspire your imagination and abilities. You can unwind preparing you for your work session.

Pick Exactly What You Would Like

Thus prepared, the next step is to decide what you want to accomplish. Do you require a dose of wealth, Magick? Are you planning for a self-initiation? Would you wish to clean up a physical area? As soon as you have decided, have a bit of a large index card or paper and then fold it in half, so that it stands out just like a tent. Compose your aim on one half of this newspaper as a simple, clear statement, describing what's at stake and what you expect to achieve:

Gather Your Tools

You are ready for a piece of paper. To think, for instance, at this early stage about the paper you are using, and you can use the notion of correspondences. This paper's color, texture, and contour may bring about your spell-craft. I have seen prosperity spells written on single dollar bills and space-cleansing spells written on paper towels, which have been used to wash the ritual area clean before being burnt as a member of this spell. The very same ideas apply to your selection of pencil pen or quill.

Ground and Center

Before working, have a moment, Energies, center, and then the floor. Understands what A hangover feels like. Writing is a way of the energies, as well as practice you control, and I'll call up needs to be

Lest you are left with a headache dealt with and exhaustion. For this reason, it is almost always a fantastic idea to center and ground on the two ends of a magickal writing session. Most spell workers take this time to predict on a or a muse patron deity for inspiration. Do not have one? Contemplate Athena Greek, Brighid Celtic, or Seshat Egyptian, goddesses connected with poetry and writing.

Establish Your Spell Components

Now the work starts. Begin with deciding when you are working the charm. Day of the lunar period, time of day, the week place, and hour are examples of time-consuming aspects which could affect your outcomes. By way of instance, a spell for wealth could be worked throughout the Moon stage and about midday, when the solar energies of the Sun would be the most powerful. A spell to get initiation would do the job nicely throw on a Monday at sunrise after the new Moon. Can you do the charm, or can others participate? Can you spell be structured and formal, or spontaneous and casual? Think about the particular materials you will use: Materials or alternative Fire craft, herbs, incense, stones or crystals, conventional altar tools, colored altar cloths, etc. Work out of your source publications with correspondence tables, fitting your goal. To remain on track Since you work, look back to be certain.

Write Your Spell!

With elements recorded and purpose, you are all set to write the charm itself. Your spell's results may differ from unstructured and conversational to rhymed poetry. The language might be ideal for uncomplicated intentions, but rituals, spells, and spells use vocabulary. Rhyming language, if spoken, and has its rhythm indicates a drumbeat that adds cadence into the words' impact. Poetry also tends to utilize a lot of imagery and metaphor, making beautiful verses, which improve the overall impact. Whether utilizing constructions that are poetic or plain, you need to begin with getting the words down. Do not be concerned about your first draft is ideal: only let your mind dump all its thoughts. You may begin with it. When the material is there, together with the notions set up, add words with a dictionary or thesaurus to locate choices. Rhythm and read the words to listen to the sound they create. Make notes to signify in which pauses or activities should happen. You might choose to compose the action into the charm, e.g., "Light incense today."

Work the Spell

For less spell function, after the words are recorded on paper, you are ready to build your stuff and perform the spell. To get even a setting between a substantial event or persons, or an official ritual, you might choose to repeat the measures twice or once. Look at memorizing the words. Memorization is not needed once you memorize phrases; you internalize them allowing them to take on energy and to input your subconscious. Additionally, not having to read out of a bit of paper frees you to be a part of the procedure, adding to your enjoyment.

Assess

After working, the spell is an essential step: the test procedure. Sit down on the process worked and take notes out. Did everything go as planned? If you replicated the spell, does anything change? File them away. Some traditions warn against speaking about spell work before a period has passed, believing this to talk of this Magick is to discharge a number of its power. Make sure you do your test, although Celebrate these customs as needed by your practices --for your eyes only. Come back into it after time has passed, including a note about the spell worked weeks or even months.

CHAPTER 4:

Wiccan Rituals

The definition of the word ritual means a religious ceremony with an order of predefined events. In Wicca, our contact with the Gods happens through rituals and also it is in a ritualistic way that we formulate our desires, build a talisman or we consecrate an object to protect us or attract positive energies.

In Wicca, a ritual does not start with the casting of the Circle and ends with the burnout and not all are formal or ideal for the magician's work. Most of the time they are devotional in character, only to honor our Gods as we do when we celebrate a Sabbath, etc.

Ritual is a way of connecting with the energies of nature, with the sun, moon or ancestors. It is our bridge of communication with the other world and we practice rituals to ensure that we do not lose contact with these forces. According to Wicca philosophy, a ritual can be performed in many different ways. Anything can become a ritual. Even tasks like reading, writing, eating, waking up or sleeping can be ritualized to give them spiritual meaning. Raise the thought to Goddess thanking her for the abundance before we feed or greet the sun for the morning is a simple ritual practice that puts us in direct contact with the sacred calling so that every moment in our lives becomes magical.

Most of the time a ritual involves communication with a deity. Through it, a psychic connection is established, bringing awareness of the Sacred closer to us, inviting him to be part of the devotional ceremony so that he may extend his blessings and presence into our daily lives.

Be aware that not all Wiccans ritualize in the same way. The rituals vary greatly from one witch to another and among the covens. This happens because for rituals to really work they need to reflect the personality of their operator and this is only possible by giving a personal touch, adapting them according to our vision and understanding of the Divine.

There are basically two classifications of rituals in Wicca:

- Devotional rituals: to honor one the Goddess, the God, a deity in special or celebrate a Sabbat or Esbat

- Magical rituals: to direct magical energy into the desired range through spells, spells, talismans, etc.

In many cases, as in the Sabbath rituals, a ritual can be magical and/or worshiping the Goddess or her Mother face at the same time as an enchantment or spell is made and cast.

From here you will learn a little about the magic that Wiccans use and by understanding its essence, you can also practice it to fill your life with the presence of the Sacred.

What is described is just a guideline for you to begin performing your rituals. The suggestions given reflect much of what most Wizards do. However, feel free to add your personal touch and develop your own particular way of performing rituals that reflect your personality and personal concepts. The best way to learn to ritualize is by practicing.

A ritual follows some guidelines to be created and performed. It is important that you know these bases because they are essential for the success of any magic operation:

Preparation of objects and ritual area

It is important to clean the objects and the space that will be used to perform your ritual. Clean the instruments of the altar, sweep the floor of the room chosen for the ritual, adorn the place with flowers, candles and incense sticks. Make the environment pleasant for your eyes.

Make sure that everything you need is at hand when the ritual begins. So, check out the herbs that will be used, the candles, instruments, etc.

Personal preparation

Personal preparation is also important because it puts us in a state of being receptive to the energy of the gods and centers us inwardly. When we perform a ritual, we carry our own energy into the magic circle. Therefore, we need to be clear of mind, body, and heart.

Take a bath of cleansing herbs like rosemary, cloves or sage before performing a ritual. Wipe off with a freshly washed towel and dress in a clean outfit. If you wish, pass an oil with your favorite body aroma and purify yourself through smoke from incense. As you do this, reflect on the purpose of your ritual, asking gods to purify your being.

The act of purification is a practice that puts us in an altered state of consciousness, preparing us for magic.

Creation of the Holy space

The creation of sacred space can be divided into 3 different stages: purifying, casting and blessing. A room like a living room or bedroom can be used for a ritual. But because they are also used for other functions, many waste energies end up staying in these places.

The purpose of purifying the sacred space is to remove all energies from the area which are incompatible with your practice. Pour some salt into a bowl of water and splash it on the floor while visualizing all negative energies being destroyed and nullified. You can also use incense and even candle flame to purify the area that will be used.

Circle the environment counterclockwise, the movement used to banish. While doing this say something like:

"I purify this place of all negative energy. May evil come out and good come in. For all the power of the three times the three, let it be so and let it be done! "

After purification, the next step is to launch the magic circle, which will sacralize the area used. An example of how the circle can be drawn has been described. Casting a circle basically consists of circling the ritual area in the sense three times with the athame while viewing a light coming from its tip going towards the ground and forming a bubble of light around us.

Welcome to elements and gods

Right after the magic circle is cast, the elements of nature and gods are invoked. The invocation of these powers is nothing less than a personal request that they are present and bless your ritual. The first to be called are the elements. The invocations to elements of nature are always made in order starting from the north, then east, south, and west invoking respectively the elements earth, air, fire, and water. Next to the Goddess, god and all the other deities we wish to invoke optionally are also summoned to the ritual.

When we invoke the presence of energy in our rituals, we expect an answer, but you will not always notice a strong presence in the rituals, especially in early experiences. Over time and practice, the invoked energies will be increasingly noticeable, and their presence may be strongly felt.

Aligning a Sabbath, Esbat or purpose ritual

If you are performing a ritual to celebrate the arrival of a season or on a full moon night, the observation of this date should be associated with your theme. While your ritual also includes a magical practice, this is the time for making a talisman or to perform the chosen spell, for example. Many are the magic practices that can be used in a ritual ranging from candle rituals to magic strings. In a further chapter, you will find some spells that can be realized for the different needs of human life. Use them as a way to align your ritual with your desire.

The banquet

The banquet marks the end of the ritual and is used to return your awareness to the normal state since eating is one of the most humane acts and it can easily refer our mind to daily activities. Foods and beverages that are part of the banquets vary greatly from witch to witch. The most common are fruits, wine, and bread. Many Wiccans use cakes, seeds, and many other food sources as part of their banquet. Food plates are usually placed on the altar or its feet and before being ingested are consecrated with the touch of the staff while saying something like:

"In the sacred name of the Goddess and God, I consecrate and bless you that by eating this food. I (we) are reinvigorated internally and spiritually, and may they bring me health, harmony, and prosperity. Let it be so, and let it be done! "

This is also the time to perform the great rite when wine, water or any other liquid present in the altar cup is consecrated. The great rite represents the union of goddesses and gods, who bring the blessings of abundance to earth.

To do this, take your athame in your right hand and the chalice in your left. Slowly dip the athame blade into the chalice liquid, watch it shine through the mind's eye and then say:

"The union of goddess and god is represented here. May this wine (or any other liquid) bring me health, success, prosperity, and harmony. In the sacred name of the Goddess and God, let it be so and let it be done!"

Finish the ritual

It is time to thank the elements, gods and all the energies that have been present in your ritual. At this time, the magic circle is unlocked. For this, the operator thanks the elements, the Goddess, the God and all the invoked energies, and then travels through the ritual area counterclockwise, while visualizing the sphere of light fading away.

The completion of the ritual is an important part and should never be forgotten, because it is what will make us return to our state of consciousness daily, to perform daily mundane necessary tasks. After completion incense and candles should be extinguished without blowing through a damper or other artifact; or they may also be left at the altar to be consumed to the end. Everything that was used in the ritual is collected and saved.

The efficacy of ritual

A ritual is an important part of the religious life of people around the world. The primary cause of a ritual is to invoke to connect with the great mystery:

A goddess or a god, a force of nature, the different spiritual worlds, or even the simple rhythms of the seasons. So, the ritual is the invocation in action.

In Wicca and other pagan ways, every ritual is a moment of transformations, a magical instant where a portal between the worlds is opened and everything becomes possible. It is through rituals that we connect with our ancient deities, for physical and spiritual change to take place.

The call to these deities is through invocations, prayers, and texts, which are recited or read during ritualistic practices as an invitation to the Divine to manifest. Such invocations call aspects and specific Divine forces to be discernible in our rites. The perception of these forces can be felt in many emotional, mental and even synesthetic ways.

Rituals help us in this connection with the great mysteries of existence. Remember, they are gateways to other realities of power, and we could make a simple analogy with television as a portal to connect with the world. The world will always exist; programs of news, soap operas and documentaries will be playing at many people's homes, whether we turn on the TV or not. But television is a channel that encodes the signals that are sent by the antennas, and helps us to see them in an understandable way to our mind and eyes. This also happens in magic: gods are always around us, and rituals and invocations are the focus for us to connect with them.

Following some simple guidelines, a ritual for the invocation of a deity or strength can be created for any kind of need.

Steps to effective invocatory ritual:

There are thirteen basic steps that must be followed to perform a successful summoning ritual. They are essential for a rite to be more well-designed and well-planned:

1. Set the goal.

2. Choose and prepare symbols.

3. Purify and consecrate objects.

4. Use symbols.

5. Choose a right time.

6. Words must have strength.

7. Invoke the gods.

8. Prepare the sacred space.

9. Create a state of relaxation.

10. Use the five senses.

11. Pronounce your desire.

12. Power is generated

13. Release the magic.

CHAPTER 5:

Wiccan Spell Casting with Candles

How to Work with Candles in Your Spells

Candle making itself became an art in the early 19th century, when more elements were starting to become known to humankind and these elements influenced the availability of candles to the public. In the previous centuries, candles were quite expensive and can only be afforded by the rich, especially colored candles. However, nowadays, candles are cheap, and there are a variety of colors that you can choose from and a variety of spells you can cast.

Each color has a different meaning and can influence a person's emotions. You know that yellow makes you feel happy, and green is associated with money. Applying those same meanings to different colored candles will promote the same meanings and many others. Color is just one layer of energy added to your ritual. Different colors represent different frequency, meanings, energy, and vibrations that when combined together affect the spell work in a positive way. The material in which the candle is made out of can also play an important role in the energy of the candle. For example, there are candles that are made out of beeswax, which signifies power and life. Adding color to this candle, such as red for passion, will give you twice the amount of energy, and it can even heighten your intentions throughout the spell or ritual. Essential oils, sigils, and herbs are also different layers that can be added on the candle to enhance the power of the spell.

The size of the candle does not affect the power and energy of the spell. However, it depends on how long your spell lasts for. There are candles that take three days to burn, and many people do not like to practice spells that are longer than one day, since it can be rather distracting than letting the candle burn straight away. Many people use votive candles or short taper candles, just because they work best when it comes to spell casting. However, often, different spells will require different candles such as a figure candle or a seven-day candle. One of the most popular candles used are the menorah candles, which can be found in any grocery stores, specifically in the kosher section. Many practitioners use them because they are white, four inches long, thin, and unscented which is perfect for any spell work.

When it comes to determining the size of the candle, look at how long your spell will take, if it is a long one and takes a couple of days, then choose a thick candle and make markings on how much to burn a day. If the spell is a one-time thing, small two-finger sized candles are perfect, since it will not take long to burn them out.

For many Wiccans, candles operate as stand-ins or symbols for practitioners who use them. For example, the candle wick is associated with the mind; the wax of the candle is the human body; and the flame itself is the spirit or soul of the practitioner. The flame releases the desires of the body and the mind into the universe through the smoke of the candle.

Candle Magic

One of the simplest forms of spell casting is through the use of candles. It is a form of magic that does not require the caster to perform any complicated ritual. It also does not require the use of any type of priceless ceremonial tools or artifacts. Basically, what this means is that candle magic is a type of magic that any average person can do.

A candle is a beacon, announcing to the universe that someone is calling for energies to unite, and to make new energy out of it. The power of all thoughts can be imbued into a candle's flame and magic, and that is what the basis of magic really is—turning thoughts and energies into realities.

Magic is the art of sending a particular thought, goal, or intention into the spiritual plane to have it take shape and manifest in the physical world. Candles are messengers who help you achieve this magical goal. They are also channels, or *mediums*, to convey your messages or intentions and goals to those Divine energies called upon to help you and guide you. The candle burns through the wick, the wax, and the air all around and slowly disappears, carrying your message from the earth plane to the ethereal plane, striking a chord of energetic intention into the fibers and vibrations of the whole universe. To see your intention, burning away through the magic of candles, is truly a helpful way for you to put your purpose further out into the world. It is a symbol of the physical manifestation of your purpose into a message for the Divine. To go a step further, the candle is thought by some Wiccans to be the perfect balance of all four elements. The wick that passes through the center of the candle and leaves the bottom, like a root plunging into the soil, is the element of Earth. It is present to keep the candle burning, without which it could not burn all the way down to the bottom. The wax of the candle is seen as the water element. As it transforms from a solid form into a melted and watery form, and then eventually evaporating as gas, it has all of the qualities of water's many shape-shifting forms. It is what gets carried away to the Spirit. Without oxygen around the candle, the flame could not burn. The element of Air, present all around you, is what calls the candle flame into being and keeps it burning. If you eliminate the air around it with a candle snuffer or lid on a candle jar, you extinguish the light and the flame. Lastly, but most appropriately, the Fire element is represented by the burning flame at the top of the candle, which rests close to the wax as it melts away and burns the wick as it continues to burn. It is valuable to consider the magic of the whole candle and how it can establish the presence of all four Elements, carrying your message away to the fifth (Spirit). When you use candle magic, you are harnessing the power of the elements and how they contribute to every act of magic you are performing in your practice. Remember those times during your birthday where you made a wish and blew out the candles on your cake? The same theory applies. However, in this case, instead of wishing or hoping for something to happen, you are actually declaring your commitment.

Thinking about it more clearly: the blowing of the candle on the cake is a ritual based on three key principles:

- Decide what you are aim is going to be

- Visualize what and how the end result would be

- Fully commit to achieve that result

Candle Colors

Along with choosing which kind of candle and what scent you may wish to use in your spells, color is another important consideration. This section will discuss the use of colors in candles. However, for an easy guide, consider referring to the back of this book for the Tables of Correspondence, which will have a quick, easy to look at the meaning behind each color without all of the frill, fluff, or explanation here.

Black

Black as a color is avoid—it is the absence of light on the spectrum, but the absence does not imply that it is bad. Despite the fact that it is black, consider that the color of blackness is avoid—it absorbs all colors, which is why wearing black is so uncomfortable on a hot day. It absorbs instead of reflecting, and as such, it also absorbs negativity. By absorbing the negative energy instead of allowing it to continue to flow, the negative energy around you is pulled from the air. You can use this to protect, repel, reverse, or even banish magic or energy from your surroundings. You can also use this color to remove negativity altogether, to overcome obstacles or blockages that are preventing you from moving forward, and to cause issues and promote chaos or dysfunction among your enemies.

Blue

Blue is a relaxing color by nature, and it is commonly used to heal and strengthen the mind in spell casting. You can use this to encourage sleep, hence, allowing your intention to sleep to flow into the candle before burning it for a few short minutes and putting it out. When you use a blue candle, you are encouraging one's inherent understanding and awareness of the spiritual world, and generally speaking, the shade of blue you use matters as well:Light blue candles tend to bring about peace, tranquility, and clarity.

Medium shades of blue candles tend to bring spiritual strength and fortitude, as well as a deep inner peace.

Dark blue shades tend to show deep thoughts and spirituality—these may cause moodiness if you are not careful in how you use them.

Brown

Brown candles are largely natural—it is the color of the dirt beneath your feet and many different animals. This color is usually applied with other colors as well in order to tie your spell to the natural world, influencing the world around you rather than you or someone else. Usually, you may use darker russet brown in uncertain situations, such as if you are unsure about your love life. Medium brown can symbolize some sort of pause or hesitancy to understand what is happening next.

Green

Green candles tend to represent growth, fortune, and prosperity in general, as well as the element of Earth. These candles are also related to healing, much like how the blue ones are. When you light a green candle, you are likely preparing for a spell that has some sort of tie to money, such as asking for help to get a promotion or to undertake a new financial venture. These candles can also help you achieve success in your business, whatever that business may be.

Gold

Gold candles are primarily associated with the God, the Sun, and masculinity. Often seen as the counterpart to silver, gold candles are also related primarily to finances and businesses, much like green. They are fantastic for attracting any sort of knowledge that you need, as well as finding fortune, money, or developing a power of influence or healing.

Orange

Orange candles are energetic and attentive—when you use orange, you are attempting to attract something, whether that is energy, influence, intentions, or other objects in the universe. If you are trying to find someone or something that is lost, for example, you may choose to use orange candles. You can also combine the orange of this candle with others in order to be a fortifier, strengthening the intention of the other color. Overall, orange is positive spiritual and physical energy and is associated with being encouraging and allowing for clear thoughts.

Pink

Pink candles are usually indicative of some sort of connection, be it love or friendship. They are nurturing, and they encourage the art of communication. They are usually used before any sort of ceremony that will link people together or otherwise emphasize the bond between two people. This means that you will often see these during marriage ceremonies, or when they are used to influence love and romance, encouraging the affection and romantic feelings.

Silver

Silver is first and foremost associated with the Goddess, the Moon and celestial bodies, and femininity. When you are using a silver candle, you are attempting to dispel any sort of negative energy that is present around you. You are encouraging good to win in its endeavor to overtake evil, and in doing so, you are able to encourage reflection and a connection to the Moon. It encourages the use of intuition, and you may use this candle if you are trying to meditate on what to do next or how best to proceed with your situation at hand.

Red

Red candles are primarily meant to convey passion and health—they are associated with energy and vitality, representing health itself. In burning a red candle, you are able to power the soul, bolstering it and allowing yourself to prevent being influenced by negativity or corruption. Along with health and passion, it is also seen frequently with lust and sexual passion, as well. Of all the colors for your candle, this is the closest one to represent the element of fire. When you use a red candle, you are filling yourself with courage—maybe you are getting ready to go into an interview, an important meeting, or even a date.

Violet

Violet candles are reminiscent of power—blue is about awareness, while violet encourages prowess in the magical world. When you use a violet candle, you are encouraging a buildup of your magic, strengthening your spells. For example, if you are attempting to cast a love spell, you may choose to burn a violet candle, while also burning a pink one to really magnify the effects of the candle's affinity for love.

White

White is pure and unifying—its purity allows for it to be used in virtually any context, though it is most commonly associated with truth and illumination. It is used primarily for defensive or purifying reasons, though you can choose white when you do not have the right color being called for, or when you feel like you are unsure which color to use. When you use white, you encourage strength and power, as well as revere innocence and purity. It can help you connect with the spiritual world and to prevent evil from taking you over.

Yellow

Yellow candles are associated with knowledge and discovery. They are meant to improve visualization and encourage movement toward innovation. These are most strongly aligned with the element of air. When you light a yellow candle to burn with you as you study, you will find that you absorb the information better, making it particularly useful. This can range from a light yellow all the way to a bright shade of lime yellow, or even have golden undertones. It is meant to convey and represent any sort of cheerfulness or attraction, and it is used in encouraging the fulfillment of dreams.

Choosing the Right Candles to Use

Many people who practice candle magic will most likely tell you that, similar to some of life's most important aspects, size really does not matter. The saying "the bigger, the better" surely does not apply in this case. In fact, making use of an over-sized candle may prove to be annoyingly counterproductive. The reason for this is because some candle-spells involve asking the spell caster to wait until the candle burns itself out before proceeding with the rest of the invocation of the spell. Therefore, making use of a tapered or votive candle is recommended.

There will also be cases where a specific kind of candle is required for a spell, such as a figure candle or seven-day candle, representing a specific individual. You would be astonished to know, however, that one of the most famous candles that are used in the invocation of spells is the menorah candle. Menorah candles are usually sold in boxes in your local grocery store. They are white, unscented candles which stand about four inches tall—great for casting spells.

One important thing to remember when using candles is always use a fresh, brand new candle for spell work, or virgin materials.

Never, ever use leftover candles from a previous spell work. Magical traditions believe that once a candle has been burned, it attracts vibrations from everything around it. It would be prudent to always use a fresh candle to have a positive or effective magical outcome.

You cannot just take any candle you see and assume it will work just right. While you may be able to create some influence in doing so, the best way to truly be successful at Wiccan magic is to know when to use which tool, and to use those tools to the best of their capabilities.

In this case, you want to learn how to pick the perfect candle. You can do this relatively simple, and while you may eventually get this down to memory, it may help you to take this list and transcribe it into your *Book of Shadows* for future reference. Doing so can provide you with a handy tool that you can reference at a glance, to ensure that you are always choosing the right candle for the right job.

Candles are used in nearly every ritual and spell you will do, though there are some that require nothing more than yourself. Because of that, you will find yourself constantly needing to select candles as you go through the process of learning how to cast spells yourself. This can be intimidating. If you have ever been in a candle aisle, you know that there are several different kinds of candles in every color imaginable. Each color and each shape will have different tendencies and meanings. If you learn how to navigate through this, learning which candles will best be used in any situation, you will be able to make sure you start each ritual and spell on the best foot that you possibly can.

Remember, candles are used representatively and to charge and begin your spell, attracting or repelling energies depending on your intention and usage. Despite how small the candle is, remember that it is incredibly powerful. It has the ability to burn down your house relatively easily if you were to knock it over or otherwise cause a problem for yourself. No matter how small it may be, it needs to be treated with the care, caution, honor, and reverence it deserves. It not only is able to pull energy around it, which adds to its utility, but it can also be quite destructive if not treated right.

One well-balanced tool that is directly symbolic of the elements is the candle. This is because each element is present throughout the use of a candle. The element of Air is ever-present in the form of oxygen, and oxygen is necessary to keep the flame alive and burning. The Earth element is represented by the wax of the candle, as well as the fibers used to make the wick. The wax also represents the element of Water as it transforms from solid to liquid when it melts, and is characterized by its shape-shifting abilities. Of course, the literal flame of the candle represents the element of Fire. By charging the candle with your intent, you create a small yet powerful tool that embodies the entire universe, because when you charge your candle, you add that last very important element: Spirit.

Types of Candles

Candles come in all shapes and sizes. You will find a wide variety among different occultist shops, body shops, or even grocery stores. It helps, however, to buy from shops that specialize in magickal intent so that if you have any questions, there will be somebody there who likely knows what they are talking about, compared to an average grocery store clerk.

The main types of candles are tea lights, votives, tapers, columns, encased pillars, and free-standing pillars. All of these types can be used interchangeably, but the best kinds of candles to use in spells that require them to be burned all the way are votives and tapers. This is because their wicks are typically short, and they are generally the easiest to control. One of the most popular candle types are the menorah candles, which are about four inches in length and are sold in bulk at easily accessed places, such as at the grocery store. They are white, thin, and unscented, which make them perfect for most kinds of spell work.Below is a short list containing the intent of a few commonly used candles in these cases.

- **Female figure:** This is used to attract or repel someone specific, but can also be used to represent someone close to you who identifies as female.

- **Male figure:** This is used to attract or repel someone specific but can also be used to represent someone close to you who identifies as male.

- **Couple:** Candles shaped like a couple are used to bring a married couple closer together.

- **Genitalia:** This one is pretty straight forward. It is used for arousal, passion, sexual desire, and fertility.

- **Buddha:** It brings Good fortune, abundance, and luck.

- **Devil:** A devil-shaped candle is used for temptations, whether to encourage or banish them.

- **The Cat:** This is used specifically for money spells, luck, or even protection.

- **Skull:** This candle shape is used to repel unwanted feelings or thoughts. It is also used for healing spells or cleansing.

- **Knob Candle:** The seven knobs that make up the body of this candle represent seven wishes.

It is highly suggested that you use a candle that has never been used for spell work. Do not just pick up a candle that you burned for your nighttime bath and use it in a money spell, because you do not have anything else. If you do not feel like going out and buying a new candle that day, you should save your spell work for another day. According to most magickal beliefs, a candle, once lit, absorbs the vibrations caused by the many items around it. It is believed that this may lead to a negative or ineffective magickal outcome, so you must exercise caution.

Using Your Candle in Ritual

After you have chosen the right candle for the spell that you want to do, you will want to apply oil on the candle before using it. This process is called *dressing*. What dressing does, is it creates a psychic connection between the spell caster and the candle. Creating a psychic connection means that you are expressing your intent by projecting your own energy and vibrations on the wax of the candle before using it.

Dressing a candle requires using natural oil. Grape seed oil is preferred by many spell casters due to the fact that it has no scent. An alternative option is to make use of special magic oils that are usually found in metaphysical supply stores. Begin dressing your candle by rubbing oil from the top part, down to the middle part of the candle. Then, start at the bottom part, up towards the middle of the candle where you first left off.

There are some variations of this process, where coating starts from the middle of the candle and working its way to both ends. If particular candle spell requires the usage of herbs, just roll the oil dressed candle in the powdered herb until it is completely covered all the way around.

One of the most basic forms of candle magic involves using a small piece of paper that has the same color as the candle itself. The color of the paper and the candle will depend upon the intent of your spell. On this piece of paper, is where you will write your intent for the spell itself. As you write down your main goal for the spell, you must envision yourself attaining that goal.

Think of the various forms in which your aim might come. Once you have written your aim on that piece of paper, fold it while still keeping your concentration on your intent. Some candle spell casters recite a little incantation in order to be more focused on their intent. The incantation does not have to be anything elaborate. A simple incantation expressing your intent would suffice.

After folding the paper, allow one corner of the paper to catch fire by putting it into the flame of the candle. Hold the paper while it is burning until the last moment without getting your fingers burned. Place the burning paper in a cauldron or fire-safe pot or bowl, to allow it to burn on its own the rest of the way. Leave the candle until it is completely burned out. Once the candle is completely burned out, do not reuse it for later. Dispose the used candle immediately.

The Secrets of Cleansing and Consecration

Selecting your candle is just the beginning. You still have to process the candle, preparing it to work for you. Think for a moment about preparing a meal—you may buy a slab of raw meat, but you would not yet serve it for dinner. You must still prepare it into something cohesive, in order for it to be delicious and nutritious. Just as you will still need to trim, season, and cook your meat before serving it to your guests, you must also prepare your candle.

When you are preparing your candle, however, instead of trimming and seasoning it before cooking like you would a piece of meat, you are going to first cleanse your candle of energy and then consecrate it. Consecrating is a fancy word, which means that you will prepare and dedicate the item to being used for your Divine purpose, declaring the intent to use it specifically for the purpose that you have chosen for it.

Consecrating the candle can come in several different forms, such as anointing, coating it with herbs, or carving it, and depending on your intent and the spell that you will be using, you will need to choose the method that works best for you in the moment. As you read through this chapter, you will build up an idea of when it is appropriate to use each of these methods and how best to go about the process.

This step is incredibly important. Remember that as you do this, you are preparing for your spell or ritual, and because of this, you want to do the best job you can manage. You want to ensure that you are able to make the spell as effective as possible. That effectiveness will come with the quality of your spell, as well as intention. This means that you do not want to rush through these steps as you prepare for your spell. Instead, take the time to slowly and carefully dedicate and prepare your candles, using it as a time to really reflect upon the purpose of your spell and ensure that you will be able to complete it exactly as intended.

How to Cleanse a Candle?

The first thing you will do to prepare is cleanse your candle. When you do this, you are effectively purifying it in some way. Remember, your candle has been out in the world before it arrived in your home or on your altar. Even if you bought it new, it was still shipped to you, handled by the manufacturer, shipped to a retailer where it was likely placed upon shelves, or packaged and sold to you, if you bought it online. It would then be handled by several people as it traveled to your location, and by the time you get it, you have no idea where it has been, how many people it has passed, or how clean or pure the area around it was. It has been handled by so many people, absorbing energy and intentions as it went, that it is incredibly important for you to go through this cleansing process.

By cleansing your candle, you will release any and all energy that has been absorbed. You essentially turn your candle into a clean slate that you will be able to use in order to make your candle far more open to the intentions that you are hoping to imbue it with for your spell. Even if you have made the candle yourself, unless you have done so just then, for that specific spell, it is a good idea to cleanse it prior to the completion of the spell, simply to safeguard it. You do not want your spell to be tainted with any negative energy at all. Instead, you want it open and accepting of all positive intentions and energy that you are attempting to project. When trying to purify your candle, you have several options, depending on which you feel is appropriate at the time. We will discuss four effective ways that can be used to purify your candle. Ultimately, you need to pick the one that you feel works best for you.

Cotton and Alcohol

One method involves little more than a tissue or cotton ball along with rubbing alcohol. Rubbing alcohol is not only good for killing bacteria. You can use it to help you expel energy from your candle as well. Starting at the bottom of the candle, take your cotton saturated in alcohol and rub it gently. Do not scrub too hard, especially if this is a narrow candle, as you do not want to damage it. As you rub the candle gently, imagine the energy within the candle releasing. Imagine it as a flame, burning at the tip of the wick as you slowly rub along the wax, working your way up slowly. The energy will be expelled through the tip of the candle as you do so.

Purified with Sage

Another way that you can cleanse a candle is by burning sage. Sage itself is deeply intertwined with the idea of purifying a room. The smoke, as you burn it, purifies the area around you, and it is often used to purify an area during an exorcism, or if negative energy is present within the setting.

Sea Salt

Salt is well-known as a preserving method— for example, you can use it when you are attempting to sanitize or preserve food. It protects the meat from going bad as you cure it. However, salt also has important ties to Wiccan culture, as well. Salt is a powerful purifier, and you can use it when you are casting circles, performing spells, or even purifying your candle. When you set out to cleanse your candle, start by pouring salt into a bowl. The bowl should be large enough to accommodate the candle, and you need enough salt to bury the candle. Place the candle into the salt and bury it, covering the entire thing in salt.

Moonlight Cleanse

Particularly during the light of the Full Moon, you can cleanse items with ease. Of course, even just a little bit of Moonlight will be enough, but the effect and strength will be far stronger if you leave it out during the Full Moon. When you use this method, you are allowing the energy of the Moon to bathe the candle overnight, slowly purifying it and allowing the energy of the Moon to draw out the negativity within it. This means that you can effectively cleanse the candle with no effort, so long as you leave it out overnight.

How to Consecrate the Candle?

With your purified candle, are prepared to consecrate your candle. This is your dedication to the purpose of the spell you are attempting to do. During this, you will fill your candle with your intention, deciding exactly what you will be doing with it and filling it with that energy. As you consecrate your candle, you will do something else with it as you think and focus your energy on it. The methods of consecrating your candle can vary—from using oils and herbs to engraving it. Some people choose to use Holy Water or Moon Water to consecrate their candle as well. The method that you use will depend on your personal preferences, as well as the intention and intensity you will need for your spell.

After you consecrate your candle, you will be ready to begin your spell or ritual, which the rest of this book will focus on teaching you to do. Make sure you really understand this process, and again, do not rush through the consecration. The more entirely that you are able to imbue the candle with your intentions and desires, the more the candle will be able to deliver the results you are hoping for. Your candle will burn, and with it, it will send out the intention and energy that you have filled it in with. With the burning energy emanating outward into the universe, you create a gap of energy, to which something else must flow in. The hope is for the energy to bring with it whatever you were attempting to obtain with your spellcasting in the first place.

Anointing and Dressing the Candle

The first method of consecration that we will discuss is anointing and dressing. This is a simple process. You use oil to cover the candle and then dressing it with herbs, which involves you covering the candle in the herbs, that will help strengthen your message to the universe.

When you are going to anoint your candle, you must first choose an oil that will work for you. This oil will be related to the intention that you are hoping to send out into the universe. You want to find an oil that really lines up with the particular goals that you have in mind for your spell. With the oil chosen, it is time to anoint the candle. At this point, you should take the candle and close your eyes. Really imagine the goal that you are hoping to imbue into the candle, focusing on your goals and wishes that you have. Imagine those goals and wishes filling your fingers. Perhaps you visualize this energy literally illuminating your fingertips. Now, dip your finger in the oil and prepare to rub it into your candle.

It is important to note that when you are anointing a candle, you want to start at the top and work your way down when you are attempting to attract something to you. This process will attract positive energies, luck, and other benefits to you. When you wish to expel something, however, you want to start at the bottom and work your way up. This direction is incredibly important, and if you can keep this in mind, you should find that you are able to send out just the right kind of energy into the universe.

As you are envisioning your hands pulsating, the energy representing your intentions, gently rub the candle with the oils you have chosen. You want to make sure you cover the entire candle in whichever direction lines up with your intentions. As you do this, keep your intentions in your mind and heart, feeling the energy and intention filling the candle in your hand. At this point, you can choose to dress the candle if you wish to do so. If you wish to dress the candle, move down to the next section.

Coat the Candle with Magical Herbs

Dressing the candle will help you build up the power of your spell. You can build up extra energy by adding herbs to the candle oil. This is simple enough; all you will do is select the herbs that will work for you. You will take the herbs, crush them onto a piece of paper, and then roll your anointed herbs into the crumbs. When you do this, you will cause the herbs to stick to the candle. You will not get a perfect coating, but the important part is not to get a perfect layer. What you want is to make sure that the candle itself is mostly coated.

Carving and Engraving

This step will involve you carving symbols into your candle. You will want to choose a symbol that really helps convey the message you are trying to send off into the universe. For example, you may make it a point to use a heart to send your romantic intentions into the world around you, or you may wish to use a dollar sign to attract money. You could also engrave names or astrological signs, or even find some runes that you think will work for you.

Spray with Holy Water

The last method that is commonly used to consecrate a candle is to create your own Holy Water and use that to prepare it. Holy Water is easy to make—all you need to do is use some water, oil, and salt that you will use to then spray over the candle.

When you are making your Holy Water, remember that salt is purifying—by adding salt, you create a protective, purifying addition to the water you will be using, and by doing so, you allow the candle to help project your energy into the world. You will start this process by taking a cup of water and mixing three pinches of sea salt into it—try to make sure this is sea salt. Sea salt is much less processed than table salt, making it much better for the use in spells. When you use this sea salt, you allow yourself to tap into the power of the ocean as well as the earth, and you will be applying this to the candle you are going to burn.

Color Magic in Candles

In addition to their elemental magical properties, candles come in a considerable variety of colors, and like with most things in this world, there is special magic behind every color that you use in your spells and rituals. Color magic helps us further direct our intentions and purposes, by clearly stating and representing what we choose to manifest.

Throughout the centuries and our history as a people, colors have carried specific meanings across cultures, and have a universal identity and characteristic associated with each one. When you see the color red, you might instantly think of love, passion, desire, blood, and heat. When you see the color green, you might think of money, luck, a four-leaf clover, and Mother Earth. Colors pull our energies in specific directions because of their symbolic associations.

Utilizing color magic with your candles helps to reinforce particular goals and intentions that are being set. You may see in your research that these candles will be referred to as 'spell candles,' but any colorful candle you find can be charged and consecrated for magical uses.

Magical Properties of Color

The list below will offer you some of the magical properties associated with each color. You may find other sources in your research that provide additional insight into various ways that color can have symbolism and meaning. Use your intuition when working within your practice, and let it guide you to the right color for your candle magic spells.

Red: Love, romance, passion, courage, intense emotion, willpower, strength, physical energy and vitality, health, root chakra, and fire

Orange: Power, energy, vitality, attraction, stimulation, adaptability (especially with sudden change), and sacral chakra

Yellow: Communication, confidence, study, divination, intellect, inspiration, knowledge, and solar plexus chakra

Green: Prosperity, wealth, growth, fertility, balance, health, luck, abundance, growth, renewal, heart chakra, Mother Earth, and Mother Moon of the Triple Goddess

Blue: Healing, psychic ability, understanding, peace, wisdom, protection, patience, truth, understanding, harmony in the home, and throat chakra

Violet: Devotion, wisdom, spirituality, peace, enhancement of nurturing capability or quality, balancing sensitivities, divination, and third eye/brow chakra

White: Clarity, cleansing, spiritual growth, understanding, peace, innocence, illumination, establishing order, purity, crown chakra, and Maiden of the Triple Moon

Black: Force, stability, protection, transformation, enlightenment, dignity, banishing and releasing negative energies, Crone of the Triple Moon

Silver: Spiritual development, psychic ability, wisdom, intelligence, memory, meditation, warding off negative vibrations, psychic development, and Divine feminine/female Goddess

Gold: Success, good fortune, ambition, self-realization, intuition, divination, inner-strength, health, finances, and Divine masculine/male God

Brown: Balance, concentration, endurance, solidity, strength, grounding, concentration, material gain, companion animals, home, Earth, and balance

Grey: Contemplation, neutrality, stability, complex decisions, compromise, binding negative influences, complex decisions, and balance

Indigo: Clarity of purpose, spiritual healing, self-mastery, emotion, insight, fluidity, expressiveness, meditation, crown chakra

Pink: Partnerships, friendship, affection, companionship, spiritual healing, child magic, and spiritual awakening; adding herbs, oils, and symbols to your candle magic

Color is vital, and sometimes you will not have colorful candles for every spell, and that is okay. There are other ways to enhance the magic of your candle spells with herbs, oils, and symbols. Anointing your candle with sacred oil is a common practice and simply involves rubbing the scented and consecrated oil all over the wax of the candle before burning it. This can be done on its own, or you can add herbs to the process by rolling the oiled candle through a selection of dried herbs that will correlate with the magic of your spells.

These two simple acts enhance the power of your candle spell significantly and can help you open up even further to Divine guidance and sacred manifestation.

As you learned in the chapters about the *Book of Shadows*, there are a variety of symbols, runes, and sigils that carry significant meaning, which can be used in all of your magical practices to empower your spells. With candle magic, you can carve the symbols directly into the wax to further carry your message to the spirit plane.

Your symbols should be specific to your goals and intentions, and you may need to do some research to decide carefully on which symbols are required for which spell. Trust your intuition, and let it guide you. You can carve the symbols before anointing them with oil and herbs, or after. You can also choose to use the symbols alone without any other ingredients. It is up to you, your spells, and your magical purposes.

Reading the Candle Flame: Divine Communication

There are many ways to read the magic of your spell through the flame of the candle. After the spell words and incantations are spoken and the candle has been lit, you can watch the flame to receive messages about the potential success of your manifestation. There are some who will view the results in the following way, but you may need to use your intuition in these matters, or research other sources:

- **High and Strong Flame**. Manifestation is proceeding quickly.

- **Low and Weak Flame.** There is not much spiritual energy invested in your intentions.

- **Wick with Black/Thick Smoke.** Active opposition exists to your work (possibly coming from ill-meaning people, or your unconscious mind is working against your intentions).

- **Dancing Flame.** It has highly energetic for your spell, but also very chaotic.

- **Flickering Flame.** Spirits are present; prayers are being acknowledged.

- **Popping/Sputtering Flame.** It signifies communication/interference with outside forces; something could be working against you; you may need to add more concentration and energy to your spell.

- **Goes Out Flame.** A flame that just goes out indicates that your work is finished, and a stronger opposing force has ended the work.

- **Candle Will Not Light** = The spell cannot help you with the results you are seeking.

- **Candle Will Not Go Out.** You are not done working, and you need to spend more time with your spell.

There are many more interpretations to consider with candle magic that you can incorporate into your research and *Book of Shadows*, including reading the smoke and its colors; or, how the wax melts or drips, etc. Always tap into your intuition for guidance on these matters, to help you align with your uses in your practice.

Once your candle has burned down, you can find fun in interpreting the melted wax, like reading tea leaves in a cup. The name for this technique is 'ceromancy,' and it will require some practice on your part. It has a lot to do with seeing beyond the reality of what is in front of you and using your power of divination and clairvoyance. You can work on identifying shapes, patterns, symbols, images, and so forth, and try to determine what the 'mood' of the candle spell might be or what is the final message from spirit.

Try not to overthink it, or you might skew and muddle the energy of your spells. Give some practice to it when you are not doing important spell work and have fun with it!

The Intent Behind the Days of the Week

Monday: Monday is ruled by the moon, and deals with fertility, insight, wisdom, beauty, illusion, emotions, and dreams. The colors best used on this day are blue, white, and silver.

Tuesday: Tuesday is ruled by Mars, and deals with victory, success, courage, defense, logic, vitality, conviction. It is a good day to cast problem-solving spells. The colors best used on this day are black, red, and orange.

Wednesday: Wednesday is ruled by Mercury, and deals with luck, change, fortune, creativity, education, insight, and self-improvement. The colors best used on this day are orange, purple, and grey.

Thursday: Thursday is ruled by Jupiter, and deals with prosperity, wealth, healing, abundance, and protection. The best colors to use on this day are purple, green, and blue.

Friday: Friday is ruled by Venus, and deals with love, fertility, birth, romance, passion, friendship, and pregnancy. The best colors to use on this day are green, pink, and blue.

Saturday: Saturday is ruled by Saturn, and deals with wisdom, change, cleansing, motivation, and spirituality. The best colors to use on this day are black, purple, and brown.

Sunday: Sunday is ruled by the Sun, and deals with promotion, success, fame, prosperity, and wealth. It is a good day to cast money spells. The best colors to use this day are gold, yellow, green, and orange.

Now that the days and the colors have been covered, it is time to choose a candle. To choose the color, it is best to correlate your intentions with the color you pick and the day that you cast the spell. For example, if you want to cast a spell that will multiply your wealth, you will want to use gold, yellow, or green candle and cast a spell on a Sunday.

The potency of your desired spell entirely depends on how you choose to organize it. The closer you cast the spell to the intended day, with the right color, the more potent it will be. This is why it is of dire importance to choose your candle with deep thought and preparation.

Most candle spells require the candle flame to burn all the way down naturally on its own, without being disturbed. However, it is hardly a good idea to leave a flame unattended, even in the form of a candle. Staying with the candle as it burns down could take hours, depending on the kind of candle one uses, and most do not have the time to spare. If you absolutely must leave your candle, simply place it in a safe place away from any flammable objects. An empty tub or a sink are examples of safe places to leave the candle, while you go about your daily business. It is also important to note that many oils used for anointing can be highly flammable, and must be used with care. Some spells require the candles to be snuffed out, and it is easy for one to forget that there is oil on their fingers as they try to pinch the candle out. Handle these oils with extra caution.

As you explore and practice the magickal qualities of candles, you will soon take note that if you exercise the appropriate cautions and keep your focus, as well as a sincere intention of doing harm to none, of course, you will begin to see your spell work flourish with success.

Practicing Safety with Candle Magic

Let us be straight and honest: fire is dangerous and can take down a whole house and the surrounding areas with one flame. It is significantly important that you practice fire safety whenever you are using candle magic or any kind of burning ritual in your spellcasting process.

Many candle spells ask that you leave the candle burning until it goes all the way out. If you are trying to conjure certain magic, this is a crucial part of your spell and needs to be considered. All you have to do is make sure that your candle is safe. Do not leave your house while it is burning or check on it periodically while it burns.

You can also find certain kinds of containers, like flat-bottomed cylindrical vases made of glass, to put your candle in to burn. In this kind of container, the flame is contained, and even if gets bumped or knocked over inside the glass, it will be safe.

Additionally, the oils can be flammable if not worked with properly, and the wax and flame can burn your skin, so take necessary precautions while developing your candle magic skills, and make sure you are practicing safe magic.

CHAPTER 6:

Wiccan Spell Casting with Crystals

What Are Crystals?

Gemstones and crystals have been appreciated throughout history for more than their esthetic beauty. Kings, queens, priests and other influences have used amulets and charms of crystals and gems for increasing their power from ancient times.

Today, people worldwide still believe some gems, even crystals, are small storehouses of healing and/or magic energy–from the ability to heal mental and physical illnesses to attract good luck and love.

There are six possible patterns:

- **Isometric crystals** have a cube pattern. They are known to strengthen your energy and improve your situations.

- **Tetragonal crystals** interior is rectangular. They are known to make something attractive to you.

- **Hexagonal crystals** receive their name because their interior resembles a hexagon. These crystals are known to help with manifestation.

- **Orthorhombic crystals** are diamond-shaped. They are best for cleansing and removing blockages.

- **Triclinic crystals** have three inclined axes. Not only will these crystals help you keep the energies you want, but they will chase away unwanted energies.

- **Monoclinic crystals** have a parallelogram structure, which is three-dimensional. They are a source of protection.

Amorphous Crystals

Amorphous crystals are a type of crystal without an internal pattern. This means while it is called a crystal, it is not a true crystal. Real crystals have one of the six types of patterns. However, this does not make amorphous crystals less unique or powerful. All these types of crystals, such as amber, opal, and obsidian, have their own special characteristics.

Common crystals

Crystal quartz is widely used for timekeeping in watches. However, are crystals and gemstones truly magic, or are they the product of the will and conviction of the New Age? The jury is out yet. Here is an alphabetical list of gemstones and the forces to be granted to their wearers.

- Amethyst: It is a gem of inner peace, strength and happiness. Amethyst has been said to improve one's psychic and creative abilities. It is also used to promote nervousness and help break certain addictions.

- Amazonite: Amazonite is a powerful gem for creative people. It promotes sincere communication with their loved ones.

- Amber: Amber, a fossil tree resin, is known to open the crown chakra, and to increase the flow of physical strength and power across the body.

- Bloodstone: Good for the lungs, increases bloodstream oxygen and facilitates relaxation and emotional stress reduction.

- Blue Lace Agate: It can be used to treat skeletal and bone disorders. The healing of bone breaks and fractures is said to be encouraged.

- Carnelian: Carnelian helps to foster feelings of love and acceptance to reduce feelings of fear, insecurity and frustration. Great also for performers and theatre.

- Citrine: Known as the merchant stone, it is thought that citrine attracts capital and develops industry. It also increases gratitude and warm feelings of hope.

- Dumorteiritis: A great gem for friendships, dumorteiritis tends to encourage positive interactions, improve tolerance and make others see the best.

- Fluorite: Good for intellectual development, higher concentration, relaxation. Helps you to consider more abstract, higher concepts. Facilitates interaction between dimensions.

- Garnet: the rock of love and dedication, Grannet helps to balance energies within the body and around it and encourages affection for oneself and others.

- Green Jade: Green jade, a pier for good luck, helps to encourage peace in and around the world.

- Hematite: A stone that encourages inner peace and happiness and growing concentration and trust.

- Honey Jade: Used since ancient times, honey jade improves psychological harmony and spiritual world interaction Iolite: it encourages accountability for money and debt reduction. It is also used to foster partnership harmony.

- Jasper: Jasper is considered a gem of security and caring to wash auras and secure them from negative energies. It also encourages a sense of community and a 'green' view of the world.

- Lapis Lazuli: It is the royalty stone, known for its power and vitality. It protects the wearer from physical and mental risks as well.

- Malachite: The shifting rock, malachite, helps to balance the power and to remain in the right direction. It is also used for treating swollen joints, broken bones and torn muscles.

- Moonstone: The moonstone is a gem of good fortune and security while traveling and called a 'traveler's stone.'

- Obsidian: Known as the 'glazing rock,' because it allows us to take a closer look and solve personal problems. Promotes pardon.

- Onyx: It is used to enhance decision-making, to encourage satisfaction and to attract good luck.

- Peridot: It provides a shield to block negativity and helps promote inner happiness and the release of anger and envy.

- Quartz: A power rock, quartz is known for fostering peace and aligning energies within and around the body.

- Quartz Rose: It helps calm energy, eliminates negativity and cures emotional pain. Well done to have noisy worlds.

- Sodalitis: It encourages mental skills and helps to calm and clear the mind. Also used to improve the lymphatic system and metabolism.

- Tigereye: It encourages cognitive insight, enhances psychological skills and facilitates wealth accumulation and management.

- Turkey: Great for innovation and promotion of open communication and friendship. Used to treat heart, ventilation and breathing problems.

- Unakite: Fosters mental stability, which also promotes healthy pregnancies and children. Used also to research the root cause of disease.

Crystal Magic

Like candles, crystal magic is a very common one, and it allows you to utilize the innate magical power of the crystal. You can use crystals in many types of spells, as protective items, and as magical jewelry. You can also use crystals as focuses for magic, which allows them to direct your raw magical potential. Hence, understanding crystals and crystal magic are very important. Crystal magic is magic that uses crystals to cast spells, and perform rituals and ceremonies. Crystals focus and store magical energy and adding gemstones increases the number of associations in the spell.

Below is a list of the most common uses for a crystal:

- Focus magical energy to empower your spells

- Store magical energy for later use

- Add additional correspondences to strengthen your spells

You might ask, however, what qualifies as a crystal. The answer is that all sorts of minerals, crystals, and gemstones are 'crystals' in pagan and neo-pagan traditions. Hence, you may see a precious gem like a diamond next to a volcanic rock like obsidian. The definition is so loose that that there are a lot of options available. Since each crystal, stone, and mineral has innate magical power, each of them is associated here and are included in the Wiccan definition of a crystal.

The Power of Crystals

Crystal cure is the use of crystals to create healing and positive changes in skin, body and mind. To me, crystals have cured illness, healed emotional trauma, helped me conquer addictions, energized me and changed my life completely!

All gemstones have their own vibrational frequencies, and you can then alter your own vibrational frequency by placing them on your body or aura. In fact, crystals serve as amplifiers. They reinforce the goal and produce the desired result much more quickly.

In all shapes, sizes and colors there are many different crystals, and they each have their own unique properties for dealing with various physical and emotional problems. You may get crazy and try to hunt for the exact crystals you feel you want.

You have to do this in the opposite direction, the crystal picks you! So, when you are in a crystal shop choosing crystals to take home, stop and come back to the very first crystal you encountered because it was probably the crystal you picked.

When you purchase your new natural products, other arrangements have to be made first before they are able to be used. I am sure you are excited, and you want to use it already, but these next steps are a crucial part of the whole process of crystal healing.

You first need to clean up any negative energy the crystals have consumed. If you were in a shop and several people may have reached you, and the crystal can easily absorb the negative energy that the shop holds, so you definitely do not want it in your field of energy. You will also need to clean your crystals occasionally depending on how you use them.

There are numerous active crystal clearing methods. The simplest and one of the most effective way to do this, is to keep the negative energy in your hands and retain it for one to two minutes under running water.

The hull works perfectly. Some other clearing methods include putting them in salt for several hours; burying them in the earth for one day or more; or simply using your breath. Phase two is to adjust the new crystal to your vibrational frequency, and to plan to only be used for you or anyone else who uses the new crystal.

You simply need to keep the crystal in your hands, close your eyes and set your intentions. You can either say it aloud or just feel it is successful either way. Third, mount your crystals. Only put your crystals for a minimum of five hours in direct sunlight. You can also place them under the light of a new or full moon overnight.

The last step is to customize your crystals for what you want them to do. You can, for instance, claim they should be used for general healing, protection or grounding, etc. This is an optional move which can be done or not.

The explanation that you can do this is because you program a crystal for a certain function to adapt it to the frequency of your needs; it can produce the desired effect even more easily.

To do this, keep the crystal in your hand and say, "I will use, " loudly (not in your head), and fill in the blanks. Repeat these terms 3 to 4 times, to program the crystal fully. You are ready to use your new crystals now!

There are many ways to use your crystals; it depends on your requirements. You can wear them as jewels or take one or two of them with you in your own pocket or purse (if you are using them like that, note that you have to wash your crystals more often as they will be easier to absorb any negative elements of the setting you are in).

You can also meditate on or around your crystals, which significantly intensify your meditation. Through putting the corresponding stones on each chakra, you will balance and clear your chakras using crystals to clear and balance them. For clearing or security, you can hold crystals around your room or in your working area.

In the night, you can even place those stones under your pillow to enhance your dreams, or to better sleep. The possibilities of crystals are endless and will enrich your life in all ways! I hope you are as happy to use crystals as I do!

Crystals are amazing conduits of energy, and can be regularly used in any of your magic spells. Like a candle, crystals are excellent channels to add even more specific energy and magic to any of your incantations and magical purposes. As you have read throughout the book, there are several spells already that contain a crystal or gemstone that can bring you additional energy and success.

Crystals collect and receive energy and hold onto it. They will carry any information you wish to implant into them for a long period. They can also collect energies that you do not want them to have.

Hence, it is common practice to cleanse and purify your crystals between spells or if they are used often for specific reasons.

Purification and cleansing can occur in a cast circle or at any other time that feels appropriate. Warm saltwater, sunlight, and smoke from and smudge stick are all ways to cleanse your stones and crystals of unwanted, old, or stagnate energies. Furthermore, once they are purified, you can then imbue them with whatever magical intentions you want them to collect and hold. Some Wiccans and witches will refer to this step as 'consecration.

All stones and crystals already have unique qualities and properties that will reflect certain energy into your spell. Some are more appropriate energies for healing and health, while others about psychic power and divination. There are stones for love and stones for protection and grounding. The list of possible crystals is long and will require additional research on your journey, so you can find all the stones that resonate most with your practice. The next section will give you a list of some of the more commonly used and essential stones.

The Energy of Crystals

Some people are better at sensing energy than other people. While some of this depends on your understanding of energy, part of it depends on how in-tune you are when it comes to vibes. A vibe is energy you recognize when it comes to another person or object. It is energy that you feel is not compatible with your own.

When someone else's energy starts to affect your own, this is called *entrainment*. For example, your friend walks into the room and sits down by you. Without saying anything, your mood starts to shift from peaceful and happy to sad. Entrainment can occur with one person or with a whole room.

Crystals have a higher vibration than humans. This means that their energy can raise our energy, which allows us to move in a more positive way emotionally, mentally, and physically. It also allows us to become more spiritual.

In order to become a crystal healer, you need to be able to feel the energy from the crystal. For some people, this is going to come more natural than other people. If you feel that you struggle to sense the crystal's energy, you should not keep this from fulfilling your dreams as a healer. Instead, you need to focus on strengthening your connection with the energy from crystals. Here are some ways you can do this:

Hold a Crystal Between the Palms of Your Hands During Meditation

If you meditate, then you can connect with a crystal by holding it through your meditation. All you need to do is place it between the palms of your hands and hold the crystal there as you breathe. You can continue focusing on your breathing as you meditate, as the crystal's energy will work its magic during your meditation. However, you should also be aware that there are some crystals you will not find yourself connecting to easily. This does not mean that you cannot become a crystal healer. It is natural for some crystals to resonate with you more than other crystals. If you find yourself in this position, try meditating with a different crystal. This is the perfect opportunity to experiment with crystals.

One of the best crystals to start out with during meditation is the amethyst. With this crystal, you can find yourself in a deeper state of meditation. The amethyst not only makes people feel more at peace but also helps boost positivity.

Create a Special Place for Your Crystals

Sacred spaces are becoming popular. This is a place within your home that you design for a specific reason. For example, if you practice yoga, you might create a space for this activity. Wiccans will create their own workspace or altar, which is where they perform their spells. If you are struggling to connect to your crystals, create a special place for them. This can help them grow within the space, and help you connect to their energies as you will begin to feel an energy shift when you enter this space. You do not have to dedicate a whole room to your crystals unless you are able and want to. A corner of your bedroom or another area in your home you are comfortable is a great place. The key is to ensure this space is for your crystals.

Place Crystals Around Your Home

Along with sacred space, you can also place crystals around your home. You can use them as décor but allow them to hold a special purpose as well. For instance, if you feel your home could use more good luck, then you will choose a Malachite crystal. It does not matter where you place the crystal if you feel it is the right place. If you are looking for a place for the Malachite crystal and find yourself drawn to an end table near the couch, place the crystal there. You can also place the crystal in the center of your home as this will allow the energies to focus on more than one area.

It is also a good idea to change the location of your crystal from time to time. For example, you can place it on a shelf in your kitchen for a month, and then move the crystal to your bedroom the following month. This will not only spread the energy around your home but will also give you a stronger connection to your crystal. When we see an object in the same spot day after day, we become used to it and can forget it is there. However, when you take the time to move the object, your mind is more aware of the object, and you are less likely to find yourself glancing over it as you walk by.

Place a Crystal Directly on Your Body

One way to place a crystal on your body is through *reiki healing*. This is usually done by a healer and helps you focus on self-improvement. If this is what you want to do, you will need to ensure you use the right crystals in coordination with your chakras. This healing is often used to heal your emotions.

You do not need to use reiki when placing crystals on your body. Find the time when you can focus on the energy of the crystals, and lay them anywhere on your body. As you do this, you can imagine the energy from the crystals going into your body. Focus on the crystal and how your body feels in connection to the crystal.

Carry Crystals with You

After Wiccans perform a spell with a crystal, they will often carry the crystal with them for a period. This allows the energy from the crystal to follow them through their situation. For example, if they cast a spell to help ease anxiety during a presentation, they will have the crystal in their pocket during their presentation. You can also carry crystals with you in order to connect with them. Of course, many people find carrying smaller crystals is easier than larger ones. However, if you are trying to connect with a larger crystal, you can place it in your car while you are driving, on your desk at work, and in your home. Even if you cannot fit the crystals in your pocket, you might be able to carry them safely in a purse or backpack.

Make Sure You Are Open to the Experience

Some people struggle to connect to crystals because they are not opening themselves up to the experience. There are many reasons for this which range from feeling judged too anxious about the unknown. The more open you are to the powers within your crystal, the more you will come to acknowledge what you feel from the crystal.

If you were raised to think crystal healing is fake, it could be hard to change this mindset. You must set aside any preconceived notions about crystals, their powers, and healing, in order to break down the barriers that keep you from feeling their energy. This can be a process, and it is important to be patient with yourself as you are opening yourself up. One way to do this is to give yourself the attitude of curiosity. In a way, you want to get into the mindset of a child looking at something new.

Another way is to go through various outcomes about how crystal healing can work and how it will not. The biggest factor to note when you are doing this is not to create expectations. Do not tell yourself that, "This needs to happen" or, "That should not happen." Instead, leave the door open for anything to happen.

Focus on the Crystal You Are Most Attracted To

People are attracted to crystals for a reason. So, when you find a crystal that you feel a connection to, you will want to use this crystal for your healing purposes. If you have a few crystals, you will be able to gauge which crystal calls to you over the others. If you are shopping for a crystal, hold a few of them and see which one you cannot take your eyes from. Sometimes the connection will be intense, and you will automatically know that is the crystal you need to choose. Do not second guess your intuition.

Charging Crystals

Before you use your crystals, you need to make sure they are prepared for use. You can do this by making sure that the crystals are charged with magical energy. The process for preparing crystals for use is similar to consecrating magical tools or dressing a candle.

To prepare your crystals for use, follow these instructions:

Magical Tools

5 white candles

White or colored chalk, table salt, or wand

Incense and censer

Herbs

Oils

Boline

Incantations

"Oh, Ishtar!

Oh, Horned King!

Oh, Moon Mother!

Oh, Tammuz!

Bless this stone with your magic touch!"

Steps in Charging

1. Dress the candles for the ritual. You can do this by carving a rune or sigil into the candle and by rubbing oil and/or herbs on the candle. Use the various charts and information in this book to find appropriate candle colors and other associations to use. Often, you want the color of the candle to be similar to the color of the gemstones.

2. Make a magic circle using table salt, white chalk, or a wand. Alternately, you can use a color of chalk that is associated with the crystal you are charging.

3. Enter the circle using a doorway.

4. Draw a pentacle in the circle using the white chalk, another color of chalk, table salt, or a wand.

5. Put a candle at each point of the pentacle.

6. Put the crystals, gemstones, or minerals in the middle of the pentacle.

7. Light the candles and incense.

8. Repeat the incantation.

9. Place the crystals, gemstones, or minerals on an altar/stang.

10. Sit cross-legged and visualize energy flowing into the crystals, gemstones, or minerals you want to charge.

11. Exit the circle using a doorway.

12. Allow the candles to burn out.

13. Break the circle and allow the energy to dissipate.

14. Remove the crystals from the middle of the pentacle.

15. Take the burned-out candles and bury them near a large tree.

16. Let the stone sit out for one night. It is better if you do this on a New or Full moon.

Crystals in Wicca Practice

Hold a crystal in your hand and look at it closely from every angle. Turn it over and over again. If you stop for a minute and clear your mind, you will be able to feel the sense of mysterious wonder that stones and crystals have. They silently speak of the living, creative, and infinite power of the Earth. For millennia people have worshipped and used crystals for many purposes. In modern times stones and crystals are used for magical purposes, for alternative healing, and for enhancing the innate energy of physical spaces.

Casting the circle is important in a ritual because it marks the line that is used to create a boundary between the ordinary world and the sacred space where the ritual will be performed. Your altar will usually be in the center of the circle. When the ritual is being performed by a coven, the altar will definitely be in the center of the circle so that everyone can move around freely and not need to worry about stepping outside the sacred circle accidentally. If you are a solo practitioner your altar is most likely set against the wall, so the sacred circle would be a semi-circle, that would encompass the altar and give you room to move freely. You can mark the parameters of the circle with candles, sea salt, herbs, or crystals and stones. Many Wiccans like to use stones and crystals, because they will aid in the energy needed to send their intentions out into the spiritual plane of the universe.

On your altar, you will find stones and crystals useful and necessary. Pentacles and wands are often decorated with crystals, and the points of the pentacle can be marked with crystals. You will also need to represent the four cardinal Elements on your altar, and you can use crystals for this.

East is the element of Air, and can be represented with alexandrite, amethyst, pumice, or topaz.

South is the element of Fire, and can be represented with volcanic lava, fire opal, or ruby.

West is the element of Water, and can be represented by blue topaz, coral, pearl, blue tourmaline, or aquamarine.

North is the element of Earth, and can be represented by quartz, jasper, onyx, or emerald.

Ether, or Spirit, is the fifth element, and is often used on the altar during ritual worship. It has no particular stones to represent its presence.

During their practice of magic a Wiccan will use stones and crystals for many different magical purposes. They are used for everything from talismans, amulets, healing, divination, and manifesting intentions through spell work. Stones and crystals can be used to intensify a spell or as the main focus of the spell work. Working magic spells focus on making one's own circumstances better, whether it be in the area of love, money, romance, happiness, health, or protection. You can also cast spells to help you develop spiritually or mentally. You can use them in meditation to reflect on the path of your life or to create intentions for balance and continued growth. Some workings of magic come from ancient traditions, and some are inspired on the spot and created then. Divination, visualization, making potions, dancing, incantations, rituals, and charms are all types of magic where stones and crystals can be used to energize and enhance the magic.

Keep in mind that no matter what type of magic you are performing with your stones and crystals, you will never create magic that is meant to harm another entity, particularly another person. Wiccans who practice magic always keep in mind the Golden Rule of Wiccans, the Wiccan Rede, that states that magic will never be used to cause harm. Your magical intentions must always be clear, so that you do not accidentally cause harm to another, or interfere with their free will. If you are casting a spell to help someone else, then you must gain their permission first. When intentions are manifested in the physical realm, they might accidentally cause harm to another, so all spells are ended with a phrase to guard against this, such as "to harm no one" or "with harm to none."

Remember that your practice of magic means that you need to practice. No one will be successful in the beginning. You will need to be patient and learn from your mistakes. Make sure you are going into your practice with an open mind and heart, because even the smallest bit of resistance or skepticism will cause your spell not to work the way in which you want it to work.

Crystals in Chakra Cleansing, Healing, and Balancing

The literal translation of the word 'chakra' means a spinning wheel or disk. When you are referring to a chakra on your body, the reference means a wheel or a spinning disk of energy that is found along your spinal column. The area along the spinal column contains seven chakras that are directly connected to your emotional, spiritual, and physical wellbeing. The chakra is a point of focus inside your body that you can imagine as a structure of energy that looks like a disk. These are located at points in your body where many meridians or channels come together.

The modern practice based on the chakras searches for a more pure and traditional way of living, by associating each chakra with various physical functions: an aspect of consciousness; a classical element; and numerous other characteristics that are used to distinguish one chakra from another.

Your chakras are the power that provides vitality to your body, and provides influence for the mental, emotional, and physical movements of your body and your mind. Your chakras are the main positions of the life energy that flows through each on a specific pathway. The main function of each of your chakras is to spin on its own axis, and use its power to pull in energy and to hold that energy inside you, in order to balance and maintain your physical, mental, emotional, and spiritual health of your mind, soul, and body.

In an effort to adopt a lifestyle that is more natural, and free from chemical and medicinal influences, more people are seeking natural ways to keep themselves healthy and well-balanced both mentally and physically. The basic belief in the power of the chakras has not changed over the years. This belief states that the energy that was released during the creation of the world, the *Kundalini*, sleeps wrapped in a coil at the base of your spine. Your goal is to awaken this energy and cause it to rise through your chakras until it reaches the highest chakra on top of your head. Then, you will be able to achieve a reunion with the higher powers of the universe.

Sometimes your chakras will be unbalanced or unhealthy. They may not open far enough, or they may be too widely open. They may close completely and block the transmission of energy through that particular chakra. Anytime any one of these things happens to you the energy that flows through you will not flow in the easy, gentle manner in which it was meant to flow. It will either be slowed, blocked, or flow through too quickly. When this happens your body and mind will be affected. This will cause mental issues, spiritual doubts, and physical ailments. Your 'chi' (pronounced CHEE), which is your life force, is unable to move through your body.

When your chakras are not right and your chi does not flow well, you can develop injuries or diseases in the area of the body that is governed by that chakra. When you spend time on healing and balancing your chakras, then you will clear these issues and restore good health to your body. When you heal your chakras, you will take control of your spiritual, emotional, mental, and physical wellbeing. Your body will send out signals that will tell you when one or more chakras need your assistance. You might be experiencing feelings of depression, isolation, poor social skills, problems sleeping, poor motivation, difficulty concentrating, or the inability to accomplish goals in your life at home or work.

There are seven major chakras, and they correspond with the different systems of your body. Your chakras are supposed to work together to provide energy and balance for you. The chakras, as centers of energy inside you, process and contain all of the energy in your body. The chakras have the power to destroy your life or to sustain it. When you have a chakra that is closed or blocked, then the energy that is contained within that chakra can be slow or stagnant, and that will affect the body parts and the organs which that chakra is attached to. However, if one of your chakras has an abundance of energy, it will absorb the energy that is stored in the nearby chakras, and it can overwhelm your energy system entirely.

At the base of your spine is the Root Chakra. This is the chakra where the energy begins to flow through the remainder of your chakras. The Root Chakra helps to give balance to your body. It is associated with your feet, legs, and bowels. It is also associated with the end of your spine, your pelvic floor, and the bottom three vertebrae in your spine. The Root Chakra is the center of your survival, security, and primal needs. When it is blocked you might experience irrational fears, anxiety disorders, and problems sleeping to include nightmares. The Root Chakra is considered to be the foundation of the other chakras and the human body.

The next chakra is the Sacral Chakra, which holds the key to your deepest emotions and sensations. This chakra controls how your feelings and emotions are held and expressed inside your body. Deep inside the lower part of your abdomen, the Sacral Chakra controls your bladder, kidneys, hips, lower back, and your reproductive system. It is responsible for your sexuality and creativity. When your Sacral Chakra is well-balanced, you will feel passionate, fulfilled, and friendly. When it is blocked, you will feel uninspired, unstable, and depressed.

Inside of the upper part of your abdomen and just above your belly button is your Solar Plexus Chakra. This chakra rules your sense of self-esteem and carries your inner Fire. People with a damaged Solar Plexus Chakra will often feel defeated, timid, insecure, or unreasonably angry. When your Solar Plexus chakra is well-balanced and healthy, you will feel confident, friendly, courageous, and optimistic. This chakra governs your stomach, spleen, gallbladder, liver, and pancreas.

The center chakra of the seven is the Heart Chakra, which is located in the center of your chest. It controls the heart, arms, lungs, and circulatory system. Your Heart Chakra will not only become imbalanced when you have been hurt by love, but also when you refuse to open your heart to love from other people. The Heart Chakra needs to give and receive love freely in order to function properly. This is the chakra where your physical being and your spiritual being meet. Your Throat Chakra, located in your throat, controls your neck, throat, shoulders, mouth, jaw, and thyroid gland. People with an unhealthy Throat Chakra have problems speaking their truth, either talks excessively or stay silent for long periods of time, and find it difficult to communicate with other people. If your self-expression is stifled you may refuse to express yourself, and this will damage the Throat Chakra.

The Throat Chakra is the first one of the three spiritual chakras; all the ones below it are physical chakras.

The highest chakra in your body is your Crown Chakra. This chakra connects you to the spiritual world. The Crown Chakra controls your cerebral cortex, which is responsible for your ability to process language, the functioning of your senses, your fine and gross motor skills, and your intelligence and personality.

It also controls your pineal gland, which is the gland that controls all of the hormone production and function in your body.

An unhealthy Crown Chakra will make you feel irrationally fearful of spirituality, be overly opinionated, and have problems understanding spiritual concepts. When your Crown Chakra is healthy and balanced you will feel spiritually awake and alive, more evolved and more exalted.

Crystals and stones have natural healing properties that can balance and activate the energy systems of your chakras. The energy of the stones and crystals resonates with the individual energy of each of the chakras. So, they can be used to activate the balancing and movement of the natural energy that lives inside you. You will use the power of your imagination and intention to use stones to heal your chakras.

Each chakra will have several stones and crystals available that you can use to heal and balance it. You will want to use the particular stone or crystal that feels right to you. Pick the stone up at hold it in your hand. Stones that are best for you will feel tingly or warm to you. They might glow or give you a special feeling. That is how you will know the crystal or stone is right for you.

There are several different methods that you can use to heal your chakras with your stones and crystals. You can lie down and place the stone directly over the chakra while meditating on your intention. You can wear crystals and chakras as jewelry to encourage your chakras to stay in balance. You can keep the stone or crystal in your pocket or simply hold it in your hand.

Your chakras are vital to the health of your body and your mind. The chakras are responsible for bringing energy into your body, and flowing it through your body to provide energy for your spiritual, mental, emotional, and physical health. Your chakras are always changing even while they remain rooted and stable in your body.

Crystals for Life Enhancement and Assistance

Even if you do not cast magic spells as a Wiccan or wish to balance and heal your chakras, there are times in your life when you will benefit from the energy that certain crystals and stones can give you. People have used crystals since ancient times for their powers to heal and provide energy. Crystals can bring you greater happiness, help you live in good health, and resolve deep-seated personal issues. Some crystals are better used to attract prosperity and abundance, and some are better for protection and shielding. Still others are good for harmony, love, and relationships.

The Best Crystals for Magic

When it comes to using crystals in magic, it is important that you understand their correspondences. This will help you to pick out the best crystals for your spells, and to find alternatives if you cannot find the crystal the spell calls for. These crystals are the most commonly used ones and tend to be some of the easier ones to find.

Amethyst

The amethyst has been one of the most admired stones due to its legendary powers, and beauty to help soothe and stimulate the emotions and mind. The ancients referred to this stone as a 'gem of fire.' It is connected to February, which was the month that the Romans dedicated to their god, Neptune. It is also the traditional birthstone for February. It is also a faithful, love stone. It has been referred to as the Bishop's Stone as well. It holds spirituality, creativity, passion, and fire, but it also bears the logic of sobriety and temperance.

Amethysts are a great stone to use when you are looking to be creative. It can help in things where original results are important. They have often been called the painter, poet, inventor, composer, and artist's stone.

Quartz

The clear quartz crystal is the most abundant and most common crystal in the world. It makes up the most diverse and the largest family in the mineral kingdom. Since ancient times, the clear quartz has been a light to mankind.

Most of the time, when a person uses the word crystal, they are talking about the clear quartz. Quartz are the supreme gift from Mother Earth. Even the smallest piece is filled with the properties of a master healer. The ancient people believed that these stones were alive and that they took a breath every hundred years. There are many countries who believed that they are the physical incarnation of the Divine.

Healers today still believe that the clear quartz is alive. They believe that they are wise and old, and will communicate to anybody who is ready and open to receive their message. Meditating with, carrying, or wearing clear quartz can open up the heart and mind to higher guidance. It gives the spirit realm the ability to be translated and transmitted into the world physically.

Jet

Jet is not made like the other crystals we have talked about. It is formed when pieces of wood are buried, compacted, and go through an organic degradation process. Once it becomes heated, it will form a coal seam. This stone tends to be black in color, but some will appear brown. They can easily be carved or cut, and its uniform texture makes it easy to carve accurately.

They can be polished and will have a bright shine. Jet can be found all over the US, Poland, France, Germany, Spain, India, and Russia. This stone can help to provide you with spiritual, emotional, and physical guidance that will help you to reach your goals and find harmony and balance. When paired with aragonite, it can help to show you how you can reach the top of any situation during tough times.

Jet allows you to focus on your life, relationships, and career. It can help to guide you through accomplishing your goals by using your natural abilities, skills, and talents. Jet also helps you to own up to any mistakes you make, make amends with others you have wronged, and right the wrongs.

Obsidian

Obsidian is often called the mirror. If you find that you are particularly drawn to obsidian and all of its intense and mysterious vibes, it could mean that you need a psychic cleanse. It is often known as the 'psychic vacuum cleaner.' Obsidian helps to work as your personal spiritual maid service, and helps to get rid of your emotional wreckage and any debris you have from your past. It helps to protect your soul.

Obsidian is known for its grounding and stabilizing abilities, which makes it a great option for reigning in your scattered energy If you start to feel as if you are being spread too thin, grab an obsidian and feel it restore all of your harmony and bring you back to Earth.

Wearing jewelry with obsidian can leave you feeling renewed and confident.

When it comes to making layouts, obsidian can help to bring in a strong presence with its grounding abilities. If you feel as if you are lost in the clouds, it can cause unwelcome side effects, which can cause feelings of isolation and procrastination. If you are feeling spiritually lost, obsidian is able to bring you harmonious balance. Obsidian helps keep you anchored to Earth.

Lapis Lazuli

Since it was discovered, lapis lazuli has been one of the most sought-after crystals. Its coloring is a celestial blue, which shows honor and royalty, vision and spirit, and Gods and power. This stone has always been a symbol of truth and wisdom.

Lapis lazuli is a great stone for psychologists, journalists, and executives. It is able to stimulate good judgment and wisdom. It will also help historians and archeologists with their intellectual analysis. It can help lawyers to solve problems. It is also able to provide writers and inventors with new and creative ideas.

It can help to stimulate the desire for knowledge, understanding, and truth. It is also able to help with the learning process and can improve your memory. It is considered a stone of truth, and can help to encourage honesty of the written and spoken word, and spirit.

Labradorite

This stone can help you to find the magic within your spirit and to connect to the universe. It is one of the best stones to help fight off a philosophical crisis. It is a shimmering, mythical light that separates the normal world from unseen realms. It is a magic stone. A crystal of healers, Diviners, *Shamans*, and anyone who travels and embraces the universe while seeking guidance and knowledge. It is great to help you awaken your psychic abilities, intuition, and being aware of your inner spirit. The labradorite reminds us to keep life magical by helping us link ourselves to the spiritual world where anything is possible.

Labradorite is considered a protector. It helps to shield your aura and to strengthen your natural energy. It will also help to protect you against misfortunes, negativity, and provides you with a safe exploration into the alternate levels of your consciousness.

Selenite

Selenite is also a cleansing stone and does not need to be cleansed like others. In fact, you can place other crystals on or near selenite to help cleanse and recharge them. A wand made of selenite can be used to cleanse your body, as well as other stones.

How Crystal Energy Works

Crystal healing is something that anyone can do. You do not have to hold special powers or be psychic. All you need to do is to open yourself up to the crystal, and allow its energy to come through you.

On the foundation, crystal energy works by fusing with your body's energy. Once the crystal's energy is within you, it transforms some of your energy. Therefore, people can place an amethyst on their desk at work and feel less stressed. You do not always need to hold the crystal in order to feel its energy. It will work when it is near you, as long as you allow the energy to come through you. The reason why you start to feel less stressed and more at peace is that the energy from the crystal helps you find your inner balance.

It is important to pay attention to your body and emotions. You want to notice what you are thinking and feeling daily. When you do this, you will learn what energies you are lacking or what crystals are best to help you find your balance. It does not matter if you are focusing on your physical, mental, emotional, or spiritual self. The energies from crystals can help you in all these areas.

However, it is important you realize in order to gain the best from your crystals, you need to focus on caring and cleansing them. When you cleanse, you are pushing out any undesirable energy from the crystals. Just like we can collect negative energy, crystals can collect negativity as well. You will not be able to find your balance or use the crystal's energy correctly if it is tainted with negativity.

Getting to Know Your Crystals

Anytime you acquire a new crystal, you would want to spend some time getting to know the crystal, bond with it, and align it with your energy. This is true of plain crystals you get, tools that have crystals built into them, and even jewelry with crystals in it.

Before bonding with your crystals, you will first want to cleanse them. Even crystals that you buy new will still have been exposed to different people's energies. Before you can bond and align with a crystal, it has to have a clean energy slate to align with your power properly.

Once a crystal has been aligned with your energy, you can then charge and program them for magical use.

There are several methods for aligning with crystal energies. One of the most popular methods is to carry the crystal with you, in your pocket, purse, or backpack for three days. This will give the crystal time to absorb your energy in various forms as you carry it with you during your daily activities.

During these three days, if you touch the crystal periodically or squeeze it in your hand, this will further deepen the bond between you and your crystal.

Another bonding method similar to carrying the crystal with you is to wear the crystal. This is easiest with crystals that are already in the form of a necklace, ring, bracelet, anklet, or any jewelry or accessory.

On the market, there are also wire-cage necklaces that can be used to hold a crystal while you bond with it, and then you can change the crystal inside as needed. Additionally, you can purchase a small medicine bag or leather pouch and keep a crystal inside as a way to wear the crystal for alignment.

Wearing a crystal in a way that allows the crystal to have contact with your skin is a great way to bond and align with crystals. Not only does it connect to your energy, but it also connects to your physical body. Contact is a powerful way to bond and align with crystals.

When wearing a crystal, you will want to wear it for three days and three nights to align it to your power.

Not all methods of bonding with your crystals have to take several days. There are methods to align with and bond with crystals that do not take as long. Another consideration is the size of the crystal. Some crystals are large or oddly shaped, and they do not make ideal candidates for wearing or carrying around.

One simple method for bonding with crystals is to hold the crystal in your hand and sit in a stationary position for 3–5 minutes. During this time, focus completely on the crystal in your hand.

When the stipulated time has passed, set the crystal on your altar overnight. Then, you can use the crystal for magic.

For jewelry, a similar method is to hold the piece of jewelry in your hand for 3–5 minutes after cleansing it. Keep your mind focused on that piece of jewelry. Once the time has passed, wear the piece of jewelry for 5–10 minutes before taking it off.

With crystals that correspond to a specific chakra in your energetic anatomy, touching the crystal to that chakra in your body and holding it there for 1–2 minutes, will help align that crystal specifically to your chakra, especially if you decide to use it in healing or chakra magic. You should use an additional bonding or aligning method with your crystal, before aligning it with a specific chakra.

Meditating on a crystal is another way to bond or align with the crystal's energy. You can hold the crystal while meditating, or set it before you on your altar. Light a few candles to set the atmosphere, and allow yourself to sink into a meditative state. Focus your thoughts on the crystal, and if your mind tries to wander, refocus on your crystal.

Meditating for 5–15 minutes with your crystal as the focal point should be enough to align and bond to the crystal. While meditating on a crystal, you might also receive information from the crystal in the form of visions, sounds, smells, feelings, etc. Anything that you experience during meditation with a crystal is worth taking note of and transcribing later.

If you are proficient in an energy-healing modality, such as *Reiki*, you can use that healing energy to help bond with your crystals as well. Crystals themselves are powerful healers, and when combined with energy healing, it amplifies that power. This allows you to create a strong bond with your crystals.

Crystals, that you intend to use for healing, can become stronger healers if aligned with energy-healing techniques.

If you have crystals that you intend to use on your altar for elemental representations, make sure to bond with them with your preferred binding method. Then, align them with the elemental energy by bringing them into contact with an element associated with the object.

For example, a feather or the wand can be used for Air. A candle flame or athame can be used for Fire. A chalice or rainwater can be used for Water. A dish of rock salt or a pentagram can be used for Earth. There are many other representations for the elements that can be used to align your crystals with their corresponding element.

If you have crystals that you would like to designate as a deity representation, first, bond with the crystal via your preferred method. Then, align the crystal to your deity as well. One option for aligning a crystal to a deity is to speak an incantation that names both the crystal and deity. Another option is to set the crystal on your altar in the space you have designated for the deity, and light a candle and meditate for a moment, visualizing the crystal representing the form of your deity.

When you use altar tools that have crystals in them, bond with them directly, and then allow the tool to sit on your altar for three days to soak up the altar's energy, along with the element the deity represents. This way, once you are ready to use the tools, they will have a sense of the energy of the other objects they will be working with.

Aligning and bonding with crystals to yourself, elements, a deity, and to your altar help facilitate a strong, energetic connection. This connection ensures smoother, balanced, and harmonious magic and ritual practices.

The more crystals you work with and bond with, the more you will find your preferred methods for bonding with them.

Even after bonding with a crystal, it is recommended that you meditate with your crystals periodically. Not only does this reinforce the bond, but it also allows you to spend time with their energy and get to know them.

Carrying bonded crystals with you is another way to keep getting to know them. Crystals are energetic entities, and keeping that bond strong is the most effective way to get the best magical results with your crystals.

Once your crystals have been bonded to you and aligned to any other energies they are meant to represent or work with, you can begin using them in spells and crystal grids.

While crystals are powerfully energetic in their own right, charging and programming your crystals before using them for spells is a way to supercharge your crystals and their magical output.

Programming crystals is a Wiccan ritual that aligns your crystal with energies, to perform or aid in a specific task. Essentially, programming is just communicating to your crystal what you need from it, so that it can assist in the task or project.

You do not need to program your crystals to use them in spells to achieve certain goals or to make crystal grids. However, programming a crystal for a specific purpose can act as a simple crystal spell or help you achieve your goals in your everyday life.

Think of a programmed crystal as a laser pointer. The programming gives the laser focus and intense direction for where the energy should be channeled.

A lot of crystal jewelry that is sold for a specific purpose, such as healing, positivity, and luck has been programmed by the maker to ensure that the wearer gets that attribute from wearing the crystal piece.

Meaning of crystals in Spell Work and Magic

Crystals are pretty to look at. For many pagans, our Magick can be carried out with the assistance of gemstones and crystals! Dealing with crystals are used because energy to be conducted by their capability. Whenever you are working using a crystal, purpose, your energy, and electricity are concentrated into the crystal clear and mix. This energy that is joining to makes workings and your spells all that powerful. The very first thing would be to wash them to rid of any energy it might hold. There are approaches: let it sit at the moon, put the crystal water, bury the crystal from the ground, or use rosemary to cleanse the power. You will read many procedures that are different. The fact is, like magic, it is private to the caster. Make certain it will not harm your crystal! If you choose to work throughout your spell function with crystals, there are a couple of approaches.

Sleep with a crystal under your pillow or in/on your night table. If you are familiar with that, you may maintain the crystal. Possessing a crystal close to your mattress as you sleep amethyst, selenite, jasper, etc. will help encourage relaxation. Some stones might help you interpret and recall your dreams!

Write out a listing of goals, or a spell, and maintain the crystal. This is an excellent way to incorporate crystals to spell bodily work. Write a goal list out and pick. You place that crystal, and the crystal will charge those goals. Keep this onto a shelf or an altar if you have one; therefore, it is not disturbed and reevaluates your listing as needed.

Use crystals. Many crystal types are good to clean negative energy out, as we will discuss below. Utilize these during a shower or a tub, and wash out any emotions that you are holding onto!

Use crystals. You can use there to guide the energy you would like of the crystal when you are using a crystal stage. Since you hold the crystal, you could feel a shake or vibration! This usually means you are in tune with all the crystal and it has possessions!

Cleansing your crystal

Once you have picked your crystals, the next thing you need to do is make sure you take care of your crystals. Crystals are like any other magical or spiritual tool you use. Before you ever use them, you should make sure that they have been charged and cleansed. Crystals have very sensitive to energies, and will take in and amplify all energies around them.

You need to make sure you are careful when cleansing your crystals. You need to make sure you know if your crystals are heat- or water-sensitive. For example, selenite, halite, and azurite are all water soluble. Some crystals are porous, like turquoise, lapis lazuli, and opal. Pink quartz and amethysts can fade if they are left in direct sunlight for too long. If you are not sure, a safe bet would be to place them outside under the light of a Full Moon. Moonlight is not going to hurt your crystals, and is a great way to cleanse them.

If you have people over and they end up touching your crystals without your permission, you will want to cleanse them once they leave. Trust me; you do not ever want to work with crystals that have been touched by other people. Their energy can end up hurting your work. The best way to make sure this does not happen is to keep your crystals somewhere others cannot find them.

The cleansing rituals we are going to go over are able to be done at any time you feel your crystals need a cleansing. You should listen to your intuition when dealing with your crystals. If they do not feel right, then you should cleanse them. It is not going to hurt them.

Sometimes people will say you should cleanse your crystals during a New Moon or waning moon, but if you know they have absorbed negativity, you should not wait. You should not let negativity hang around for any longer than it has to.

These cleansing rituals are very simple. Before doing these, you can cast a circle, but you do not have to. Beginners tend to do better if they are working in a circle so that the energy is contained. None of these require an incantation, but if you feel like you need to say something, then follow your intuition.

Air Cleansing

Cleansing crystals with smoke is one of the oldest methods of cleansing. To do this, you are going to need incense or a smudge stick. The best options are copal, sage, or rosemary. Begin by lighting your incense, and then pass your crystal through the smoke. As you do this, start to picture all of the impurities and negativities inside of them start to be burned away. This can be done as many times as you feel you need to. Let the incense burn out completely, or you can stub the smudge stick out in the Earth.

Earth Cleansing

This is the easiest cleansing method. With this, you are giving the energies back to the Earth. It works best when this is done outside. If you do this inside, you should use a bowl of salt, dirt, or sand. First, you will dig a hole and put your crystal inside of it. You should make sure that your crystal is not going to dissolve in the dirt, because some will. Let the crystal stay there and picture the Earth receiving all of the unwanted energies within your crystal. Leave the crystal is the Earth for as long as you feel like you need to.

Fire Cleansing

This is considered an aggressive but powerful cleansing method. Be careful not to burn yourself or your crystal. You will need a red candle for this. A fireplace will also work if you have one.

Light the candle and state your intent of cleansing your crystal; summon Fire into your space. Next, quickly pass your crystal through the flame, and imagine that the fire is burning away all of its impurities and negativities. Do this for as long as you feel you need to. After you are done, let the candle burn out.

Water Cleansing

Water has long been viewed as a purifier. Any can of water can be used, and some people will even use oil. It is okay to use tap water, but if you are on city water and not well water, you may want to find water that is pure.

There are two ways to do this. You can either plunge the whole crystal into the water, or simply drop a few drops on it, if it is on the fragile side. After you do this, take some time to picture all of its bad energies being washed away. Let the crystal dry and get rid of the water you used.

Singing Bowl Cleansing

This is a fun way to cleanse crystals, even though singing bowls do tend to be on the expensive side. You can also use YouTube videos to get the same effect. Using your own singing bowl, if you can, place the crystal inside of the bowl. If it will not fit in the bowl, simply place it on the altar, and sit the singing bowl on top of it so that it will be touch by its vibrations. Now is the time to play your singing bowl. As you hear the sounds echoing, really feel its vibrations. Allow the sounds to capture all of the unwanted energies within the item. Once the sound fades away, all of the bad energies will disappear with it.

Personal Energy Cleansing

You do not have to have anything special to cleanse your crystals with. Your mind is a great tool. This is a little more advanced, so beginners may have a hard time with it. In order for this to work, you need to be able to feel and use the energetic fields. If you are not sure how to do this, then you need to start out practicing alone before you try to purify your crystals. Once you are ready to move up to your crystals, here is how:

First, picture a ray of light emanating for your hands. Take some time to really feel this light. Next, place both of your hands over the stone and picture that all of the unwanted energies are little black bubbles. The light coming from your hands is an energetic vacuum and is sucking up all of those energy remnants. Once everything is sucked up in your hands, picture all of the energy falling to the ground. To help you do this, you can touch the floor with your hands. This is very important because you want to get rid of all of that energy. Push it all back into the Earth.

Connecting to Your Crystals

Once your crystals are cleansed, you will need to take a bit of time to connect with them. The best way to do this is to meditate with your crystal to help connect you with its energy. This will help them to work more efficiently, and it will help to improve your psychic abilities. It is also relaxing.

Take the crystal in your non-dominant hand. Get into a comfortable position, and then gaze upon your crystal for a few minutes. Look at all of the little details in the crystal until you can accurately picture it in your mind. Close your eyes. Now, focus on the sensation of your crystal. Tap into all of your senses to really feel the crystal. Now, take it beyond your physical senses and see if you can feel its vibrations. This will be a personal experience and will be different for every crystal you do this with. Once you feel you have been in meditation for long enough, you can open your eyes and move into programming your crystal.

Programming your crystal

You will have produced a sharp picture of your target and aim before using your Crystal, as mentioned above. It is better to use a different crystal for each of your purposes, so that each time you hold the crystal you can fire the specific vision.

The crystal must be programmed for your intent or intention. Here is how this can be done:

1. Hold the crystal as above in both sides. Be mindful of the crystal energy field between your two sides.

2. Reflect carefully on your dream, aim and objective. Imagine a deep simplicity in it, as if you had already accomplished this goal. Experience the strong emotions of success and accomplishment correlated with your goal.

3. Release your goal photo with a sharp breath.

Now you have put in the crystal the way of thinking and that feeling. This will enhance the area of perception; keep you tuned into the world and ask for what you want. You also plant an anchor for your dream in your energy field, which will keep your unconscious mind attuned to your sight.

Eventually, sit down, hold your crystal a few times, and imagine again how good it will be when your goal is reached. Plunge into these thoughts. That is what I regularly call 'firing up' your vision. This will increase your intensity and allow it to flow towards you.

According to the Law of Attraction, you must be available, responsive and at the right frequency to allow your wishes to flow to you. Crystals are a strong tool to aid the manifestation cycle, as they help you increase your intensity and stay responsive to your desire.

Spoil yourself with the cycle and enjoy the constant appearances of a beautiful crystal.

CHAPTER 7:

Crystal and candle spells

Growing Luck Spell

What You will Need:

A green candle

The seed of a plant native to your area

Casting the Spell:

Cast your circle and invoke the Divine.

Light the green candle and watch the flames as you hold the seed gently in your hand.

Visualize good luck coming to you. Think as positively as you can and remind yourself of all that you have to be thankful for. Try to think of something joyful.

If you would like, ask for a little bit of luck. For example, "Candle of green, abundance and wealth… please bring me luck. Seed of growth, please bring me good fortune."

Blow at the candle when you are ready. Take some time to meditate and clear your mind of negative thoughts.

If possible, bury the seed outside. Ensure that it is a native plant to your area if you do so.

Close the circle (you can do this twice – once after blowing out the candle and again after burying the seed) and give thanks.

Repeat this spell whenever you are feeling unlucky. Take some time to reflect on all you have or be thankful for, including your inner strength and the beauty of nature. Keep your head up, and luck will find you.

Healing Physically Spell

This spell is designed to help and support the healing process of your body, and to give you the energy to increase the rate of which it heals. Please be aware that you should still be taking your medicine or prescribed treatment; this is merely a way to speed up your healing process without any complications. With this spell, your treatment will be effective, and you will be as good as new within a couple of days. The best time to perform this is spell is on Monday or Thursday, by the waning moon. You can perform this spell every Monday or Thursday until the person is completely healed, but you must start on a waning moon.

You will need the following ingredients:

Matches or a lighter

2 blue candles

A small plate or bowl

Something sharp that will be used as a carving tool (a pin, a nail or a knife)

Sweets, nuts or fruits, that can be used as a sacrifice

Start off by creating a protection circle. You can meditate for a few minutes to clear your mind and further strengthen your intention. Take the two blue candles; on one of them, write the name of a God or the deity that has the power to heal you, such as Loco or Jesus, with your carving tool. On the other candle, write the name of the person you wish to heal, whether it is yourself or someone else.

Light both candles and ask God or the deity for their help. Then offer the sacrifice and pray for the health of that person. Visualize the person being healed, the smile on their face when they are no longer sick or in pain. Add your own feelings and emotions into the visualization to activate its full power, you have to visualize as strongly as you can.

Wait until the wax of the two candles becomes liquid. You do not have to wait until the entire wax turns into a liquid, just a small bit is still fine. Take the first candle, with the name of the God or the deity written on it, and pour the wax into the bowl. Take the other candle and pour that wax into the bowl. Repeat these words once:

"As the wax from both candles unities,

The healing power of (name of the God or Deity)

And the energy of (name of the person that requires healing)

Shall become one."

When the wax on the bowl fully solidifies, take it when it is still warm and place it on the part of the body where there is a problem or illness. Visualize the healing energy from the wax and as it sinks deep into the body. If you feel that you have completed it, the finish of the ritual and close the circle. Leave the candles to burn completely. Make sure to keep them away from pets or children and do not leave unattended with the risk of causing a fire. After the ritual has been completed, go out into nature and burry the wax within the earth. You should never eat the food that you used as a sacrifice, instead, leave it in nature or burn it and leave the ashes in the soil. Let the earth consume the remaining energy and let the forces to work its magic.

Relationship Healing Candle Spell

You will need the following items:

3 Royal blue candles

1 Red candle

1 White candle

1 Green candle

Yarn or thread, preferably white

2 sticks (from outside)

Begin by choosing the location for your spell and cleansing the area whichever way you prefer, either with incense or sprinkling moon water. Take a moment to clear your mind by meditating, in order to set pure and positive intentions. Make sure you have enough space to perform this spell.

On an altar or a table, place the green, white and red candles together, side by side forming a line. Place the other three royal blue candles together, forming a triangle. This triangle formed with candles should be facing the other three candles with the angle. While performing this spell, think about the person whose relationship you would like to fix or the heartbreak you would like to accept and move on. Take out the two sticks, which you can find outside, the size or thickness does not matter. Using the white thread or yarn, wrap the two sticks tightly together with a few rounds to make sure to keep them together.

Proceed by lighting the candles, start off with the white, then the green, red, and all the royal blues. Continue to wind the thread around the two sticks while you repeat the following passage:

"I am earth and I am water, ever since my birth.

These two figures, bite and leap, from within my view.

Draw them close and take them up close.

Dissolve the fear and hate, into harmony and love, which shall now rule.

Leave behind the foolishness, to the fool.

Light and tranquility, come to me now.

Banish the fear and hate that is within!"

Once you finish saying the chant, stop winding the thread and tie a knot so it will not undo. Hold the stick with two of your hands and close your eyes, think of the person that you wish to mend the relationship with, visualize how happy you would feel if you and that person were on talking terms. Visualize and think about that person for at least two to three minutes. Leave the candles to burn for at least thirty minutes; you can even let them burn out further if you would like, but do not leave them unattended if you have children or pets. While waiting, just leave the two sticks horizontally in between the line of different colored candles and the candle triangle. After thirty minutes or after the candle burns out, go outside into nature and bury the two sticks at least two feet deep into the ground while saying the following:

"Go back to Mother Earth, Harmonize and heal,

This new beginning!"

Good Luck Candle Spell

This spell requires the use of an orange-colored candle.

Dress the orange-colored candle in oil; preferably clove oil, lotus oil or cinnamon oil.

Light up the orange candle, and say this incantation verbatim three times:

"Brimstone, moon, and witch's fire, candlelight's luminous spell, better fortune now I shall acquire, work your power well. Midnight come, the Wiccan's hour, bring forth the fortune I seek. By wick and wax now work your power while these incantations I speak. This rite be done, while harming none. I invoke thee, so let it be!"

Make sure that this is performed at exactly midnight.

Here is one candle spell that aims to stop whoever is harassing the spell-caster. Similar to the Wealth and Prosperity Spell, this spell should be casted only during a waning moon. However, there is no specific day required for this spell to be casted.

Flaming Finances

Everyone can always use a good money spell, for this one you will need:

1 Gold candle

1 Green Candle

Patchouli Incense

Pine Incense

A Handful of Acorns

1 Piece of Paper

On the bottom of both candles, carve the rune FEHU (ᚠ this symbol). Set the candleholders up across from one another. Place the patchouli incense holder next to the gold candle, and the pine incense next the green candle. Light the candles then get all of the incense smoking.

Draw FEHU on your piece of paper, and then put some acorns on top of the paper. You can substitute smooth stones for the acorns. Both are symbols of wealth and Earth energy when you are casting spells.

Let both of the candles burn out completely by themselves; leave the acorns (or stones) on your altar until the extra money comes into your life.

Burning Away All Negatives

This spell is used to rid your life of negative energy that is causing tension in your life. To perform this spell, you will need:

1 Black Candle

Sandalwood Oil

Dried Mint

Dried Basil

White Sage

Crush the dried herbs into really small pieces. Big flakes are not going to work for this spell. Rub the oil all on your candle, until it is nice and slick with sandalwood oil. Roll the candle in the herbs so the candle is coated in herbs.

Set up the candle in a holder and light it. You could see some sparks a as the oil and herbs begin to burn, so perform this in a safe location. while it burns say aloud:

"I banish all negative energy,

I banish any bad attitude,

I banish the poor spirit,

I invite happiness and peace."

Repeat three times; let the candle burning itself out completely. Bury any remaining wax in the yard.

General Luck Spell

What You will Need:

A green or gold candle

Frankincense – either essential oil or incense (or both)

Casting the Spell:

Cast your circle and invoke the Divine.

Take a dab of the frankincense oil and run it softly along the candle, moving your finger up and down the candle three times. If you are using incense, light it and turn the candle through the smoke three times. Note: the candle should not be lit.

As you are dowsing the candle with frankincense, visualize the fortune you already have. Imagine new doors opening and challenges being conquered.

Light the candle and allow it to burn for as long as you wish.

If you would like, you can chant something like, "Green candle/Gold candle, please turn my luck around so fortune can abound." Chant, sing or meditate until you feel comfortable and accomplished.

Blow out the candle when you feel the time is right.

Close the circle and give thanks.

Repeat this spell if you feel the need. Save the candle you used for luck or fortune spells.

Love Candle Spell

You will need:

A sampler bottle of a scent that you really love

A tool for inscribing and one pink candle

How to:

Begin by carving a heart on your candle. Light it after and place it by the window, where it might receive some moonlight.

Put your favorite scent by the candle and recite:

"Venus, send me the love that I need.

Through this scent, may he or she be attracted."

Get your candle burn out after and carry the scent with you. Spray it on whenever you are out meeting people. If you repeat the incantation while you spritz it on, it will help increase its potency.

Protection Candle Spell

You will need:

A red candle

Your choice of protective herb

How to:

Begin by encircling your candle with your protection herb.

Light the wick after and gaze into the fire, make sure that you are not too close to it. Focus your energy and once you feel ready, recite your intentions.

Let the candle burn out while you meditate on your incantation.

Basic Money Spell

Choose a small, unused, brand-new candle and dress it with oil. Make sure that the dressing oil is natural. Charge the dressed candle with your personal intent for the spell.

Take a small piece of paper and write down your intent to have an abundance of money, good fortune and prosperity. Focus on your intent as hard as you can as your write in all down on the paper. Also, make sure that the paper is of the same color as the candle that you are using.

Light up the candle. Make sure that as you light up your candle, you are visualizing that your wish is coming true.

Once you have spent a certain amount of time visualizing the different forms your wish may come as, fold the colored piece of paper and light it up with the candle's flame.

Hold the burning paper as long as possible but make sure that you do not burn your fingers in the process. Place it in a fire-proof bowl or cauldron and allow it to burn out completely.

Leave the candle burning on its own until it completely burns itself out as well.

Below is another variation of a candle spell that improves one's financial situation. This one does not only provide wealth but also prosperity.

Clearing Out Spirits Candle Spell

You will need:

A white candle

Sea salt

How to:

Begin by putting all of the salt in a small bag that you can carry around. You will be sprinkling this in every room.

Hold the candle with your right hand then light it. Take some of the salt with your left.

Start walking backwards through your house and go into every room. Sprinkle just a bit of salt in the corners of each room while you repeat your intention: "Ghosts and spirits, leave this place and be gone. Never return."

Once you reach the northernmost part of your house, snuff out your candle.

Prosperity Candle Spell

You will need:

A green candle

A white candle

Any oil of your choice

How to:

The green candle represents money and the white one would represent you. Start by anointing the candles with the oil. As you do this, focus on your intent to prosper financially.

Once done, set your candles on an altar or any table available. Make sure that they are nine inches apart. After you are done, recite your intentions out loud.

Repeat this process for nine days, at the same time every day. Whenever you do, make sure that you also move the white candle an inch closer to the green one. By the time your spell is finished, they should be touching each other.

Attract New Love Spell

What You will Need:

A red or pink candle (Red if you are looking for long-term; pink if you are not ready to commit to long-term)

A rose with a stem and thorns

Jasmine incense and/or oil

Casting the Spell:

Cast your circle and invoke the Divine.

Anoint the candle with the incense or oil.

Light the candle breath in the jasmine and rose scent, imagining attracting a lover who is stable and deserving of your attention.

Take the rose and carefully remove one of the thorns. Push the thorn into the candle or drop it into the wax as it melts.

Visualize attracting a new love unexpectedly. Imagine yourself meeting someone charming and respectful.

Blow out the candle. Leave the rose on your alter if possible.

Close the circle and give thanks.

As long as you are open to it, love may find you wherever you go. After the rose wilts, recycle it or use it as an offering so the energy is not wasted.

Wiccan White Candle Blessing Spell

This spell requires the use of a white-colored candle. You can use a plain or a figurative candle that depicts the individual's gender that you desire to bestow blessings upon.

Before dressing the candle with Holy or Blessed oil, make sure that the name of the person to be blessed with the spell is carved on the white-colored candle.

To increase the spells potency, you may put a piece of white paper with the person's name or photograph, or any kind of personal item, either next to the candle or under it. That person's personal item may come in the form of a piece of hair, clothing, finger nail, etc. To make things easier, you can put all of the aforementioned items under an upside-down plate or saucer, and then place the white-colored candle on top.

Let the candle burn for a little while every day for about seven days, snuffing it out between burnings. Every time you light the candle up, recite this incantation verbatim:

"(Person's name), may you always be blessed. Let all desirable matters come your way. May you forever be away from harm. Let your heart be light. Let your journeys be free from trouble. Let your wellbeing be always in good condition. Let your mind be at peace. Let your personal relationships sustain you. May all aspects of your life be blessed."

Take note, however, that this incantation is not set in stone. You can also add your additional requests for the recipient of this spell in the incantation.

This spell ends as soon as the candle is completely burned out. Therefore, if you or the recipient of this spell requires blessing for an extended amount of time, use a big pillar-type candle so that burning it for a little while each day takes longer. In cases where a large tower-type candle is used, re-dressing the candle with oil one time each week is required.

Cleansing/Purification Candle Spell

You will need:

A white candle

A cup of salt.

How to:

Place your candle in the middle of the room you wish to cleanse.

Sprinkle your salt, clockwise, around your candle.

Light it and focus your energy before reciting your intentions.

Garden Blessing

This is the perfect spell to bring more power to your plants by harnessing the power of the elements.

You need:

A green candle

A compass

A Brown candle

Amethyst – Air

Jet – Earth

Garnet – Fire

Lapis lazuli – Water

Pick a place in the middle of the garden and then use your compass to find the four corners or cardinal directions. Pick up your amethyst and then walk to the East point of the garden. You should walk until you are just outside the boundaries of your garden. Bury the amethyst as you say, "By the four powers, my garden flowers."

Go back to the middle, and then walk to the North edge of your garden with the piece of jet. Bury the stone, saying the same thing you said earlier.

Once back in the middle of the garden, walk to the West, and bury the lapis lazuli, saying the same chant. Again, go back to the middle and then walk to the South edge, and bury the garnet, saying the same thing as before.

Once all of the stones have been buried, place the candles at the center of your garden, away from anything that could catch fire.

Light the candle. Say the following, "By the four powers, my garden flowers," four more times, and then picture your garden surrounded by a glowing white circle. Let the candles burn for a little bit and then snuff them out.

Now, give your garden the best care possible for the rest of the season to make sure that it grows.

Simple Home Protection Spell

You need:

4 Stones from your property

Black paint or permanent marker

A shovel

Start by cleansing the area, tools, and yourself with sage or Palo Santo before you start. Then cast your circle.

With the paint or marker, draw the ALGIZ rune on each of the stones. You can look up a picture of this rune, but it looks like a stick figure of a person with their arms raised but no legs.

Picture in your mind every harmful person, and watch as they run away from your home, returning to where they came from. Understand deep down in your heart that your home is completely safe from all types of harm.

Close your circle. Head outside and then dig a hole at each corner of your property. Place a stone into each of the holes and then cover them up. After you have placed them, picture an electric fence of white light around your property. Once again, picture all the harmful entities leaving your property. If anybody with evil intent comes near your property, they will forget why they are there and leave.

Sore Throat Spell

What You will Need:

A small candle of your choice

Chamomile tea with honey

Casting the Spell:

Cast your circle and invoke the Divine.

Light the candle and begin to drink your tea.

Take a deep breath. Visualize the pain in your throat becoming softened by the drink.

Imagine a ball of white energy surrounding the pain. Slowly move that ball upwards and out of your mouth.

Visualize the ball falling into the flames of the candle and dissipating.

Allow the candle to burn out and finish your tea.

Close the circle and give thanks.

Lemon tea can also work for this spell. Make sure to stay as hydrated as possible and drink lots of water to lubricate your throat.

Banishing Bad Thoughts Spell

What You will Need:

A black candle (used for banishing negativity)

A wand (or your finger)

Rosemary incense

Make sure to shower or bathe before performing this spell

Casting the Spell:

Cast your circle and invoke the Divine.

Take a minute to meditate. Ground yourself and clear your thoughts. Focus on your breathing and immerse yourself in the moment.

Light the candle. Use it to light the incense. (Note: if you cannot find rosemary incense, use essential oil to anoint the candle or rub fresh rosemary on the candle).Take out your wand. Draw a pentagram in the air and say a few words to banish negativity and bad thoughts. For example, "In the name of the lady and the lord, I banish these dark thoughts that haunt my mind."

As you are drawing the pentagram and speaking, imagine yourself being shrouded in a white, purifying light.

When you feel that you have become fully immersed in the white light, blow out the candle.

Close the circle and give thanks.

If you have been depressed or have unwelcome thoughts, using this spell with meditation is a great way to focus your mind and cleanse your personal energies.

A Crystal Love Spell

You are going to need:

Pink yarn

Red cloth

Rose quartz

Moonstone

2 Apple seeds

Ground cinnamon

Dried basil

Pink candle

Red candle

This spell is best done during the Full Moon.

Before you begin, make sure you take a moment to clarify what type of relationship you are looking to have. Make sure that you are clear on what your desire is. This can take some time. It is also a good idea to figure out how you feel about it and not allow yourself to get hung up on the details. For example, instead of listing out all of the traits you want them to have, write down that you want to be attracted to them. Also, think about how you want to feel in the relationship.

Get your items together and then cast your circle. Light the candles and spread the red cloth out in front of you. Pass the moonstone through the flames of the candles and then sit it on the cloth. Repeat this for the rose quartz.

Pick up the apple seeds and say: "By the light of the moon, I now plant these seeds of love."

As you sit these seeds onto the cloth along with the crystals, start seeing all of the soft pink energy coming from the crystals and nourishing your seeds with their loving energy. Sprinkle everything with some cinnamon and basil. Pull the four corners of the cloth together so that everything is wrapped inside, and then wrap the pink yarn around the bag three times. Tie the bag with three knots and say: "So mote it be."

You can close out your circle and then keep the bag you just made with you to attract love.

Energizing Spring Spell

What you will need:

A patch of newly bloomed flowers (if you do not have any in your garden, go to your local park or a meadow of wildflowers)

A safe and private place somewhere outside (it should be at or close to springtime)

Casting the Spell:

Cast your circle and invoke the Divine.

Take deep breaths of the fresh air. What do you smell? Rain? Flowers? Something unknown? Focus on the moment and clear your thoughts with meditation.

If possible, take off your shoes and dig your toes into the earth. Ground yourself. Feel the Earth's power underneath you. As it gives flowers the nutrients to grow, imagine it giving you the energy to grow and bloom.

Turn your attention to the flowers around you. Notice the way they look and how they are all unique. Talk to them if you wish. Do not be afraid to be silly!

Speak, chant or sing if you wish. For example, you could say: "Youthful flowers of spring, ancient earth of wisdom, nourish me and allow my thoughts to bloom too."

Spend some time meditating or relaxing next to the flowers if possible. Be sure to thank them!

Close the circle and give thanks.

Cold Hard Cash Spell

This is a cold spell, which means that it will work slower than the previous hot spell. This is great if you need to save some money for something.

You need:

A few silver coins

Pinches of dried calendula

Black or green handkerchief

At night, turn off all of your inside lights, and spread the handkerchief out in a patch of moonlight. If clouds are blocking it, you can use an outside light to light your way. You need to use some light that is associated with the night.

Add the calendula to the handkerchief. Lay the coins over it, and tie the ends of the handkerchief together tightly so everything is safely held inside.

Hold your bundle in your hands tightly and speak your intentions to save money out loud. Let the universe know that you want to keep the money that you have in your pocket and that you are going to keep it safe. Once you finish the spell, place the handkerchief into the back of the freezer. Do not touch it or untie it until you have gotten what you need.

Charming Kitchen Blessing

This is a great little herbal spell that will help bless your kitchen. Kitchen witches often use herbal magic spells, but they are full of power.

You need:

A sprig of rosemary – fresh

A long piece of twine

A bay leaf

A strip of orange rind

If you want to, you can start things by casting a circle.

When you are ready, tie the orange rind and bay leaf to the bottom of the rosemary sprig using the twine. You need to make sure that you wrap the twine around it enough so that everything stays secure but leave enough of the twine to use later on. You can take a few minutes to meditate on what you would like to accomplish with this spell. What would you like to bless your kitchen with? Once you feel charged enough, you may continue with the rest of the spell.

If you chose to start the spell by casting a circle, then you can now close the circle and thank everybody that you have called.

Then, take the rosemary sprig and hang it someplace in your kitchen to fill that space with lots of positive energy and purify the energy of the kitchen.

Money Charm Spell

What You will Need:

Conifer twigs—at least five of the same size (pick them up off the ground) – and let them sit on your alter for a few days next to a monetary note, before beginning the spell.

A piece of ribbon or yarn, silver and green colors

Patchouli oil

Casting the Spell:

Cast your circle and invoke the Divine.

Anoint the twigs with the patchouli oil.

Combine the twigs and the monetary note together, and begin to wrap them together with the ribbon or yarn.

As your wrapping, declare your desire for money luck. For example, say, "With this charm for my home, make money shown."

Make a loop for your charm and hang it around your house. Next to a door is best.

Give thanks to the tree from which the twigs came (leave it an offering or simple acknowledge it with a thank you spell).

Close the circle and give thanks.

You can create more charms if need be, but allow some time to pass before doing so. You can get creative as you would like with these kinds of charms, as long as you remember to anoint them and give thanks to the source.

Charm for Attracting Quality Relationships

You will need:

13 whole coriander seeds

A small rose quartz

A small drawstring bag or piece of cloth

A red or pink ribbon

A work candle (for atmosphere—optional)

Instructions:

Light the candle, if using.

Arrange the coriander seeds in a circle around the rose quartz.

Close your eyes and visualize the feeling of being completely at peace with a partner who loves you for exactly who you are.

When you have a lock on this feeling, open your eyes, focus on the rose quartz, and say the following (or similar) words: "I draw to me nothing less than healthy, balanced love."

Now, collect the coriander seeds, placing them one at a time into the drawstring bag or cloth. (It is best to start with the seed at the southern-most part of the circle and move clockwise.) Add the rose quartz, close the bag or cloth, and secure with the ribbon.

Bring the charm with you whenever you are feeling like taking a chance on love—especially when you go out in public.

Repay A Debt

This is specifically for calling money into your life to repay someone to whom you owe money, not for prosperity or wealth. You will need:

A green candle

Patchouli oil (or cinnamon oil)

Incense (the same as the oil you are using)

A piece of paper

Draw a representation of the bill on the piece of paper. Draw any words or logos that are on the bill onto the paper including how much the bill or debt it is for. If you photocopy the bill it will lack any personal energy. So even if you are not the best artist, do not worry about it. You will be burning your piece of paper; so, do not use the actual bill.

Anoint your candle with the chosen oil, fold the piece of paper and place it under the candleholder. Light your candle and your chosen incense. Stare at the flames and say:

"While the candle burns

It lights the way

The money coming

This bill I'll pay"

Visualize paying this bill and keep in mind why it is important for you to pay. Allow the candle to burn for around 15 minutes, and then snuff it out. Let the candle burn for 15 minutes every day, until 7 days have passed (be sure you use a candle that is big enough). On the final day, remove the paper representing the bill and light it with the flame and burn it completely. Let the candle burn until it goes out on its own.

The next part is up to you. You need to be honorable and use any unexpected money that comes to you to start paying off the debt.

Sleeping Peaceful

Help get good night's sleep and keep your dreams happy and positive with this blend of herbs.

10 Whole Cardamom Pods

A tablespoon of sea salt

15 Whole cloves

1/2 Ounce of dried mint

1/2 Ounce dried rosemary

A white candle

A pink candle

A silver candle

A small pouch and a short length of string

Light the candles in the area you are working on the pouch. Mix the ingredients (except the candles) with your hand in a small bowl. Be sure to keep your thoughts focused on peace while you work. Do this spell when you know that there will not be any distractions. Turn off your cell phone ahead of time.

Repeat this, while you are stirring the herbs with your fingers:

"Sleep, dream, peace

Peace, dream, sleep

Dream, sleep, peace"

Put the herbs your bag and use the string to tie it closed. Keep the close to your bed. You might want to sleep with it under your pillow, but if it is to strong smelling or lumpy, just keep it near you at night.

Fast Results Spell

If you are having trouble completing a task, or if some aspect of your life seems stuck, you can perform this spell to speed up the process and see quick results. You will need:

An 8-oz glass of organic juice

A piece of pound cake

A white candle

Sit in one place, close your eyes, and visualize how your life will be after your task is complete. See everything being completed and working out for the best.

Next, say out loud "St. Expedite, I ask you to help me (say whatever you are asking for) quickly. I offer you food and drink for this request. After completion, I will offer you more…so be it, it is done."

Light the white candle in homage to St. Expedite, again say aloud the task you need completed.

After the task is complete, be sure to make the offering you promised of food and drink.

Banishing A Ghost Spell

If there is an unwanted or unneeded spirit linger in or around your home, here is a way to help him/her move on. For this you will need:

A white candle

A cup of sea salt

Put the salt in a satchel, small bag or in your pockets. You will be going from room to room spreading the salt as you go.

While holding the candle in the right hand, light the candle. Grab some salt and hold it in the left hand.

Start in the southernmost part of your home. Sprinkle a small amount of salt in the corner of each room as you walk backward through the house. As you are walking speak loudly, saying, "Ghosts and Spirits leave now, never to return."

When you reach the northernmost place in the home snug out the flame of your candle.

Magic Motivation Morning Potion

This very simple potion is really an enhanced version of the morning ritual that most people already engage in, though perhaps not very consciously—the all-important cup of coffee! However, non-caffeine drinkers can also make a pleasant morning brew for themselves, ideally with an herbal tea that goes well with cinnamon.

Use this potion as an extra, magical boost for days when you feel lagging but have a lot to do.

<u>Note:</u> If you are lagging due to illness or being run-down, it is best to stick to an herbal version, rather than ingesting caffeine. The

visualization and reciting of the spell is ideally done outdoors, but facing a window is also perfectly fine.

You will need:

A fresh brewed cup of coffee or tea

A pinch of cinnamon

A teaspoon or more honey

Instructions:

Stir the honey, if using, into your beverage, using clockwise motions. (If not using honey, stir it clockwise anyway.) While the liquid is still turning circles, sprinkle the cinnamon into the center.

Take your potion outside or to a window, and thank the morning light (no matter how cloudy the day may actually be) for showing you the way into your day.

Take a relaxing breath and begin sipping your beverage.

Visualize feeling energy and clarity as you forge ahead with your day, and the satisfaction of meeting your goals.

When you are ready, say the following (or similar) words:

"I greet this day in gratitude.

I sail through this day on my positive attitude.

As my energy now rises, I know I will meet

All of my tasks until they are complete.

So, let it be."

Now get moving and enjoy your day!

Creativity and Focus Spell

This spell is designed to achieve a clear mind and mental focus in order to bring creativity and inspiration to the caster. You have to ground yourself first otherwise this spell will have an opposite effect and drain your energy instead of giving it to you. It is the best to cast on a Monday and will take around seven to fifteen minutes, but the time varies for different witches.

You will need the following:

Rose quartz and/or aventurine, (used for creativity)

Clear quartz (used for mental focus and as a fuel to increase the effects)

2 light blue candles

Lighter or matches

A purple candle

A writing utensil

A carving tool

A piece of paper (lined if possible)

Peppermint/mint for focus (something with strong odor)

Cleanse your working area, with incense or crystals. Take out your carving tool and on both light blue candles, carve words, signs or sigils that represent creativity on one candle and inspiration on the other. You can choose to just carve the words 'creativity' and 'inspiration' on the two candles. Place the candles in this order, the 'creativity' candle, purple candle, and the 'inspiration' candle. Proceed by lighting the two light-blue candles and the purple candle.

Take out your rose quartz, clear quartz and/or aventurine, and hold preferably the dominant one it in your hand, for projective energy.

While holding the crystals, look into the flame of your 'creativity' light-blue candle, visualizing the flames as sparks of energy, flowing from the candle and into you. Imagine yourself being filled with the feeling of creativity, urge to do something and work. Then look at the flame of your 'inspiration' light-blue candle, and imagine being filled with new ideas, an inspiration for your business or your life and a new way of thinking, coming up with all new techniques and plans for whatever you are working on.

Finally, look into the purple candle. Ask yourself what does creativity mean to you? Project the energy from within you to your crystals and then into the universe, all while looking at the purple candle. You are asking for imagination, new perspectives, and creativity to be brought to you. Close your eyes and meditate for a few minutes while holding onto the gems. Meditate your intentions and direct your energy into them. Feel the tingling sensations as you are holding onto the crystals and feel the energy tangling with yours.

Now direct your attention to the flames, keep your eyes closed, but feel the heat radiating from the flames. Visualize the flames as if your eyes were still open. Then, watch the flame dancing as if it is performing its own ritual or spell to bring your wish to you. Direct your attention back to the crystals, the clear quartz is a crystal of amplification, which will tell the universe your intentions and wishes.

Open your eyes and blow out only the purple candle and set the crystals down. Place a sheet of paper right in front of you, you can choose to move the two candles aside or a bit further to give space for the paper. Make sure the paper is placed horizontally. Take out the mint or gum that you will be using to stay focused, smell it and feel it within your non-dominant hand. When you have finished, set this mint down and take out another one, this time placing it into your dominant hand. Using the other hand, hold the clear quartz.

With the dominant hand that is holding the mint, crush it and sprinkle it across the paper, letting it fall. Visualize as your attention, concentration, and perception skills as enhancing as the mint falls, awakening your mental focus. Using your dominant hand, grab the clear quartz from the non-dominant hand, and place it in the middle of the paper. Do not move the mints aside, instead place the crystal on top. Meditate on the light blue candles, bringing creativity and inspiration and joining them together, creating a sense of focus from all the new ideas emerging.

Continue to visualize your mind becoming more open and sharper at all the focus coming in. Meditate for a few minutes before opening your eyes. Place the mint and the clear quartz aside. Take out a writing utensil, preferably a marker, and go over every line that you have on that piece of paper, if you do not have lines then you will have to draw them yourself. The point is for you to create as straight lines as possible, indicating your mind being focused, concentrated and perceptive. You can choose to draw at least ten lines, do not stress too much if they do not look perfect, it is simply an exercise for your mind to focus.

After you are done, take a moment to repeat your intentions and with one push, and send them out into the universe through the clear quartz, to the candle and to the universe. When you have finished, you can let the candles burn themselves out while you are working on something. The purple candle can be reused for future spells, as long as it is cleansed. You can choose to burn the paper or tear it into pieces before burying it. You may throw the mint away or eat it.

Potion for Dreams

This spell is meant to help provide you with dreams from your spirit guides, or any other power you would like to get guidance from. This should be done 30 to 60 minutes before you plan on going to sleep. Make sure you have a journal next to your bed.

You are going to need:

Light or matches

Water

Athame or wand

Graveyard dirt – you can also use dirt from a place that you feel a connection with, or you can omit this ingredient

Lavender oil

A cauldron

Black tealight candle

Add water to the cauldron that equals about a half of a cup. You do not have to measure it; you can eyeball it. Sprinkle the dirt inside and then say what your intention is. It works best if you come up with your own intention, but to give you an idea, you could say: "A bit of dirt to bring me closer to a world full of luster."

Stir some of the lavender oil into the water. Light the candle and put it underneath your cauldron. You will need to have your cauldron on a stand so that the candle simply sits under it so that the flame warms the bottom of the cauldron. You will start to smell the potion as it heats up. Let your muscles relax and allow your thoughts to start drifting around.

Sit with your cauldron until the candle has burned all the way out, the water evaporates, or you feel as if the spell is finished. Make sure you record any dreams that you have as you sleep that night.

Fix a Friendship Spell

You are going to need:

Ground dry basil

A white candle

A thin lavender candle

You will want to be patient with this spell because it can be tricky to put together. Crack the lavender candle in the middle but keep the wick intact. This crack represents the rift between you and another person that you are trying to fix. As you perform this spell, focus on this problem that you would like to overcome, and how you could help to improve things between the two of you if you were given a chance.

Rub a bit of basil on the rough ends of the broken spot of the lavender candle. Then push them back together. Light the white candle and allow the wax to drip over the broken piece until the lavender candle has been mended back together.

Sit the lavender in a holder and light it. Let it burn until the flame gets close to where the break is. Now, sit with the candle and watch the flame as it burns through the joined break, thinking about different ways to improve your relationship. Once it has moved through the split, let the candle continue to burn out all on its own.

Better Sleep Spell

What You will Need:

Lavender incense

Lavender oil

Fresh sprigs of lavender

Calming music

Casting the Spell:

Cast your circle and invoke the Divine in your room where you sleep.

Light the incense and sit on your bed.

Take the lavender oil and dab a small amount on the inside of your pillowcase. Then, take the sprigs of lavender and stuff them into your pillow.

Spend some time meditating and allowing the sweet scent of the lavender bring you peace and calmness.

Play some calming music, preferably music that is instrumental or rhythmic.

Allow the incense to burn out. Keep the lavender springs under your pillow.

Close the circle and give thanks.

Avoid using electronics an hour before bed. Instead, take some time to read a book, be intimate with your spouse or write in a journal. Replace the lavender sprigs after a few nights if you are still struggling with sleep.

Inner Power Candle Spell

What you will need:

A white, brown, or blue taper candle

A mixture of clove, juniper, and rose oils to anoint the candle. Handle the clove oil with care—only one or two drops of each are needed. A small, thin, paintbrush. A small dish on which to burn the candle.

Pink or kosher salt.

Matches to light the candle—preferable over a lighter, as metal should not strike a holy flame, but in a pinch, use what's available.

Cast your circle and draw the energy down from the universe. With the paintbrush, anoint the candle in the oil mixture, using brushstrokes that move from the back of the candle towards the front, and you. Work from the base of the candle towards the wick. Imagine yourself in moments of great personal power.

Light the candle and say:

"As it burns, so I learn. As it dances, so I turn. As it flickers, so I grow. As it melts, so my troubles go."

Move your hands above the candle as if you were drawing the healing energy of the flame towards you. Do this, as you repeat: "Flame of power, imbue me with your strength."

Sit in quiet contemplation for as long as you are comfortable, imagining yourself overcoming obstacles, and obtaining happiness, and a peaceful heart. When you are ready, open the circle and allow the candle to burn down. After the candle is burned you can dispose of the wax and salt either by tossing them in a crossroads, or by burying them.

Spell to Nourish the Heart

What you will need:

Pink quartz

Rose petals

lemon balm

lemon essential oil

Do this spell on a new, waxing, or full moon.

Cast your circle in the bathroom. Fill a bath and add five drops of the lemon essential oil to it. Add the rose petals and lemon balm. After you have gotten into the bath, add the pink quartz. As you sit in the bath, close your eyes and imagine a pink, healing light gleaming on the water. Imagine your body soaking up this healing energy. Feel your heart glowing with happiness and warmth that radiates throughout your entire body.

When you are ready, repeat these words:

"I am worthy of love, and I am capable of love.

I am worthy of peace, and I am capable of peace.

I am worthy of happiness, and I am capable of happiness.

All good things are possible. May they come into my life as blessings."

When you are finished with the bath, allow the water to drain and pat yourself dry (do not rub or wipe) with a towel from your feet up to your head. Discard the herbs and return to the quartz to your altar.

Spell for Personal Success and Achievement

What you will need:

A piece of sunstone

An orange candle

Pink or kosher salt

Juniper berries

Some soil

A small bowl, or cauldron

Benzoin incense

Myrrh oil

Small, slim paintbrush

Matches

Cast your circle and anoint the candle with the myrrh oil. Light the incense. In the bowl or cauldron, place the salt, soil, sunstone, and juniper berries. Mix these with your athame or wand, in a sun-wise direction.

As you stir the ingredients, say:

"As the Sun warms the Earth and encourages the harvest,

So does my ability for success grow every day.

I will achieve my goals and dreams, step by step,

As sure as the sunflower and the wheat grows tall."

Picture the sun shining down on a field of wheat and sunflowers: these represent your success and finances. Picture the wind swaying the tall stalks. See how the field spans out endlessly towards the horizon. This is your success; it is tangible and real.

Say:

"As the candle burns its flame, so does my success increase."

When you are ready, open the circle and allow the candle to continue burning down. Sprinkle the spell ingredients except for the sunstone in an open field at your earliest convenience.

Green Candle Money Spell

You need:

Green candle

Favorite oil

Six coins

Cinnamon

Green cloth or pouch

Set up your altar and then take a few minutes to meditate before you begin your spell, so that you are mentally energized.

Anoint your candle with your chosen oil and place it on your altar. Form a circle around the candle with the coins. While laying the coins out, picture yourself with the money you want, and project all of this gratitude out into the universe. As you light your candle, repeat the following three times:

"Money flows. Money grows. My money shines. This money is mine."

Place the cloth down on your altar and sprinkle some cinnamon over it. If you choose a pouch, sprinkle the cinnamon inside of it.

Next, place the coins on the cloth, or place them in the pouch. Wrap the cloth around the coins if not using the pouch. While you are picking up the coins, say the following three times:

"Bring me money three times three as I will it, so mote it be."

Bring the corners of the cloth together and tie them closed. If you have a pouch, tie them closed. Carry your bundle with you at all times, and picture yourself receiving all of the money that you desire.

Business Success Spell

What You will Need:

A piece of paper with the name of your business written on it and the amount of income you would like to gain in a given amount of time

A green candle

A monetary note

Casting the Spell:

Cast your circle and invoke the Divine.

Light the candle.

As you wait for the wax to melt, visualize the success of your business. Think about how you began, how far you have come and your goals for the future. Remind yourself what drove you to this business and what you love most about it.

Take the piece of paper and drip a few drops of the candle wax onto it. Allow it to dry.

Set the monetary note on top of the paper, and then the green candle on top of that.

Blow out the candle and picture your business rising along with the smoke.

Close the circle and give thanks.

Keep the candle on top of the note and paper on your alter if possible. If you develop new goals, write them down and perform the spell again, using the same candle.

Stomach Relief Spell

What You will Need:

A cup of chamomile tea with lemon

Peppermint incense

Casting the Spell:

Cast your circle and invoke the Divine.

Light the incense and get into a comfortable position.

Take sips of the tea as you wish. Make sure it is warm and free of any artificial sweeteners.

Focus on breathing naturally, listening to your breath as you inhale and exhale.

Touch your hand to your stomach and say something like: "With healing chamomile, rejuvenating lemon and refreshing peppermint… relieve me of this pain, so mote it be."

Allow the incense to burn out and finish your tea.

Close the circle and give thanks.

You can try this spell with lemon water, mint water or plain chamomile tea.

Bless Some Ones Health

The items used for this spell are not a physical cure, but they are meant to represent health. For this spell you will need:

A cup of organic apple juice

A glass

A cinnamon stick

A white candle

After pouring the apple juice in the glass, stir the juice 4 times with the cinnamon stick. Light the candle, take a drink and then say the following:

"Goddess bless my body and soul

Health and vitality is my goal"

Drink the rest of the juice, and then snuff out the candle. You can repeat this spell whenever you feel like you are starting to feel ill, or you can repeat it every morning.

Argument Clearing Spell

When a relationship with a close friend or loved one is strained, or when resentment has stopped you from making up with someone. This will help you clear the air. You will need:

A bay leaf (fresh and organic is always preferred, dry is ok)

A small envelope

A yellow candle

Before you start, have a glass or metal bowl nearby to put the envelope in. On one side of the envelope write you own name, on the other side of the envelop, write your friends name. Place the leaf inside the envelope and seal it. Light the yellow candle and hold the envelope in the flame until it burns. Drop the envelope into the bowl if it starts to get to hot.

General Happiness Spell

No need to let yourself start feeling down. Start putting some joy in your day, and start looking at everything is a positive light. You will need:

2 Orange Candles

Dried Lavender

Place a pinch or two of lavender on an altar or a table in the middle of the two orange candles. Light both candles and place your hands so you can feel some heat from the candleflame. Say this seven times:

"With this spell please bless

For my life full happiness."

Allow the candle to burn and you will soon see happy days.

A Confidence Candle

We all need help feeling confident in the decisions we must make every day. This candle spell will help you learn to love yourself. What you will need:

A pink candle

White and pink rose petals

Spring water (rain water if available)

If you do not have spring water, and rain water is not available, you could use tap water.

On a table or your altar, place the flower petals in the shape of a ring and place the pink candle in the center. Right before lighting the candle, concentrate of your best traits keep thinking of only those traits for a few minutes. Light the candle and say the following:

"Allow my light to shine

Only with love Divine."

Drink some of the water, to help cleanse your mind of all negative thoughts of yourself. Allow the candle to burn all the way out by itself.

Marriage and Relationship Healing Spell

Needed for this spell:

A white candle

A pink candle

A glass or metal bowl

Matches (lighter)

Pen and a piece of paper

2 pieces of string

To Prepare:

You will need about 30 minutes to prepare.

Start off by writing two letters. Address the first one to the God of the universe, and the second to the Goddess of the universe. In your first letter, write in detail all of the problems you have in your marriage and how you feel about it. Only you will ever see this letter, so put everything out there. Express all of your true feelings as honestly as you can.

After expressing all of your feelings you have about your relationship, write what would happen if your marriage or relationship were perfect. How would you and your significant other act toward one another? Would you like them to be a better listener, and pay more attention to you? What do you need to be happy? Make this letter longer than the first letter. Be as detailed as you can.

Take a few minutes here to meditate and center yourself again before going back to the spell.

To perform the spell:

Get together all of the spell components (including the letters you just wrote) and cast a circle. Light the white candle (which represents spirituality and peace). Next light the pink candle (which represents love and affection).

Place the first letter that you wrote in the bowl and light it on fire. While the letter is burning, let yourself feel the negative energy in your marriage or relationship burns off with it. Say the following:

"Sacred flames carry my problems away,

Let our relationship start anew this day."

Get the second letter and pieces of string. Read over the letter again, and visualize for a few minutes the desired picture of you and your loved one living together and living in harmony with one another.

Take the two lengths of string, and tie them together at one end so they form one longer piece of string. Ensure the knot is strong. The knot will represent the bond between you and your partner. Fold the paper in half and in half again. Wrap the string around the paper while you say:

"Goddess and God above,

Please help unite me with my love,

Bring us sacred harmony and peace,

Allow the strength of our bond to increase.

So be it."

Close the circle and bury the paper and string near an apple or a birch tree (they symbolize love). If an apple of birch is not available, substitute anther nearby tree.

Divination with Many Candles

Use this spell to help see what is in your future. You will receive different signs during the spell. You will need to interpret what each sign means. For this spell you will need:

3 candles that are exactly the same

Start by placing the three candles on your altar in the shape of a triangle. Light the candles starting at the top of the triangle and light the rest in counterclockwise direction.

To read the signs you receive:

If you see one flame burning brighter than the rest, you are entering a time of good fortune

If one of the candles flames extinguishes suddenly, you have negative energy headed toward you. You will need to perform a protection spell

If the candle flames burn bright and then start to suddenly dim, stay on guard. You are entering a time of uncertainty and sudden change

If the candle flames appear to twist and turn or have a spiral appearance, someone close to may be harboring a grudge or have some secret resentment for you. They are not deserving of your trust

Wiccan Anti-Harassment Candle Spell

Make sure to begin casting this spell during a waning moon. Take a brown-colored candle to symbolize the particular individual who is incessantly harassing you.

Write this individuals name on both sides of the candle (front-side and backside). If you are using a round candle, just imagine dividing the candle vertically into two parts the write the person's name on each side accordingly.

Write this small incantation down on a tiny piece of white paper:

"From this day forward, (individual's name) only say sweet and endearing words towards me. Through the power of the Goddess Aradia, so let it be!"

Put one honey drop on the white paper in the middle and make it into a small ball.

Using a small knife or pin, make a small slit or gash in the candle and insert the ball of paper into it.

Light up the candle and allow it to burn for one, three, six or nine nights. Do not exceed nine nights.

Find flowing water and throw the candle's remnants into it. Save a small amount of ash or candle drippings to be sprinkled in your oppressor's path.

The next spell involved blessing someone, may it be you or someone else, with good vibes. The recipient of this spell reaps a lot of good benefits, may it be in health, wealth or both.

Wiccan White Candle Blessing Spell

This spell requires the use of a white-colored candle. You can use a plain or a figurative candle that depicts the individual's gender, whom you desire to bestow blessings upon.

Before dressing the candle with Holy or Blessed oil, make sure that the name of the person to be blessed with the spell is carved on the white-colored candle.

To increase the spells potency, you may put a piece of white paper with the person's name written on it, a photograph, or any kind of personal item either next to the candle or under it. That person's personal item may come in the form of a piece of hair, clothing, finger nail, etc. To make things easier, you can put all of the aforementioned items under an upside-down plate or saucer and then place the white-colored candle on top.

Let the candle burn for a little while every day for about seven days, snuffing it out between burnings. Every time you light the candle up, recite this incantation verbatim:

"(Person's name), may you always be blessed. Let all desirable matters come your way. May you forever be away from harm. Let your heart be light. Let your journeys be free from trouble. Let your well-being be always in good condition. Let your mind be at peace. Let your personal relationships sustain you. May all aspects of your life be blessed."

Take note, however, that this incantation is not set in stone. You can also add your additional requests for the recipient of this spell in the incantation.

This spell ends as soon as the candle is completely burned out. Therefore, if you or the recipient of this spell requires blessing for an extended amount of time, use a big pillar-type candle, so that burning it for a little while each day takes longer. In cases where a large tower-type candle is used, re-dressing the candle with oil one time each week is required.

This next spell helps you get that one job that you have been yearning for.

Candle Spell To get a job

This particular spell needs to be casted only after you have submitted your application or resume.

Casting this spell requires using two large candles; a red and a green one. Using a small knife or a pin, carve the names of the companies that you would like to work in on the side of the large green-colored candle.

Carve the symbol of the Tiwaz victory rune together with your full name on the side of the red candle. The Tiwaz victory rune looks like an arrow pointing upwards.

After the sun sets on a Thursday, burn the two candles for about 30 minutes while envisioning getting the job you want.

Once you reach the 30-minute mark, snuff the candles out. Remember, snuff instead of blowing them out.

After that, continue burning the candle for about 15 minutes every Thursday night, until it completely burns itself out or you get the desired job.

Throw away the used candles and leave a bowl of fresh milk outside until morning as an offering.

Improving oneself is everybody's main goal. However, doing this proves to be much more difficult for some people due to the fact that they lack self-confidence. Confidence is a very important aspect in a person's life. This candle spell helps you have confidence in yourself.

Cinnamon Money Magnet Charm

You will need:

A cinnamon stick, 2-3 inches in length

12-18-inches of green or gold ribbon

Instructions:

Thread the ribbon through the hollow of the cinnamon stick and tie the ends securely.

Hold the stick in both palms and close your eyes. Imagine a storm of dollar bills flying at you from all directions.

Gently touch the stick to the pulse points at your wrists, elbows, neck, and temples as you say the following (or similar) words:

"Sweet wood of cinnamon,

Draw to me my fortune.

In record time, more money is mine,

Attracted with this talisman."

Hang your 'money magnet' somewhere visible and try to touch it at least once every day.

Youth Preservation Spell

What You will Need:

A candle of your choice (yellow or green are good choices for youth and growth)

A native flower or plant seed

A small flower pot

Fresh soil from the earth

Your favorite essential oil (patchouli or jasmine are good choices for beauty)

Fresh water

Casting the Spell:

Cast your circle and invoke the Divine.

Light the candle and reflect on the qualities you love about yourself. Imagine yourself remaining a beautiful individual for years to come, with your beauty continuing to grow like a blooming flower.

Take your flowerpot and anoint it with your favorite essential oil. Blow out the candle.

Fill the flowerpot with fresh earth and plant the seed inside of it.

Water the flowerpot. Visualize the seed growing and flourishing, along with your beauty. Acknowledge the youthful life force within the seed and borrow it for yourself. In turn, take care of the plant.

Keep the flowerpot somewhere safe where it can be exposed to sunlight.

Close the circle and give thanks.

Continue to take care of the plant as you would yourself, with natural nourishment from water and sunlight. If possible, plant a native flower outside to attract honeybees and birds. Take time to appreciate the youthful, ever cycling beauty of nature and your inner self.

Red Beauty Spell

What You will Need:

A fire opal

An athame or ritual knife

A red candle

If possible, where red and/or black clothing

Casting the Spell:

Cast your circle and invoke the Divine.

Sit at your alter or sacred space with your back straight. Take three deep breaths and hold your head up. Try to relax; you do not want to be too tense.

Light the red candle and hold the opal in your hand. Invoke the spirit of fire. For example, say: "Spirits of fire, help guide me to passion and vitality."

Next, take up the athame and hold it against your chest gently. Invoke the spirits of Air. For example, say: "Spirits of air, help guide me to playfulness and confidence."

Take some time to visualize your inner power and brightness. Imagine a wildfire and a windstorm in your heart, giving you energy. Touch the athame to the fire opal.

Blow out the candle when you are ready. Ideally, you will feel strong and empowered at this time.

Close the circle and give thanks.

A Simple Spell for Abundance

What you will need:

A cauldron or a silver bowl

3 Silver dollars

Collected rain or river water

Perform this spell only on a full moon. Fill the cauldron or bowl halfway with the collected water. As you drop each coin into the water, say:

"Abundance, come to me,

By river, road, air or sea.

I am grateful for this abundance, eternally."

Place the cauldron or bowl where the moonlight can reflect upon the surface of the water. The next day, remove the coins and keep them in your pocket, billfold, or purse. Never spend them.

A Treasure Chest

What you will need:

A wooden box with a latch

A coin of every denomination, some foreign coins, and a paper bill of each denomination

Green jade

Pyrite

Clear quartz

Rose quartz

A bundle of alfalfa, tied with green string

Freshly picked basil leaves

3 Bay leaves

A piece of ginger root

Abundance oil

Florida water or orange blossom water

A spray bottle

A bundle of sage

Matches

Perform this spell under a Full Moon. A Blue Moon (the second full moon in a month) is a particularly good time for this spell.

This is an expensive spell, obviously, but a powerful one. Save it for a time when things are going well, or save up for it to build up your abundance and help keep it going strong. In the spray bottle, mix some Florida or orange blossom water with a few drops of the abundance oil. Light the sage bundle and gently smudge each coin, bill, and stone. Take the spray bottle and lightly mist each coin, bill, and stone, setting each one inside the box as you do so. As you place each object into the box, say: "By the power of three times three, this treasure box brings abundance to me."

When you are finished placing all the objects in the box, close the box and place your hand upon it. Say:

"This box is now a magnet for wealth and prosperity

Which then flows from this box to me,

That it harm none,

So, mote it be."

Set the box in the light of the moon, either outside (where it will not be detected or stolen), or on a windowsill, and say:

"Bella luna,

Cast your light

Upon this treasure box tonight

And let my magic take flight."

Recharge the box every full moon for continued flow of wealth and abundance.

Note: If you ever find you are in a situation where you must spend the money in the box, do not worry over it. Use the stones in new ways for continued prosperity, and when you are able, refill and recharge the box.

Wiccan Anti-Harassment Candle Spell

Make sure to begin casting this spell during a waning moon. Take a brown-colored candle to symbolize the particular individual who is incessantly harassing you.

Write this individuals name on both sides of the candle (front-side and backside). If you are using a round candle, just imagine dividing the candle vertically into two parts the write the person's name on each side accordingly.

Write this small incantation down on a tiny piece of white paper:

"From this day forward, (individual's name) only say sweet and endearing words towards me. Through the power of the Goddess Aradia, so let it be!"

Put one honey drop on the white paper in the middle and make it into a small ball.

Using a small knife or pin, make a small slit or gash in the candle and insert the ball of paper into it.

Light up the candle and allow it to burn for one, three, six or nine nights. Do not exceed nine nights.

Find flowing water and throw the candle's remnants into it. Save a small amount of ash or candle drippings to be sprinkled in your oppressor's path.

The next spell involved blessing someone, may it be you or someone else, with good vibes. The recipient of this spell reaps a lot of good benefits, may it be in health, wealth or both.

A Confidence Candle Spell

For this spell you will need the following:

White and pink rose petals

Pure/Fresh water – Natural is best in this case. However, if you are not entirely comfortable drinking rainwater, a bottle of spring water would suffice. You may use tap water in a pinch; however, it is not ideal.

A pink-colored candle

With the rose petals, make a right of them on top of a table or an altar.

Set the candle in the middle of the right of rose petals.

Think of your best characteristics as a person and focus on it for a bit before lighting up the candle.

Light the candle up, and then repeat the following incantation:

"May my personal light glimmer, with true love Divine."

After reciting the incantation, drink the natural water in order for you to get rid of any negative vibes or thoughts.

Allow the candle to completely burn down on its own.

If you have been separated from your significant other, sexual partner or something of the sort, below is the perfect candle spell to case to reunite you with each other.

Double Money Spell

You will need some type of money on hand to perform this spell

Pick an amount of money and get it ready for the spell. It should be physical money, not a check. The more money you have on hand for the spell, the more money you are going to get once the spell is over. You can use as many bills as you need to.

Place the money inside an unused white envelope and seal it. Fold the envelope in half. The fold should be made toward you, and as you do so, say:

"Powers that be, to me shall bring the means to double this sum. Hear me, you spirit which sing, quickly and gently come."

This should be done once a day for a week. When you say the chant, have the envelope in your hands and stretch it out in front of you. Imagine that the envelope is becoming heavier. While working the spell, the envelope needs to be kept someplace safe in your bedroom

Once the money has come to you, you can take the money out of the envelope and deposit it or spend it.

If you ever do this spell again, you must use different money and a new envelope.

Bringing Love Back Spell

What You will Need:

A pen and paper

Jasmine incense or oil

Casting the Spell:

Cast your circle and invoke the Divine.

Write down your name and the name of your lover that you have lost or are afraid to lose. Draw a square around your names.

Light the incense and hold the paper over the smoke (do not burn it). If you are using oil, put a small dab in the middle of the paper.

Breathe deeply and meditate on your relationship. Is it healthy? Is it genuine? If so, focus on your relationship growing and lasting.

Say a few words if you wish. For example, "Jasmine of love and luck, bring my lover back for they are away from me stuck".

Burn the paper if you wish or keep it in a safe place.

Close the circle and give thanks.

Love is never easy, especially if you have lost love of fear your love may be fading away. Keep moving forward and allow the strength of the Divine energies fill you with the will to withstand your challenges.

Headache Relief Spell

What You will Need:

Peppermint oil

A cup of clean water

A white candle

Cinnamon incense

Casting the Spell:

Cast your circle and invoke the Divine.

Light the candle and then use it to light the incense.

Mix in a few drops of the peppermint oil in with the water. Massage it onto your temples and the back of your neck.

Breath in the scents of peppermint and cinnamon. Breathe in and out deeply, but naturally. Focus on your breathing and continue to do so until you feel you are more relaxed.

If you are able to, lay down and rest as the white candle and incense continues to burn.

Blow out the candle when you are ready.

Close the circle and give thanks.

This spell is meant to soothe you and relieve you of pain. Lavender oil and your favorite incense can also do the trick. Try to control your breathing, drink lots of water and lay down until the

Beauty Charm Spell

What You will Need:

A pouch, preferably leather

3 Herbs of your choice

A small shard or stone of your favorite crystal or gem

Your favorite essential oil

Casting the Spell:

Cast your circle and invoke the Divine.

Gather your herbs together. If need be, dice them with your boline.

Sprinkle the herbs inside the pouch (you may need to put them inside of a smaller cloth to ensure they are contained).

Insert the small piece of your favorite crystal or gem into the pouch.

As you are performing these activities, visualize the crystal as yourself and the herbs as beautiful qualities that you love about yourself.

Close up the pouch and anoint it with your favorite essential oil.

Close the circle and give thanks.

Keep this pouch on you whenever you wish to recall or bring forth your inner and outer beauty. Let it remind you of who you are as an individual and ensure that it is geared toward your personal interests and passions.

Calling in the Cash

You will need:

A gold (or green) spell/votive candle

Wealth Attraction Oil

A $1, $5, $10, or $20 bill (or higher, depending on how comfortable you feel carrying cash with you)

A green or gold ribbon

Instructions:

First, anoint your temples, third eye, and pulse points with the oil. Then anoint the candle, starting at the base and working your way up to the top.

Anoint the bill at each corner on both sides. Then fold the bill into a triangle shape and bind with the ribbon.

Light the candle and tilt it over the center of the folded bill so that a little wax drip onto the ribbon.

Place the candle in its holder, and when the wax on the bill has dried a bit, place the bill gently between your palms.

Say the following (or similar words) three times:

"Essence of abundance, I call you forth into my life in the form of solid currency."

Leave candle to burn out on its own. Carry the magically charged bill with you in your wallet for at least one month.

Pyrite for Prosperity Change Jar

You will need:

A medium-sized raw pyrite stone

Jar for keeping change

Several coins of different denominations

Decorating materials (optional)

Instructions:

If you are decorating your jar, it is nice to do this as the first step of the spell, but you can do it ahead of time if need be.

When you are ready to start, charge the pyrite by holding it between your palms for several moments, focusing on the feeling of balance and prosperity.

When you can feel a strong energy running through your hands, say the following (or similar) words: "In wealth and wisdom, my life grows."

Place the pyrite at the bottom of the jar, and gently drop in the coins.

Whenever you add coins or remove them from the jar, acknowledge the pyrite in some way, either by thanking it, or by repeating the words of the spell.

Be sure to also honor your own capacity for creatively influencing your financial life.

Desire Spell

What You will Need:

A red candle

Opal

Patchouli oil

Musk incense

Casting the Spell:

Cast your circle and invoke the Divine.

Anoint the candle with the patchouli oil.

Light the candle and stare into the flames. Use it to light the incense.

Hold the opal in your hands and imagine the stone amplifying your emotions and the emotions of your lover (or potential).

Visualize yourself with your lover in an intimate situation. Imagine yourself feeling confident as they gaze upon you and begin to touch you.

When you are ready, blow out the candle and put away the opal. Your body should be buzzing with energy and emotion. Take some time to meditate and focus your energy.

Close the circle and give thanks.

Remind yourself that desire and love may take time, and infatuation should not be mistaken for desire. Energize yourself with positive thoughts by acknowledging your desirable traits. If you attract the desire of your lover, be sure to consider what follows.

Purified Luck Spell

What You will Need:

Four green candles

One white candle

Quartz crystal

Sage or bay leaves

A photo of yourself

Sandalwood or frankincense incense (optional)

An offering bowl

Casting the Spell:

Cast your circle and invoke the Divine.

Place the green candles at each cardinal point (north, west, south, east) with the white candle in the middle. Place your photo in front of the white candle.

Place the quartz crystal and sage or bay leaves into the offering bowl.

Light each of the green candles, and then the white candle. Light the incense with the white candle.

Carefully pour a couple droplets of wax on your photo from the white candle.

Focus on your photo and imagine yourself being lucky and successful. Ground yourself to the earth and imagine prosperity flowing into you. Slowly blow out all the candle, allowing yourself to be immersed in clear, positive thoughts.

Close the circle and give thanks.

Leave your photo and offerings overnight if possible.

Quick Good Luck Spell

What You will Need:

A sealed four-leaf clover (you can just visualize one if need be), OR

An acorn, OR

An item or talisman that you cherish

An incense of your choice (optional)

Casting the Spell:

Cast your circle and invoke the Divine.

Take up your luck item in your hand.

Take three deep breaths. Visualize happy, positive energies interacting between your hand and the item.

If you wish, say a simple chant. For example, "Please bring me what I need, give me luck to help me succeed".

Place the item on your alter or somewhere safe and contained.

If you wish, light your favorite incense and allow it to burn completely while you meditate or rest.

Close the circle and give thanks.

If you are traveling or wish to carry luck with you, keep the item on your body in your pocket or as a necklace. Try not to let self-doubt enter your thoughts. If it does, remind yourself of something positive in your life and consider the strength of your inner power.

Utilize This Spell for Banishing Stress and Stress

You Require:

A Black candle

A Piece of paper

Something to light your candle

Method:

Cleanse your distance and throw your circle of security.

Draw on a pentacle.

Set the paper in the middle of your sanity or area at which you are working.

Lighting the candle

Since the candle is burning, chant the following:

"I call on abilities far and close to

To banish, that is not welcome.

Use this candle, utilize this allure,

To banish that would lead to harm.

Send undesirable injury away."

Envision all the negativity, fear, and anxiety-dissolving since you are chanting.

Create a Magickal Anti-Anxiety Bath

You Require:

1/4 Cup of chamomile blossoms

1/4 Cup of hibiscus blossoms

1/4 Cup of lavender blossoms

1/2 Cup of black sea salt

Method:

Run and a bath combine it with the components that are above mentioned. Get in and revel in the vibe! If you would like to take this up a degree, chant some positive affirmations if you are able to make the thought, even better!

Note: Hibiscus Blossoms can stain; you can try infusing the blossoms and then placing the infused water in your tub.

Conclusion

Do you want to change your life? If so, how? Start with small details and see if one area of your life needs more attention than the rest. Once you have decided what aspect you would like to focus your first spell upon, start to look up the phases of the moon, the times of sunrise and sunset where you live, and which days of the week would be best to perform this spell. See what ingredients are needed and go about collecting them. Take your time and enjoy the process of preparing to cast your first spell.

Once you are ready to create magic, remember to relax and have fun with it. A mistake is not a deal breaker—whatever you do, do so with good, strong intent, and you will see the results better than you imagined.

You may instead choose to pick a spell in this book and just go for it. That is okay too! Curiosity in magic leads to miraculous things. Learning keeps us alive and filled with the energy of the god and goddess. Therefore, test the waters, explore, be brave, and know that every spell in this book has been crafted keeping the new witch in mind.

Finally, if you want to go slow and gradually build your altar, gather and purchase your tools, grow a magical herb garden, and wait until the time is right for you to delve into the world of Wiccan magic. That is okay, too. There is no wrong way to honor yourself in Wicca. Choose the path that is right for you.

Try out the various techniques in this book to find the right ones for you, or combine the various techniques into your own spells. Let us hope that you found everything you need in order to begin casting your own spells or to grow into a more powerful witch.

The other thing you can do is keep reading. There are many books on this subject and your skills and magic will only grow the more you read. One thing that other books will give you is access to more spells and more magical techniques. Reading more can only improve your various magical skills.

Connect with other Wiccans and embrace the community. There may be a coven in your area that you could join, or you could create one. If not, there are plenty of online resources to chat with other practitioners. It is easy to become a hermit when practicing solo, especially if you are surrounded by people who are unsupportive of Wicca. While it is growing in popularity, there are people who still view it poorly. Do not let yourself become isolated and alone. Find a Wiccan community you can relate to and communicate with them. Even if you prefer to be alone most of the time, a group of like-minded individuals you can share ideas with and occasionally talk to is an invaluable resource.

Keep up with your magical practice and continue to mold it to suit you. You might find some of these things difficult as a beginner, but the more you do it, the easier it will be. It will not be long before you consider yourself a full-blown witch, even though you became one the moment you decided to start.

Be blessed.

WICCA MOON MAGIC

LEARN THE POWER OF THE MOON AND THE MYSTERIOUS LUNAR ENERGIES.

ILLES ARIN

Table of Contents

INTRODUCTION 212

CHAPTER 1: WHAT IS WICCA? 214
   WORLD OF WICCA 214
   HOW TO BECOME A WICCAN 216
      Peruse 216
      Think 216
      Pray 216
      Observe 217
      Build 217
      Magic 218

CHAPTER 2: THE HISTORY OF MOON WORSHIP 220
   THE MOON AND THE GODDESS 222
   THE STORY OF MOON MAGIC 225
   SHADOW WORK AND THE DARK OF THE MOON 230

CHAPTER 3: HOW MOON MATTERS TO WICCANS 232
   MAGIC AND THE PHASES OF THE MOON 232
   DAYS OF THE WEEK 233
   DAILY MEDITATION OR DEVOTION 235
   DEVELOP YOUR BOOK OF SHADOWS 236
   EXPAND YOUR WICCA COMMUNITY 236
      Connect with Fellow Wiccans 237
      Join a Coven 237

CHAPTER 4: THE IMPORTANCE OF THE MOON 238
      Connection between the Moon and Women's Cycles 241
   HOW THE PHASES OF THE MOON CAN IMPROVE YOUR LIFE 243

CHAPTER 5: PRACTICAL WAYS TO HARNESS THE POWER OF THE MOON 254
   THE FIVE MOON TIDES 254
      Ocean Tides 255
      Earth Tides 255
      Fire Tides 255

    Air Tides 256
    Blood Tides 256
  THE TIDES AND REPRODUCTION 256
  THE TIDES AND MENTAL & EMOTIONAL BALANCE 257
  HOW TO GARDEN BY THE MOON 257
    Planting in the New Moon 258
    Planting in the Waxing Quarter Moon 258
    Planting in the Full Moon 259
    Planting in the Waning Quarter Moon 259
  ZONES, SEASONS, AND PLANTING 260
    Region 1: Southern United States 260
    Region 2: Coastal United States 261
    Region 3: Northern US and Canada 261
  POSITIVE CHARGING UNDER THE NEW OR FULL MOON 262
    What Is Positive Charging? 262
    Charging Your Object 263
  PREGNANCY: BIRTH RATE AND THE FULL MOON 265
  THE FULL MOON AND CREATIVITY 266
  WAYS TO TAP INTO YOUR INTUITION 268
  LIVING IN THE PRESENT 268
    Ignore the Ego 269
    Do not be Afraid to Ask 269
    Meditation 269
    Making and Using Moon Water 269

CHAPTER 6: THE PHASES OF THE MOON **272**

  FIRST PHASE: NEW MOON 272
  SECOND PHASE: WAXING MOON 274
  THIRD PHASE: FULL MOON 275
  FOURTH PHASE: WANING MOON 276

CHAPTER 7: TOOLS FOR MOON MAGIC **280**

  PENTACLE 281
  SWORD 282
  CHALICE 283
  SOIL, SALT, AND HERBS 285
  SMOKE AND FEATHERS 287
  CANDLE AND CAULDRON 288
  BATH SALTS 291
  PENDULUM 291

- Black Moonstone...........292
- Labradorite...........292
- Eclipse Stone...........293
- Oracle Decks...........293
- Grimoire...........294
- Selenite Crystal...........294
- Wand...........295
- Jewelry...........295
- Besom...........296
- Boline...........296

CHAPTER 8: MOON MAGIC 298

- The Power of the Moon...........298
- Herbal Magic...........299
- Spell Casting...........299
- Candle Magic...........300
- Practicing Moon Magic...........300
  - *Moon Baths*...........*301*
  - *Moon Harvesting Time*...........*302*
  - *Moon Planting*...........*302*
  - *Clearing, Charging and Consecrating*...........*302*
  - *Fires and Candlelight*...........*304*
  - *Spells and Rituals*...........*304*

CHAPTER 9: THE TRIPLE GODDESS 306

- The Maiden...........307
- The Mother...........308
- The Crone...........308

CHAPTER 10: MOON RITUAL AND SPELL BASICS 310

- Preparing for the Ritual...........311
  - *Ritual Bathing*...........*312*
  - *Ritual Garb*...........*313*
- Creating a Circle...........314
- Calling the Quarters...........316
- Performing the Ritual...........317
- Ending the Ritual...........317
- Cleaning Up...........318

CHAPTER 11: HOW TO FIND YOUR FAVORITE SPELLS 320

Read.. 320
Study the Traditions.. 321
Finding the Right Circle or Coven 321
Resources for Solitary Witches 322
Online Articles, Blogs, Videos, etc. 322
Online Forums and Message Boards.. 322

CHAPTER 12: RHYTHMS OF THE MOON... 324

LUNAR ENERGY AND MAGIC 324
TRACKING THE MOON 324
Light and Shadow 324
Measuring Time 325

CHAPTER 13: CREATING A LUNAR GRIMOIRE 328

CHAPTER 14: THE MOON'S INFLUENCE ON THE WICCAN YEAR 334

CHAPTER 15: MOON SIGNS 340

LUNAR EVENTS 341
The Blue Moon... 341
The violet Moon 343
The Blood Moon 343
Blood on the Moon 345
The Harvest Moon 345
ECLIPSES 347
The Lunar Eclipse.. 347
The solar eclipse 349

CHAPTER 16: MOON MAGIC SPELLS 352

WAXING MOON SPELLS 352
Money Spell Bottle... 352
Get a Job Spell... 353
Waxing Moon Vitality 353
A Spell for Positive Mental Health 356
Hair Growth Spell 357
Mix a Bath Spell for a Ritual Happiness Bath 360
A Spell to Banish Jealousy 361
Cast a Spell to Banish Feelings of Jealousy 362
WANING MOON SPELLS 363
Tea Cleansing Spell 363

A Spell to Remove Obstacles to Good Sleep *363*
Broom Purification Spell *364*
Self-Purification Spell *366*
Negative Energy Cleansing Spell *366*
Banishing Bad Habits Spell *367*
Waning Moon Banishment *367*
NEW MOON SPELLS 369
New Moon Ritual for a Job *369*
New Moon Love *371*
Tea Cleansing Spell *375*
Broom Purification Spell *375*
New Moon Ritual to Release a Past Love *376*
Self-Purification Spell *377*
Cast a Spell to Open Up Your Spiritual Pathways for Spell Work *377*
New Moon Ritual for Romance *379*
Cast a Spell Designed to Attract Success and Abundance to You *380*
Self-Purification Spell *381*
FULL MOON SPELLS 382
Tea Cleansing Spell *382*
Self-Purification Spell *382*
Full Moon Journal Ritual *383*
Cast a Love Spell to Bring Love to You *384*
A Husk of Harvest Spell for Wealth *385*
Full Moon Divination Bath *385*
Full Moon Smudging Ritual *387*
Full Moon Magical Infusion *388*

CONCLUSION **390**

210

Introduction

In this guide we will learn the beginnings of the practice of Wicca, and how it is still a relevant practice in modern times. We will see the powers that the Moon holds over the Earth and how the Moon can effectively energize your magical intentions. The Moon has marvelous energies waiting to be bestowed upon you. If used in the right way, Moon magic can be a very powerful addition to your practice of magic.

The Moon is magical. It always has been, and as far as we can tell, it always will be. Since the dawn of humanity, we have gazed at the Moon and looked for answers in its luminous orb-to-crescent transitions. It has governed how we plant our food and harvest our bounty. The Moon has pulled the tides and continues to pull the internal Waters of our bodies as well.

The following chapters will discuss the basics of Wicca and its connection to the Moon. They will also cover the way the Moon moves, how these changes affect its connection to Wicca, and the history of Moon worship in the British Isles. Finally, this book will also provide several rituals based on the Moon and discuss how to tailor your magical practice to align with the Moon's energies.

CHAPTER 8:

What is Wicca?

In Wicca, Gods and Goddesses are within us and with us. Portrayed as much more mild and nurturing entities, they are not vengeful towards their children, they do not hold grudges and punish and do not create Heaven and Hell. Instead, they are ever loving, understanding and promote love and equality.

Wicca teaches us to accept Full responsibility for our actions and does not support behavior and claims of an external entity such a Devil manipulating us into doing something bad.

This is where the teaching of Karma comes in that what you put out in the world comes back to you in the form of energy, people, and circumstances. Wiccans do not believe in Satan or any other representation of Evil. Such concepts are usually part of Christian teachings. Also, there is no claim of any exclusivity in terms of it being the only path to knowledge, peace, wisdom and divinity. Instead, the teachings of Wicca encourage the individual to seek out and choose his or her own path in life. This philosophy is based on the belief that Nature is sacred and that Life deserves respect regardless of the form through which it is manifested.

World of Wicca

What many people all around the world do not understand is that Wicca is an actual religion, also known as 'Benevolent witchcraft', 'The Old Religion', and 'The Craft'. This ancient craft is a part of our modern paganism or is also known as nature spirituality.

Paganism is a name for those who follow a religion or practice which is not Christianity, Judaism, Buddhism, or Hinduism. The Wiccan religion is a part of paganism along with Pantheists, Heathens, Goddess Spirituality folk, Ecofeminist, Unitarian Universalist pagans, Animists, Druids, Christo-pagans, and any other Nature related spirituality practices.

However, within those religions, there are a variety of groups, all with different purpose, practices, size, orientation, structure, and symbology. There are many different types of practices within the Wiccan religion, such as Shamanic, Alexandrian, British Traditionalist, Gardnerian, Faerie, Hereditary or Family tradition, Celtic, Circle Crat, Dianic, Eclectic Craft, and many other paths and traditions.

Certain of those groups have other different specific practices and groups. Some of the Wiccan religion groups are initiatory, while there are others who are not. Many of those initiatory practices vary from different traditions; several of those groups have initiations by spiritual helpers, teachers, groups, and deities within dreams, visions, and vigils quests.

In this Wiccan religion and other paganism religions, it is a belief that every human, stream, animal, rock, tree, and other forms of nature possess a Divine Spirit located within. This is why in many traditions, apart from paganism, they have a monotheistic dimension, in which there is only one Divine God that they worship. In paganism and some other traditions, they have a polytheistic dimension in which there are a variety of Divine forms including gods, goddesses, and many other spiritual forces. Nature and the universe play a big role in the way the Wiccan religion is shaped.

How to become a wiccan

Peruse

Before you even consider changing over to Wicca, or before you settle on any concluded choices or statements, you ought to invest some energy contemplating. Sorry to learn this—however if you do not care for perusing or considering, you are most likely not going to like Wicca without question; or possibly you are not going to get much of anywhere. Wicca is a non-dogmatic religion; as opposed to disclosing to you what to accept, it tosses the ball in your court and guides you to think fundamentally. This requires information.

Think

When you genuinely start finding out about Wicca, it is beliefs, it is precepts, and so forth., it is time to think about whether your beliefs are a match. Are your own beliefs something that can fall inside a Wiccan system?

Wicca is certainly not a dogmatic religion, and this is valid; so, anybody coming into it searching for a book of a sacred text or a rundown of charges is moving toward it from an inappropriate edge. In any case, Wicca is additionally not, as some more unfortunate sources have generally been putting it, "anything you need it to be." The issue with saying Wicca is anything is that you are saying it is nothing. There are a few things that do not fit very well under the definition.

Pray

When you come to the heart of the matter at which you realize you need to adore as a Wiccan, it is time to begin reversing. Start going to your Gods. Acquaint yourself and ask them to uncover themselves to you — request direction, for clarification, for comprehension.

Start ruminating—for as is commonly said, if supplication is conversing with your God, reflection is tuning in. An everyday reflection system can be gainful for wellbeing and health purposes, yet spiritual advancement.

Observe

Start monitoring life from a Wiccan viewpoint. Watch the cycles of the seasons and the cycles of the Moon. Start recognizing them in little ways. Consider Wiccan precepts and morals when you are looked with decisions. Think about your life, and territories in which exercises can be gained from Wicca.

Watch your general surroundings; the transaction between every living thing. Begin to see the cycles of the seasons, of the Moon, of life. You may wish to get into an increasingly ordinary everyday practice with your reflections and supplications or start some extremely straightforward, casual rituals to observe Esbats and Sabbats.

Now, perusing and learning '

When you stop it is important to begin using what you have learned, the standards of Wicca.

Build

A misstep many individuals make right off the bat is hurrying out to gather tools—however, Wicca is not a scrounger chase. In any case, now, when you have started to practice, you might need to begin moving towards progressively formal practice. You may wish to begin gathering special raised area tools—you do not need to get them at the same time. It is a smart thought to examine a tool and its motivation, at that point, search for it, begin to utilize it, doing this each in turn.

Many books will guide you to get various things; however, remember that you need each tool that each book refers to. This is why it is critical to comprehend a tool's capacity before you even stress over getting it—it might end up being something you needn't bother with.

Start pondering a standard opening and shutting, summons, throwing a circle. Once more, it is not something you need to do across the board night. However, every couple of months consider and include another component.

Magic

Enchantment is not the focal point of Wicca. However, it is positively a noteworthy segment. In the end, you are going to need to join some into your practice. Somebody intrigued by simply learning enchantment need to be Wiccan and ought to go directly to learning The Craft; however, if Wicca as a religion is the thing that premiums you, invest the energy acclimating yourself with the religion first. When you come to the heart of the matter at which you are gathering tools and holding standard rituals, it is a decent time to begin rehearsing this intriguing and charming component. Begin including some minor mysterious functions in your hover, just as beginning examinations in expressions of the human experience.

CHAPTER 9:

The History of Moon Worship

The practice of Moon worship goes back much further than the current incarnation of Wicca. Wicca, as it stands today, was created in 1954 by Gerald Gardner. And though Gardner created the modern Wiccan religion, he rooted it in English and Irish beliefs that predated the presence of Christians on either island. Moon worship has existed across cultures and continents for millennia. It has likely existed since humans first looked up at the Moon and felt the same awe that people still feel when they gaze up at Her today. However, Gardner modeled Wicca largely on the practices of the ancient English, Welsh, Scottish, and Irish. This makes sense, given that Gardner himself was British.

Unfortunately, many of the pre-Christian religious rites in both Britain and Ireland have been lost over time. This was, in part, due to intentional action by Christian conquerors that invaded the islands long ago. Many pre-Christian traditions were seen as threats to the power of the Catholic church. In order to remove the threat, Catholic conquerors outlawed most of the practices.

This was not restricted to Britain and Ireland, of course. It was the standard practice of the day. As Bishop Elegius of Noyon, in what is now present-day Western Europe said in a sermon, "Let no Christian take note... of the Moon, before commencing any work." Elegius went on to say that people should no longer 'shout at eclipses' nor refer to the Sun and Moon as Lords or make oaths using their names.

Elegius railed against many things in that same sermon. However, none appeared as often or in as many different contexts, than the Moon. Ancient Celts even dedicated an entire festival to the power of the Moon, known as Samhain. It was held at the beginning of November, around what is now All Saint's Day for many people. Ancient Celts would light bonfires and pour out offerings to spirits and gods so that evil would pass the village by during the coming winter.

Samhain was also the night when the spirits of the dead rose from their graves to visit the living. Plates of food were set out for these lost loved ones. And, in some cases, people used the thin veil between the living and the dead to communicate with those that had passed on.

The Sun also had its own holiday, known as Beltaine or Bel-Tane. These two holidays were the largest in any given year. They were so important to ancient Celts that blessings were often phrased as 'the blessing of Bel-Tane and Samhain.'; this to worshipers, meant the same thing as saying "the blessing of the Sun and the Moon."

Gardner adapted all of this into the Wiccan religion. Both Samhain and Beltaine appear on the Wiccan Wheel of the Year. This Wheel marks all eight major holidays of the religion. And, even to this day, Samhain is one of the largest and most widely celebrated.

The Moon and the Goddess

Wiccans seek balance, this is true; but they also understand that change is inevitable. Hours, days, and seasons all spin on regardless of what humans do. Rather than rebel against this, Wiccans try to move with the flow of change and find their balance in the change. They try to celebrate it. And this is part of why the Triple Goddess and her connection to the phases of the Moon are so important to Wiccans.

Because the phases of the Moon run on cycles, it is hard to say which is the Moon's first phase. However, many Wiccans start with the waxing Moon, since it is connected to the aspect of Goddess Maiden. The Maiden Goddess represents all new growth. She guards newborns regardless if they are plant, animal, or human. And She watches over all new endeavors. It does not matter if the new venture is a business plan, a relationship, or a piece of art. The Maiden looks over the fresh wellspring of energy that guides nearly every new venture.

Unlike the Maiden, the Mother Goddess has only a few short days to bestow her energy on Wiccan magical workings. However, what She is not given in time, she more than makes up for in the abundance of Her energy. The Mother Goddess is the most fertile face of the Triple Goddess. To Wiccans, the fullness of the Moon represents the fullness of a pregnant belly.

However, the fertility of the Mother Goddess is not limited to the specific act of carrying a life or giving birth. Rather, the Mother represents all that is fertile and all that nurtures life. If the Maiden is the eager beginning of a thing – whether that is life or a creative project – then the mother is the patient middle point. The Mother has seen the benefits of optimism, but has also known failure. She has grown and matured. And along the way she has learned how to nurture.

The energy of the Full Moon is best suited for spells that help people through a tough time. Maybe someone is running out of steam on a painting or they are struggling to finish a lengthy work project. Perhaps life has been unkind, or someone is out of options and needs help. The energy of Mother Goddess can help all of these situations and more.

She can be called on during the Full Moon, as well as the day before and day after. Spells cast in Her light are those that leave people feeling safer, more secure, and more confident in themselves. They are the spells that seek to lift up and nurture, as well as those that urge people to complete their goals.

That is not to say that the Mother Goddess does not have her sharper side, of course. Anyone who has threatened a mother's child knows what sort of fury a mother can call down. And the Mother Goddess is no different. Although, because of the Wiccan Rede order to "Harm None," the fury of the Mother Goddess is less about retaliating during an attack and more about protection.

Full Moons are the best time to set wards and protections. These protective spells can be for people or homes, or they can be for ventures either magical or mundane. With the energy of the Mother Goddess, Wiccan protections spells are awesomely powerful and fearsome for those who try to cross them.

Nonetheless, what of spells that seek to banish or remove things from a person's life? Neither the Maiden nor the Mother, in their eagerness and their fullness, have energy suited to banishing. They are still young, still learning that there are some things that cannot be healed, cannot be completed. For those situations, Wiccans call upon the Crone Goddess during the waning Moon.

The Crone represents the last phase of the Moon, known as the waning Moon. She also represents the later years of life, when mot adventures have already been completed and wisdom is in more abundance than energy. The Crone is the calmest of the goddesses, content to sit with her knowledge and consider all possibilities before making a choice. She has lived her brash years. Now is the time for her caution and introspection.

With this introspection also comes the knowledge that some things should not be borne. While the Maiden seeks to explore and the Mother seeks to nurture, the Crone seeks to protect. She has seen the darkness in the world and has lived through enough of it that she has learned when and how to end something.

Wiccans call on the Crone during the waning Moon when they must banish something or someone from their lives. They also call upon Her when an end is near. This could mean the passing of a loved one, at which time the Crone can act as a guide for the soul of the beloved to reach the afterlife. Or it could mean the end of a project when the wisdom of the Crone can help practitioners overcome any final hurdles and reach their goals.

Finally, there is the new Moon, which is also referred to as the Dark Moon or Dark of the Moon. There is no aspect of the goddess associated with this lunar phase. Instead, this is the phase that reflects the absence of the goddess. Spells cast during this time either call on the unknown that comes after death, as this phase comes after the phase of the Crone. Or, viewed the other way, the new Moon is also a time of unknowable potential because it precedes the birth of the Maiden goddess.

Each phase of the Moon brings unique energy to Wiccan spell work. This is true whether the phase calls on the unknown space between lives or on the power of a goddess aspect. Every night is a new opportunity for Wiccans to bring the power of the Moon into their work. And, as with all energy, this lunar boost can take their spells to new heights.

The Story of Moon Magic

The Moon is a part of our world. We have never been without it, as far as we can tell. The most interesting parts of our story with the Moon have come from all of the different ways that we have adapted to its glowing and wild magic as it teaches us when to do things and how long we need between Moons before something is ready or right. In witchcraft, the Moon has always been a representation of the feminine. The Moon was often seen as the aspect of the Goddess, as depicted in various styles of pagan worship and all of these ideas have transferred into the modern rituals, spells, and practices of Wicca.

So much of this worship, that has been related to Wicca, was already a huge part of early witchcraft and the various pagan religions of the past. The pagans worshipped the Moon in deep and laborious ways. Their entire realities were supported by the waxing and waning of the Moon, as well as the seasonal waxing and waning of the Sun. Traditional pagan worship was surrounded by the effects of the push and pull of the rotation of the Earth and the relationship of the Earth to the Moon. When in doubt, they would say, ask the Mother Moon for her prophecy.

The research of today can tell you much about the science and physics behind why the Moon shines so brightly, how it becomes Full and then seemingly disappears again in similar cycles throughout the year, and how it manages to coordinate the tides of the oceans all over the planet. Nonetheless, the truth of our story with the Moon is much more magical and spans centuries of dancing beneath it, calling out to it, and following its guidance in all of our personal and spiritual lives.

pagans had their own way of worshipping the Moon that was never allowed to be spoken of, keeping their secret ceremonies to themselves. Druids have been some of the most highly misunderstood of all the ancients, because so little can be understood about their practices from archaeological digs and artifacts. What we do know about them is that they were very magnificently connected to the Sun and Moon and worshipped deities that represented each. They built their entire communities and sacred ritual spots (Stonehenge) in areas where they could see the most Moonlight and starlight.

Places all over the world have similar sacred ritual places and temples devoted to the worship of the Moon. Moon temples are still standing today, built by ancient civilizations in Peru, Teotihuacan, Sumerian, China, and other places around the world. It is a cross-cultural and historical truth that the Moon has mesmerized us all for centuries and millennia as we have evolved into a higher-minded group of beings. Without this work we have done to embrace the magic of the Moon over the centuries, we would not be as understanding of the richness of her power.

Witchcraft found the sacred art of Moon worship through the presence of utilizing its cycles for casting spells or for reading omens. In fact, many witches and Wiccans today will still feel the shock of seeing a Blood-red ring around the Moon. Scientists will explain this as being a matter of light and the rotation of the Earth at the time of its appearance; but to a witch, it is an omen or prophecy of dangerous or ill-fated things to come. It can also mean that there is something circling your power or your purpose with magic that is unwanted and should not be present in your rituals. For others, it can simply mean that the magic of the Moon is amplified.

Other Moon-related omens were associated with the timing of an eclipse, and how the Moon would pass in front of the Sun, completely blocking it and creating an image of a bright, white ring in the sky. The power of an eclipse was celebrated by many who worshipped the Moon and her power and feared by others who were not as devoted and connected to her mystery and magic.

There were also matters of luck surrounding the Moon, and that it was considered unlucky to have a Full Moon land on a Sunday, or that it would be lucky to give birth on a new Moon. Others believed that is you held your newborn baby in front of a waxing Moon it would give them strength, while others believed that the darker Moons were needed to protect the family or the wintering lands. There are a lot of different opinions on the omens of the Moon and for many Wiccans and witches, intuition is the best prophet.

Intuition is the magic of the Moon as well. It is one of her many gifts and so while people learned how to read the energy and lunar cycles of the Moon, they learned also to develop their knowledge of the world around them. A waxing crescent Moon was a good time to plant your crops, rather than when the Moon was waning . Crops that were planted before the Full Moon would often thrive well, and much more than the crops planted on the other side of the Full Moon.

There were also the stories of when animals would begin to have their madness when the Moon became full. Stories of people going mad or losing their minds were often associated with the Moon. The word lunacy comes from the word lunar, which is a word associated with this celestial body. We have always welcomed the power of the Moon and even worshipped it, knowing that her power over us is strong.

The planet is moving on her own axis and while the Moon orbits the Earth, we are able to see her rise and fall every night, disappearing in the dawn light. This regularly occurring cycle has always existed and so has our powerful connection to the Moon. The beginnings of Moon magic are no surprise when you consider how early humans must have experienced this strange, bright eye in the sky that changed shape over time like it was winking in slow motion.

The lessons of the Moon extend to a greater depth than just observing cycles and tides. The Moon has let us become more of ourselves through the symbolic discovery of the power of the feminine. In Wicca, a religion of nature worship, the Sun is a Masculine god and the Moon is a Feminine Goddess.

The male Sun and female Moon are represented through the worship of the seasons and are portrayed in different ways during festivals and ceremonies. The Woman of Earth is also the feminine aspect of the seasons worshipped in Wicca. Gaia, Mother Earth, and others are names given to the feminine aspect of the seasonal shift and urge of the birth of spring, the fecundity of summer, the harvest, and the falling leaves time that lead into the waning Sun and the darkest nights.

The Moon serves her purpose throughout every cycle of the seasons and represents the gateway of change. Every month she glows to fullness and darkens again, preparing us for the next cycle. Our history with following this pattern is as far back as we can recall through our cave paintings and ancient rituals as we were beginning our evolution as people. We learned how to understand our bodies, how to feed our livestock, when to harvest, when our menstrual cycles were likely to flow when there would be a birth or a death, and so much more. As we have become a more technologically advanced society, we have become less engaged and enthralled with the mysteries of the Moon and what she does to influence us every day.

The power of the Moon has not changed, we have. The power of the self is linked closely to this great energy and force and as our ancient ancestors have shown us through their megalithic pyramids and temples devoted to the Moon, there was a very good reason for its worship.

The best ways to understand Moon Magic are listed in these pages and as you begin to understand more of this history and background, you will see why these spells and rituals are so simple and easy to practice.

Through the ages, the enhancing power of the magnetic Moon has given us additional power and energy to the spells we cast. The energy of the Moon is obvious to you when you begin to sense her cycles, and feel the pull of her lunar magic. There is a reason that we all flow in accordance with the Moon; we are 70 percent Water. Water is the element of the Moon. Understanding the element of Water will also help you empower your Moon Magic rituals.

There are plenty of different ways that you can appreciate and understand the way the Moon will affect your life. As our ancestors did, start by watching and observing the Moon. Spend time seeing her every stage and notice the intricacies of the world around you. Notice the synchronicities or similarities involved in all of the matters of your life and other people's when the Moon is at her peak fullness, or when she is at her darkest moment.

Use the observation of the Moon to show you the path to truly seeing her magic. Consider the ways that the witches before you have looked at the Moon and known exactly what kinds of seeds need to be planted, or what kind of spell must be cast. The Moon will tell you everything you need to know if you will listen.

The Moon has had power over our beliefs, psyches, intuition, and dreams for as long as we have had an awareness of its pull. As you read through more of these pages, you will learn a great deal about the Wiccan way of Moon Magic and how it can positively impact your life.

Shadow Work and the Dark of the Moon

The Dark of the Moon has already been touched on, but shadow work is its own field entirely separate from the Triple Goddess. And, as such, it must be discussed separately. The Goddess can be involved, of course; but shadow work is much more about the practitioner than the powers around them. This is why it is more easily done during the Dark of the Moon.

Wiccans foster connections to the world around them. Most of the time, this means nurturing new connections. However, there is always deeper work to be done. And one such form of work is called shadow work. This term refers to magical soul searching. It is the process by which Wiccans and witches look at the connections they already have, and try to understand them fully. This could mean intense meditation, self-reflection spells, or mundane research to discover the who and where of their roots.

No magic should be undertaken lightly. However, this is truer of shadow work than nearly any other magical field. Witches who undertake shadow work must be prepared to learn things – about themselves, about others, and about the world – that may challenge their world view. They may expose secrets that are hard to process and upend beliefs they have held onto their entire lives. Shadow work is about knowing. And sometimes knowledge can hurt.

However, knowledge can also heal. And this is why so many witches choose to undertake shadow work. Everyone has small thoughts in the back of their minds that they do not want to face head-on. Shadow work requires practitioners do just that. And, in the end, they come out knowing themselves better than they ever would have otherwise.

The nature of shadow work means that it is best suited for the Dark of the Moon, or the new Moon. Though some practitioners may want the aid of the Goddess, shadow work is ultimately something that must be undertaken alone. And the new Moon, when the Goddess is either leaving this life or waiting to be born back into it, is a time when practitioners are most alone.

Shadow work is considered advanced magic, due to the possible repercussions. It should not be undertaken lightly. No summary can do it justice. However, when the Moon is dark in the sky and there is no Moonlight to be found, all witches know of shadow work and its potential. It is another journey, another path, waiting in the dark space, between one Moon and the next.

CHAPTER 10:

How Moon matters to Wiccans

When working with magic, it is important to plan your spells according to many factors. Additionally, it can be helpful to understand the symbolism and magic inherent in the plants and animals we see either in our dreams or waking life. This is a practical guide to understanding the meaning behind the aspects of the natural world, when to plan your magical work, and which plants and flowers might be useful to you in the circle.

Magic and the Phases of the Moon

The great part of following the Moon for your magical work is that you get a chance each month to manifest what you truly need. New Moons are a perfect time for beginnings, though they require a certain degree of courage and faith for you to move forward. Think deeply about your desires and plan ahead—imagine your future success. Magic involving purification, initiation, beginning a project or new union, are all excellent workings to be undertaken beneath the new Moon. The new Moon is pristine, pure in spirit—if you are planning to detox, discard a negative habit or begin a new diet or fitness routine, the new Moon is also suitable for affirmations concerning these things.

Waxing Moons are when the new Moon is growing towards the Full Moon, and are wonderful times to do magical work concerning abundance, growth, strength, physical and mental health, and striving towards a long-awaited goal. Magic regarding career and finances are best undertaken beneath waxing Moons; however, there is a time when an emergency dictates the action. Just understand that the energy of the Moon, combined with your spell-craft, will yield a result of a particular kind. Magic to aid in the search for a new job may find you opportunities during the waxing Moon; the same magic may cause you sudden, unexpected job loss during the waning Moon—but such upheaval might also reveal an opportunity you would have never seen, had you been at the office that day.

Full Moons are the culmination; the Moon is at its strongest now, and psychic abilities are at their most sharp. A spell you begin several days or a week before the Full Moon can now be realized fully. Full Moons can be time for celebration, concentration, and manifesting your dreams.

Waning Moons are times of recovery, rest, and cleansing. Spell work undertaken beneath a waning Moon will be about getting rid of what is not necessary in your life or shaking off whatever is holding you back from realizing your goals. Banishing or protection spells can be useful at this time as well.

Dark Moons are the best times for spells of reflection, regarding personal growth. Do you crave to rise like the phoenix and shake off the binds of old habits and ways? A spell for renewal and personal insight during the dark Moon can help lead the way.

Days of the Week

Sunday is a perfect day to do magical work regarding health, finances, fortune, and abundance—anything that you can imagine growing bigger with sunlight can be done on this day. Sunday's colors are orange, yellow, white, and Blue. On this day, Mother Goddesses and Sun gods can be called upon to aid you in your work.

Monday is a tricky day for magic, but it is a good time for beginnings. It is the day of the Moon—and by the Moonlight, we do not always see things accurately with our eyes, but we can often intuit them with our heart. The colors of Monday are Blue, red, and black—the Nigerian god Papa Legba—an African version of Mercury—is honored this day. Give him an apple, some coffee or cola, and some candy, and ask for his guidance or to help with an endeavor.

Tuesday is a day of battle and strength. Today is best for spells of protection or strength. Tuesday's colors are red and gold, but it is best not to wear red on your person this day.

Wednesday is a day of communication and being bold. Wear red somewhere on you to attract good fortune and luck. Magic involving trade, the arts, making beneficial connections, and receiving good news can be performed on this day.

Thursday is a day blessed by lucky Jupiter. The wheel of fortune tarot card favors this day. It is an excellent day for magic involving self-love, rejuvenation, manifesting wishes, and luck in business.

Friday is a day of love but can also be a day of justice. It is ruled by Venus, but is also a day thought to be sacred to Oshun and Oya. Magic involving trust and fidelity, healing, love and friendship, and justice for the innocent can be handled on this day.

Saturday is ruled by Saturn, and can be a heavy day to work. However, it is the best day for spells of protection. Keep in mind that in some practices it is also a day of love goddesses, which goes to show that magic involving romance must be utilized with great precaution.

Whether what you are seeking is a deep and dedicated incorporation of witchcraft into your life or merely to learn more of the mystical tradition, learning the practice into great depth is the way forward. This is so because the field of witchcraft is often a very poorly understood and a much-maligned mystical tradition, given many of the practitioners are highly private and secretive about their beliefs.

Whether you choose to join a community or decide to incorporate the practice of magic into your life on a private level, you can straight away begin weaving powerful spells into your life, thereby transforming your day to day experiences and life. Many novices have managed to practice practical magic with little effort and time investment. You too can get the powers also!

Daily Meditation or Devotion

Visualization and meditation exercises and total devotion of the spirit help enhance concentration for the practice of magic. Make your place for meditation a peaceful speak place that you can enjoy solitude and quietness. It is good that your meditation and visualization exercises are done when there is not too much distraction. One way to incorporate Wiccan beliefs into your daily life is by a regular reflection on your desirable achievements as a Wiccan and your religious path. Wiccan beliefs help to allow a connection to nature, connection to the physical, creative freedom, the divine feminine, family bonding and spiritual self-empowerment.

You can easily integrate these Wiccan ideals into your daily life by having a regular time for meditation, increased time with your family and a close engagement with the environment and all of nature.

Many Wiccans do well to start with just a few minutes practice of centering exercises by feeling your weight and feet against the floor, deep breathing, 10-15 minutes meditation or even the lovely act of thanksgiving for a meal. You may also want to perform a brief ritual to one of your gods thanking them for a blessed life or asking for help and support for a few problems you may be facing in your life. There are still more practices that can take more time. You can take a walk in a natural setting to get closer to nature. You may also create writing or wall arts that reflect your religious beliefs or build a sacred altar to one of your deities

Develop your Book of Shadows

When walking the path of Wicca, it is a good idea to keep a clean track of your journey as a witch practitioner in a journal or diary. As you go deeper into studying and learning more about Wicca, you will soon begin finding preferences and natural inclinations within yourself. Make a note of these observations in writing helps you configure the realizations and the connections about your own self. These noted in your journal soon grows into your Book of Shadows, a journal every Wiccan keeps tracking progress and use as a reference for spell, rituals, ceremonies **etc.**

The Book of Shadows is inseparable from a Wiccan since it is the complete record of the Wiccan's practice and progress. This book follows a number of templates and being personal each person's book can ever be the same. Each Wiccan tailors the Book of Shadows according to different personal experiences. The common themes in the Book of Shadows include a page for the Wiccan Rede, mythology, rituals, ceremonies, spells and incantations, description of the deities the Wiccan follow and many others.

Expand your Wicca Community

As you get deeper into the Wiccan practice and get more comfortable finding how the religion fits into your daily life, you need to become an integral part of the wider Wiccan fraternity. This should however never imply that you should try to recruit anyone to become a Wiccan. The religion does not proselytize or try to convert non-followers. Nonetheless, you can be a Wiccan leader within your local community, offering mentorship and guidance to new members.

Connect with Fellow Wiccans

Apart from performing ceremonies and rituals with Wiccans in your local community, you may want to join a large population. Joining online discussion groups and forum can take you a long way. Those are the places to share beliefs, spells, incantations and personal chronicles with practicing Wiccans and get more insight into this powerful religion. The conversations will offer you a great chance to understand the finer details of the Wiccan faith and help you find support and wealth of knowledge from veteran Wiccans.

Join a Coven

You may also want to join a coven after a year and a day of study. The formal Wiccan gatherings called 'covens' require that you have studied the beliefs of the Wiccan religion for a year and a day before you can be considered serious and knowledgeable enough to attain a membership. Research if you have one in your local community. You might find closed membership covens that do not accept new members or open covens that welcome new members. However, it is good to note that joining a coven is not mandatory in order to be a true Wiccan and to follow this path you can do your practice as an individual activity or in a group setting. The choice is largely yours. In certain cases, you might not find a community in your locality. This should not stop you from practicing Wiccan beliefs. However lonely it may seem, it can still be greatly rewarding and liberating.

A circle is a small Wiccan group meeting periodically, but a coven is more formal. Both of them give some kind of support, but again, the choice is yours.

CHAPTER 11:

The Importance of the Moon

What is it about the Moon that evokes curiosity, awe, and even a twinge of dread? Why is it that the specter of wolves or wild dogs baying at the Moon sends chills down people's backs? And what happens to the minds of unstable people at the Full Moon to have made the word lunatic associated with insanity?

How did a lunar mystique evolve that can be seen in mythology of all eras and on all continents, including among the Greek, Roman, and a variety of native cultures? Lunar images appear as a powerful symbol of human consciousness throughout world literature from ancient to modern times.

We will explore the beliefs of our ancestors about the Moon, the suppression of such beliefs by the knockout team of the Church and science, and the natural principles scientists are now rediscovering. We will look at some controversial research findings and some ways that modern life may have masked or altered our natural rhythms, causing tension and stress. In doing so, we will draw on the work of two painstaking and pioneering researchers into the Moon's history and the scientific evidence for its power.

The Moon was once an object of worship for people the world over. As explorers from the West traveled throughout the Earth's islands and continents, they found people everywhere sharing a fascination and reverence for the Moon and even many identical beliefs about it. There was a linkage of the Moon with fertility and childbirth, and some connection was made between women's menstrual cycles and the cycle of the Moon. Was the universal reverence for the Moon an example of primitive superstition by ignorant people, or did it reflect centuries of observation of the powerful effect the Moon had?

Before Christianity became the dominant religion in Western civilization, there were many gods. Among the most commonly worshipped was the Moon Goddess, who was known by many names, including Diana, Artemis, and Hecate. People looked to her to insure fertility, safe childbirth, good crops, and success in hunting. In those days, there was a high rate of infant mortality and death in childbirth, so her temples were popular ones. No woman who wanted a child and wanted to live through her pregnancy would neglect Diana.

Throughout Europe, in the millennia before Christianity, the Moon religion was the dominant one. Rituals, ceremonies, and revels were held routinely at the Full Moon. Certain Full Moons were considered especially powerful and holy; perhaps these so-called primitives were attuned to the fluctuations in the energy and power of the Moon, which we will become familiar with as we work with the processes in this book. The Full Moon revels may have constituted a safe and possibly even healthy outlet for the emotions that build up throughout the monthly cycle and tend to need release around the Full Moon. Halloween and Easter are actually holdovers from celebrations of that era that were shrewdly preempted by the Church fathers.

Now known by the names of Wicca, paganism, or witchcraft, the Old Religion was not a matter of witches and goblins and was certainly not a matter of devil worship or Satanism. Instead, it was a spiritual practice based on centuries of observation of how the Moon and other natural forces interacted with plants, animals, and human beings. The old Angle-Saxon word Wicca simply means knowledge, and it embodied knowledge of when to plant, hunt, and fish, and of how to heal using plants, herbs, and other natural means. Even now good farmers know to watch the Moon for planting and harvesting. They find, as the ancients did, that seeds sprout far better just after the New Moon, especially the New Moon in Taurus, which falls in late April or early May? Likewise, avid fishermen buy Moon calendars telling them the times when fishing is best.

The Moon corresponds to the more feminine side of people, whether male or female, and the Old Religion itself was a celebration of the feminine aspect of nature, with a goddess and priestesses rather than priests. As Christianity grew more powerful, the Moon religion came to be regarded as dangerous and wicked, along with the corresponding, more feminine side of us that is in touch with the Moon and with emotions, natural rhythms, and instincts. The decline of the Old Religion paralleled a period in history when society became strongly patriarchal and women were put in an inferior and powerless position.

The Old Religion was suppressed by religious persecution, by forceful conversions, by witch-hunts and witch burnings, but it was once the religion of the people. Perhaps you have seen statues of Mary with a crescent Moon under her foot. This symbolizes the stamping out of the Old Religion. And yet, in places where the Old Religion was strong, Christianity won out only by establishing the worship of Mary, in which the cult of Diana persisted, thinly disguised. In forcibly suppressing Wicca, we unfortunately also suppressed much of the knowledge of healing and natural rhythms that accompanied it.

I am not for a moment suggesting we go back to worshipping the Moon; but at least we can stop ignoring it and start paying attention to the rhythms and cycles it represents. As we will find out in the course of this book, there is a cost to ignoring this part of ourselves, in terms of stress, fatigue, frayed nerves, and exploding tempers. This ignorance leaves us feeling deprived, as well as out of touch with ourselves and our needs. We can relieve stress by not working against the grain. We can come to know the periods when our bodies, minds, and spirits need rest, as well as the periods most productive for work. In order to do that more consciously, you will find information here about the best uses of the signs and cycles of the Moon, as well as tables to help you keep track of the daily and monthly course of the Moon.

Connection between the Moon and Women's Cycles

As noted earlier, the ancients prayed to Diana, the Goddess of Fertility, for safe childbirth—not something to take for granted in those days. Among many different peoples the world over; there was a common belief that the Moon had her own menstrual cycle. Even those not involved with Moon worship spoke of the Moon as having her period when the Moon was dark. Many different tribes, ignorant of the facts of life, believed that women were impregnated by the Full Moon. Where did such beliefs originate? Were these beliefs the products of confused, primitive thinking, or was there in those times a close, readily-observed connection between the Moon and women's cycles that would cause them to leap to that conclusion?

Research seems to indicate an actual connection. As long ago as 1898, the Nobel prize-winning scientist Svante Arrhenius made careful studies of the menstrual cycles of twelve thousand female patients of a Swedish maternity hospital and found that the Moon did have a special effect on their cycles. In 1936, ten thousand German women were charted by Guthmann and Oswald, and more of them were found to have their periods at the New and Full Moon than at any other time. A study of over seven thousand women in 1962 by the Czech scientist Dr. Jeri Malek showed that the onset of bleeding occurred at the Full Moon more often than any other phase.

Folk wisdom also held that there were more births at the Full Moon. So did hardworking nurses in maternity wards. Doctors began to be fascinated with the question and to compile statistics. The foremost French medical journal, La Presse Médical, reported that the birth rate doubled just after the Full Moon. A German physician, Dr. H. Gunther, reported increases in birth rates in Cologne around the Full and New Moon in 1938. Studies continued, and in Roanoke, Virginia, and Tallahassee, Florida, reviews of several hundred births found peaks of deliveries at the Full Moon and New Moon. Some researchers felt that the prevalent practice of induced labor, to avoid weekend deliveries cutting into gynecologists' free time, might be distorting the natural pattern of births. Thus, they eliminated induced births from their study.

After reviewing a number of older and smaller studies that seemed to support a lunar effect on births, Dr. Walter Menaker decided to take a very large sample. He reviewed the records of over half a million live births in New York City from 1948 to 1957, and found that the highest frequency of births occurred at the Full Moon. A second study by Dr. Menaker of another half-million New York City births from 1961 to 1963 again pinpointed the peak rate of births around the Full Moon. It was speculated that perhaps the pull of gravity on the amniotic fluid increased with these lunar phases.

Research such as this inspired a woman named Louise Lacey to speculate that in ancient times, most of the women in the tribe were fertile at the Full Moon and that their menstrual cycles were synchronized with one another. It has been seen that women who live together tend to adjust their menstrual cycles to one another. Biologists postulate some sort of subliminal olfactory perception of the released hormones as an explanation. Imagine living in an encampment or tribe where most of the women were ovulating at the same time and at their most responsive sexually, while overhead the Moon was Full, and emotions were at their peak. The connection between the Moon and fertility would be strong, in this worldview, and so would the link with childbirth, since nine lunar months later, also at the Full Moon, children would be born.

How the Phases of the Moon can Improve Your Life

When a lot of people imagine a witch, they will usually picture a shadowed figure who is performing magical rituals under the light of the Full Moon. This image is false in a lot of ways, but in other ways, it can also be somewhat accurate. As you might have learned while reading this book, a lot of witches will actually gather under the fool Moon, because of the strength of the energy that the Moon provides during this time, taking advantage of this energy in order to strengthen their own energies and their spell work. The reason that a lot of witches will be attracted by the Moon is because of the power that the Moon possesses and that it can give us, especially during the Full Moon.

The Moon is a very powerful body, and has a very strong impact on all areas of life on Earth. It controls the ebb and the flow of the ocean tides, the emotions and feelings of humans and other living beings, and even the menstrual cycles of human women. The Moon can also affect the magic that we perform, as well. A lot of witches will tend to ignore the phases of the Moon, and will form their own habits, which are centered on themselves and their own energies, as opposed to the energies of the Moon and the Sun. A lot of people will even center their magic primarily around the Sun, instead, focusing on the power of the god to empower their magic. Every individual person will be different, and not everyone will consider the same things to be as important as others and as other people do. The techniques that will work for one person might not necessarily work for other people.

However, the people, who do align their schedules and their magic with the phases of the Moon, will probably find that their magic is empowered during the Full Moon, or during the phase of the Moon that is best aligned with the intentions that they have and the kind of magic that they perform, or that they are performing. This can be thought of as similar to swimming with the tide in the ocean or the flow of a river, as opposed to trying to swim against it. One way, you will find yourself moving forward much more quickly and easily, is if the Water is pushing you back at a faster pace than you are able to push yourself forward. Otherwise, if you try to move in the opposite direction, you might find it much harder to move forward, or you might even continue to move backward instead.

A lot of people who practice Moon magic still might perform magic rituals or spell work to achieve the same or similar effects regardless of the particular time of the month. However, this is possible because of the different kinds of energies that the Moon will produce throughout its cycle and the different ways that we are able to use those energies. For example, if you are trying to lose weight or become healthier, then there are a lot of different ways that you can do that, and there are a lot of different kinds of spells that you can perform in order to achieve that effect, based on the phases of the Moon. This is very similar to the kind of thinking that you might need to perform if you are making wishes that will be granted by a genie. You will need to phrase your requests very careful, in order to achieve the best effects. If you want to perform a magical ritual to help you to be healthier during the waxing phases of the cycle of the Moon, then you might go into it with the intentions of increasing your will power or strength, and helping you to overcome your cravings or temptations toward certain kinds of unhealthy foods. However, if you want to do this during the latter half of the cycle of the Moon, when the Moon will be waning, you will want to cast a spell to help you to dismiss those cravings or release negative energies, that might be indirectly causing you to succumb to those cravings or temptations.

In the same way, certain kinds of goals that you might be trying to reach will be better for different kinds of energies and different phases, which means that you can change the purpose of your spells instead of the specifics of the spell work that you perform, in order to create the strongest effects in your magical rituals. With any kind of spell work, it will be very important to consider your intentions and the reasons for the spells that you are performing, and plan your magical work around those intentions and the kind of energies that will be best suited toward the kind of intentions that you have during that time. The more specific you are with your intentions and the time that you keep with the Moon, or other sources of strength that you utilize, the more effective your spells will usually be. A lot of people will keep a much more meticulous kind of schedule with the Moon, even doing things like visiting planetary, or by calculating the specific positions of the Moon and the Sun, to help them with their magical spell work. Some people will simply experiment and see what works for them based on trial and error, and will use the results of their spells and the ways that the energy that they produce from the Moon and the Sun in order to fine tune the times that work best for them, and the kinds of spells that they perform during those times. This can be very helpful, if you want to be more exact in the timing that you use for your Moon spells.

However, it is also very important to remember that magic, by definition, is not an exact science. In order to achieve the best results, you should try to use these positions in a general sense, while allowing for some variation with the specific timings and energies that you will be using. In this way, Moon magic is a lot like cooking or other kinds of art forms. A lot of the things that you will do with regards to your Moon magic will be based on feelings, and you can usually intuit the specific kinds of energies that you will be able to use more effectively. Sometimes these energies might not be what you might have calculated on paper, which can actually make it more difficult to achieve the desired effects with your magic, if you rely too much on those kinds of calculations and expectations. You should try to experiment as often as you can, playing around with different timings for your spells in order to find out what will usually work best for you, and picking out any patterns that you notice based on that experimentation.

The Moon has always been seen as a source of power and strength, and humans have always seemed to be inspired by it, using it for a number of different purposes. The word 'moon' comes from a Greek word, which means 'measure.' It was often used to count the days and the months because of its consistent cycles. A lot of different holidays around the world are based on specific dates that are significant because of, or to, the Moon, or come from celebrations that were started as celebrations of certain lunar events. The reason for the duration of the two months of the typical Gregorian calendar is the duration of the cycle of the Moon as well, and this structure for calculating the days and months of the year by the Moon has been used for many centuries, and possibly even millennia. Even a lot of animals will use the light of the Moon in order to help them to remember when they should do certain things. Sea turtles will lay their eggs on the beach to hatch, and the newly hatched turtles will follow the light of the Moon toward the ocean, where they will begin to grow. A lot of fish and other kinds of aquatic creatures will use the different phases of the Moon to do things like mating and spawning as well, depending on the particular phase that the Moon is in. A lot of animals, both in the oceans and on land, will simply be more active during specific phases of the lunar cycle, as well.

A lot of ancient cultures used to use the Moon to help the to predict things, like the weather based on the patterns of the Moon, and how they correspond to different kinds of weather, a practice which was also sometimes referred to as magic in the past. This was because of the lack of understanding that a lot of people had of these effects and the gravitational fields that were produced, and how they were related to the Moon and the Sun, which were thought to orbit around the Earth.

Seven things like natural disasters will usually come during times when the Moon and its influence on us are particularly weak, like tornadoes and hurricanes, which are usually recognized to be a little bit more common during the new Moon and the Full Moon. There is also usually a slightly higher chance of rain during these times as well, because of the varying distance that the Moon will have to the Earth. It is also due to the ways that the gravitational pull, coming from the Moon, which can affect the water in the clouds, causing them to be more likely to fall as rain in some cases.

A lot of people will even perform specific chores or tasks during certain parts of the month as well. Some people will deliberately wait until the final two quarters of the lunar cycle to perform tasks like building fences, because it was often said that a fence would last much longer if the posts and their foundations were set during the waning stages of the lunar cycle. Some people will also set their fishing lures during the waxing stages of the lunar cycle as well, and will do their fishing during the waning stages as well. Some people have even scheduled their weddings, so that they are within about two days of the Full Moon in order to assure that their marriages are healthy and happy. The different phases of the Moon and the specific kinds of effects that most people will find that they are able to achieve the greatest effects with will be listed here:

- **New Moon**: This is, of course, the first phase of the lunar cycle. This is often considered to be a time of renewal, when spell work that is meant to help with the beginnings of new relationships or endeavors will be especially strong. Other kinds of spells that have a similar purpose will also be especially helpful. The new Moon is a time of change and new beginnings, and you will find it a lot easier to find and embrace new opportunities as well.

- **Waxing Moon**: When the Moon is beginning to wax, it is growing in power, as it literally appears to grow in size. As it moves forward from the new seeds that have been planted during the new Moon, spell work that is aimed toward an increase in power or strength will also be especially helpful. This stage of the lunar cycle is a time for growth, and you will find that you have a much easier time learning new things or gaining new knowledge during this time. The waxing Moon can also symbolize fertility, and will be a very beneficial and healthy time for pregnant women. However, the emotional states of a lot of people will also be amplified, and they will be especially sensitive during this time. Because of this, communication is very important in both the personal and professional lives. Magical work that helps with these things will be much more effective than it otherwise would be during the waxing Moon.

- **Waning Moon**: When the Moon is beginning to wane, it will begin to appear to decrease in size. As it does, it will also begin to decrease in power as well as it moves past the Full Moon, when it is at its strongest point. This is the time to perform spell work that is aimed toward letting go of certain kinds of energies or negativity. If you wish to change something within your life, this will be the perfect time to try to do it. If certain things that you have been doing have not been working particularly well, then the waning stages of the Moon will be the best time to let go of those things.

- **Full Moon**: This phase is when the Moon is at its strongest, and produces the strongest energies. The Full Moon enhances our perceptions and our awareness, and gives us more insight than we would normally have. The Full Moon is very helpful for introspection, as well as for emotional awareness. You will also be able to use this time to begin to accomplish your goals and to finish projects that have been left unfinished.

A lot of people will also believe that the ten days that come immediately after the Full Moon, or sometimes the new Moon, will also be significant in their own ways. People who are aware of the specific energies that these days have will also be able to use these energies for the benefit of themselves or for other people.

The first day can be very similar to the new Moon. It will be very useful for things like beginning new projects. A lot of people will say that these are very lucky days for new babies to be born on, as they represent renewal and beginnings, as with the process of birth. However, the first day is also a very unlucky day for people who become ill during this day. Usually, if you contract some form of sickness during this first day, it will be much more difficult for you to recover from that illness, and it will usually take much longer to do so as well.

The second day can be compared to the waxing phases of the lunar cycle, similarly to the way the new Moon can be associated with the first day. During the second day, rising or growing energies will be particularly strong. This is a good time to encourage growth and progress.

The third day is often associated with more negative things, and is commonly considered to be a day wherein a lot more theft will occur than usual. However, thievery that happens on the third day will also result in negative consequences, as well. A lot of thieves who act during this day will be caught very quickly as well.

The fourth day is very commonly associated with structure. Building or constructing things will be very successful on the fourth day. Children who are born on the fourth day are also often thought to be attracted to things like politics or law as future career paths, due to their rigid stances on those kinds of topics and stable senses of morality.

The fifth day is often thought to be another very lucky day for new life, in a similar way to the first day. However, the fifth day is more commonly associated with conception. A lot of people will believe that the weather on the fifth day will also be a good indication of the way that the weather will be for the remainder of the month. This is also a very good time for coming up with new ideas or concepts for future endeavors.

The sixth day is a very good day for doing things like introspection and meditation. A lot of people will often consider the sixth day to be very good for indulgence, or for rewarding yourself for your accomplishments. This day is also commonly considered to be a good day to begin a holiday or vacation, as well a s a very good day to begin an adventure or to explore new things.

The seventh day is often considered to be a very lucky day, as with its association with a number that is very commonly considered to be lucky itself. This is a very good day to find luck or to have faith in yourself or in the world around you.

The eighth day is commonly considered to be a very calm and mild day, which possesses a very low and weak kind of energy. Similar to the first day, if you get sick during the eighth day it might be particularly difficult for you to return to good health. It can be very easy to become sick on the eighth day, if you have been neglecting your physical health. If you do become sick, you will want to take time to allow yourself to relax and recover. You might also notice that you are very sensitive during this day, as well, both physically and mentally.

The ninth day is often considered to be a somewhat unusual in comparison to the other days on this list. A lot of people will tend to advise you to try to avoid looking toward the Moon during the ninth day, because the energy that is produced on this day will be somewhat unsettling and uncomfortable. Some people will even say that looking toward the Moon on this day can be bad for your skin as well.

The tenth day is also considered to be somewhat unusual and have a little bit of a slightly different energy similarly to the Full Moons of the ninth day. The energy that is produced during the tenth day is also often considered to make people feel uncomfortable or on edge. A lot of people will become anxious, or will experience a lot of stress during this day. Children will be especially erratic and energetic during the tenth day. Because of this kind of wild energy that is often produced during this day, it is often very important to be patient and to avoid rushing the things that you do. You will want to take time and make sure that you are doing things right on the tenth day.

When you are casting spells or performing magical rituals, as well as other kind of magical acts, it will also be very important to take note of the days of the week, as they will also have their own kind of energy that is specific to that day, and which can either help or harm the spell work that you perform depending on the day and the spells.

Monday, for example, is very similar to the new Moon or to the first day, as it is often considered to be the first day of the typical work week. The energy that is produced these days can be very helpful for building inspiration, or for allowing yourself to be much more aware or awake. You will find it much easier to come up with new ideas and to be creative on Mondays, as well as starting new projects.

Tuesday is a very stable day, and is often considered to be helpful in building confidence or strength, both physical and mental. Tuesdays are also often associated with healing energies.

Wednesday is often considered to be a very planning heavy day, and possesses a very careful energy. This is usually thought to be a very good day to schedule a job interview or to handle matters related to work or to the future. Research and other similar tasks will usually go especially well on Wednesdays. If you are planning a vacation, then it is usually best to do it on a Wednesday.

Thursdays are often considered to be very helpful to taking care of spiritual matters. They are also often considered to be good for things related to psychic energies or the occult. A lot of people will tend to be much more mentally keen on Thursdays than on Fridays, which makes it a very good day to take care of things like finances or mental tasks.

Fridays are often considered to be very good days for things like recreating things or reimagining things that already exist. These are very good days to do things like redecorating your house or rearranging furniture, because of the energy that is produced on these days, and their ability to help change. Fridays can also be very good days for new beginnings in your romantic life. If you are trying to find a good chance to take a leap with a person who you are interested in romantically, Fridays are great days on which to do so.

Saturdays are commonly considered to be good days for planning, especially if you are planning things related to your home or personal life. Saturdays are very good days for things like making plans for the next week or for doing things for yourself. Things, like abandoning habits or patterns that might not be very beneficial to you or forming new healthy habits, can be very successful on Saturdays. This is also a very good day for change for similar reasons, so if you are planning on kicking a bad habit, then Saturday is a very good day to start on.

Sundays are usually thought to be very spiritual days. This is the day that Christians will go to church for worship, and that is often referred to as the Lord's Day. Christians will usually take Sundays to relax and practice quiet introspection, and will visit their church for the weekly sermon. This is because the energy that is produced on Sundays is very closely related to the Spirit and the mind. A lot of people will find that they have a much easier time making difficult decisions on Sundays, and that they will be much more insightful on these days than they might normally be. Sundays can be very good days to find answers to issues that are troubling you, as well as recognizing your relationships with other people, and acknowledging your bonds with them. If you are struggling with a personal issue that you cannot seem to understand, then Sunday will be a very good day to try to figure it out.

CHAPTER 12:

Practical Ways to Harness the Power of the Moon

And now it begins! You are going to start developing an understanding of how best to harness the power of the Moon.

The Five Moon Tides

Most people know about tides—you say the word, and they immediately think about the ebb and flow of Water in the ocean. The ocean rises and falls daily, thanks to the influence of the Moon. However, there are several other tides as well—the influence of the Moon pulls on all substances, not just the Water within the ocean. Despite the fact that the Earth pulls the Moon to it, the Moon is also constantly exerting a gravitational force onto the Earth as well. It is commonly accepted that the Moon is able to pull on the Elements, but it is also able to impact life itself.

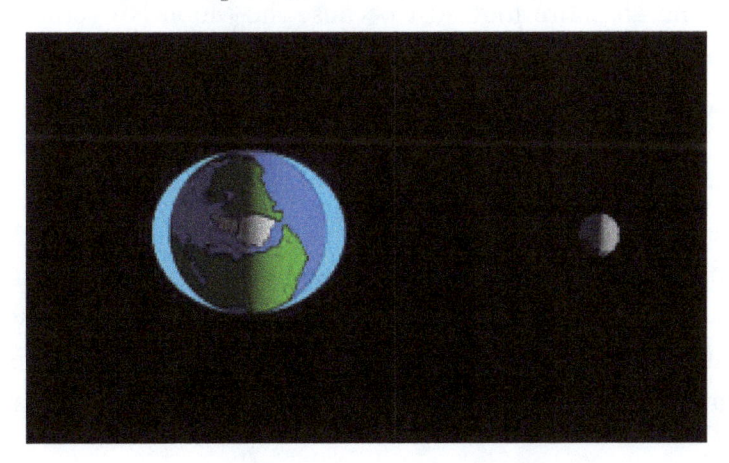

When you are talking about tides, it is important to understand how they work—there are two tides every single day. These tides correspond to the location of the Moon in regard to the area that is being looked at in the moment. These tides occur when the Moon is overhead and when the Moon has traveled to the opposite end of the Earth. These are not necessarily exact—the orbit is not perfectly round, nor is the Earth or Moon. However, after billions of years of orbit, it has established enough of a pattern that the Earth follows this same shift.

Ocean Tides

This is the tide that everyone thinks of—the ocean tides push Water, causing it to recede and grow depending on the time of the day. These tides are at their most extreme during the Full and New Moons, and these are known as 'spring tides.' When these tides occur, you will see a more drastic fluctuation in the depth of the Water.

Earth Tides

Just as the ocean shifts with the orbit of the Moon, the Earth itself shifts. As the Moon rises up over the horizon, it pulls the very Earth with it, causing the surface to expand somewhere between four inches and an entire foot, just because the Moon is overhead. The gravitational force of the Moon is strong enough to move mountains, forcing the crust of the Earth to move similarly to the tide.

Fire Tides

The center of the Earth is comprised of a molten core—it is so hot that the stone that makes up the planet has melted and exists as a liquid center to the planet. This molten core moves with convection currents, with magma rising and falling based on temperature. This is what causes continental drift. And this is still unable to escape the power of the pull of the Moon. The core of the Earth is also subject to the pull of the Moon as the oceans, causing ebbs and flows.

Air Tides

Our planet is surrounded by air. This is well-known—it is what allows us to breathe. The Moon is able to influence that pocket of air, causing it to change and bulge as the Moon passes it by. As the Moon lingers over any given area, its gravity forces the atmosphere beneath it to move upwards. This shift is not as subtle as the Water or Earth tides—the atmosphere will bulge outwards upwards of fifteen miles in some areas.

This change in atmosphere, then, influences the weather itself. Because it changes the air pressure so much, it influences the weather, and it actually has been found that most significant weather events have lined up with specific positions of the Moon itself. As the Moon enters certain positions in its orbit, it seems that it is able to cause the weather itself.

Blood Tides

While people try to reject this notion: if the Moon is capable of shifting the very core of the Earth and literally pulling the crust of the Earth up, why would it be so hard to believe that it can influence Blood as well? Nevertheless, there has been evidence to show that the Earth can, and does, influence the tide of Blood within life itself.

The Tides and Reproduction

The Moon, particularly when full, has been linked to ovulation and breeding cycles, and women tend to menstruate most frequently around the New Moon. Have you ever wondered why the Full Moon became such a romantic object? It is thanks to the fact that women ovulate around that period, peaking their sexual desire as well. It is noticeable in several species of animals beyond humans.

The Tides and Mental & Emotional Balance

Beyond just that, however, it has been found that people hemorrhage more frequently when the Moon is full, and it has had an impact on surgery. Beyond just that, there seems to be some tie between the Moon and the human mindset. People drink more, commit suicide more, become violent more often, and become mentally disturbed more often with the Full Moon. Ask any emergency room worker—they know that the Full Moon will bring far more problems than any other period in the month.

The connection between the Moon and emotional wellbeing has been believed to be linked for ages. After all, look at the word lunatic—it is antiquated now, but it was originally used to describe those of unsound mind, or those who were otherwise emotionally disturbed. The word itself literally means 'of the Moon.' Nevertheless, this notion is largely frowned upon and denied these days, despite the fact that the Moon can influence everything else around it in the world. It almost seems remiss to say that it is irrelevant to human life if it can raise mountains, move oceans, and even create weather.

How to Garden by The Moon

Gardening by Moonlight may seem difficult or even unpleasant to those who would much rather be sleeping, but it actually could influence the successes of your plants growing well. By tapping into the natural cycle of the Moon, you can make the chances of your plants surviving and thriving significantly better with ease. All you need to do is learn what to plant at which points in time.

Thanks to the gravitational field that is constantly being acted upon by the Sun and the Moon, Water, in particular, is shifted extensively based upon the positions of both celestial bodies. Just as the tides rise up with the Full Moon, groundwater is pulled upwards as well.

As the Water rises upward through the ground, the seeds you plant are more likely to absorb that Water, allowing for them to grow better.

Planting in the New Moon

During this period of time, when the Moon is dark, gravity pulls Water up toward the surface of the ground. As seeds that are planted absorb readily available Water in the ground, they swell—this is what prepares them to grow, and they eventually burst into a sprout. Because your plants will go through the initial swelling and bursting stage with the darkness, they should poke through the soil right as the nighttime light starts to increase, thanks to the swelling Moon.

During this period of time, you should consider growing your annual crops that will bear above-ground crops, particularly those whose seeds are external. This means that you will want to take a look at lettuce and leafy greens, cruciferous vegetables such as broccoli and cauliflower, cabbages, and grains.

Planting in the Waxing Quarter Moon

During the Waxing Quarter Moon, you will not find the pull of the Moon to be as strong—its gravitational pull is less than what you would see during a Full or New Moon. Nevertheless, thanks to the extra light from the Moon, leaves grow well, creating healthy plants. The best time to plant during this period is the two days prior to the Full Moon. This will give the plants the added benefit of the extra Water that will be brought upward by the Full Moon.

When growing plants during the Waxing Quarter Moon, you want to plant other above-the-ground crops that will grow with their seeds inside rather than externally. For example, you may choose this period to grow tomatoes, peppers, peas and beans, melons, and squash.

Planting in the Full Moon

By planting under the light of the Full Moon, you do have one inherent benefit—you have more light to use! Nevertheless, there are plenty of plants that will thrive being planted into the Full Moon, despite the fact that energy and light levels will begin to decrease as it all peaked with the Full Moon. As already mentioned, gravitational pull does draw Water higher into the soil to allow the plants to get the moisture they need. However, as the light is decreasing, this means that more of the energy needs to be drawn from the ground and roots of the plant to sustain it.

This is not a bad thing, however—because the roots need to be active, this is the perfect time to plant crops that are harvested for their roots. This can be any root vegetables you will need—garlic, onions, carrots, and beets, for example. This is also the perfect time to plant perennials or other bulb plants. It is also a good time to transplant anything that you would like to move, thanks to the emphasis on root energy.

Planting in the Waning Quarter Moon

During the Waning Quarter Moon, you will notice that both Moonlight levels and the gravitational pull from the Moon lessen. Because of this, you are usually best served to treat this period of time as a rest period rather than one to try to plant more crops. During this period of time, you should instead tend to your plants, giving them the care that they need to thrive.

This is the perfect time of the month to use for harvesting your crops that have grown successfully. Beyond that, you can also take advantage of this period of rest to fertilize and prune your plants, ensuring they are at their healthiest or transplanting them since the nights will be dark, and the plant can redirect energy toward establishing a solid root system.

Zones, Seasons, and Planting

One important factor to consider when gardening, whether in the Moonlight or by day, is zoning. When you plant your crops, you want to make sure you are considering your own weather patterns. After all, you might be able to grow tomatoes throughout the winter in Florida, but if you tried leaving that tomato plant out in Montana in November or December, you would most likely wake up to a frozen plant.

Very briefly, let us go over the zones in the United States, and how these will alter your growing patterns for a handful of common crops.

Region 1: Southern United States

This is the southernmost portion of the US and involves warmer climates. In these states, you can start planting much earlier, either in late winter or late autumn to see early spring crops. Try following this guide, especially in relation to the Moon phases:

- **Feb 7-14:** Plant beets.

- **Feb 15-Mar 1:** Plant broccoli and other cruciferous vegetables.

- **Mar 17-20:** Plant peppers and tomatoes during this period of time.

- **Mar 17-31:** Plant cucumbers during this time.

- **Aug 1-10, Aug 27-Sept 7:** Plant carrots during this period.

- **Sept 9-24:** Plant collard greens during this period.

Region 2: Coastal United States

This region encompasses both the east and west coasts of the US. As you can see, these areas are just a bit further north than the Southern areas, and the dates are pushed out accordingly to accommodate for cooler spring temperatures for longer.

- **Mar 7-16:** Plant carrots.

- **Mar 17-31:** Plant broccoli and collard greens.

- **Apr 15-29:** Plant cucumbers, peppers, and tomatoes.

- **Aug 27-31:** Plant beets.

Region 3: Northern US and Canada

Now, you are in the northernmost parts of the country, as well as the southern areas in Canada. As you can see from the dates, these are pushed out significantly compared to when you could start gardening in, say, Florida compared to northern Washington.

- **May 1-14:** Plant your beets.

- **May 15-20:** Plant peppers.

- **May 15-29:** Plant broccoli, collards, cucumbers, and tomatoes.

- **Jun 13-20:** Plant another round of cucumbers.

- **Jun 13-28:** Plant another round of peppers.

- **Jun 29-Jul 11:** Plant carrots.

Positive Charging Under the New or Full Moon

At this point, you get it: the Moon is powerful. How would you like to start harnessing that power for yourself? You can do so with a handful of simple steps. The Moon is powerful, regardless of the phase that it is in at any given moment, and because of that, you can utilize its energy with ease, particularly during a New or Full Moon. However, the energy emanating from the Moon is super-powered—when you use this energy, you will see the best end results.

When you want to capture this power for yourself, you will charge your items. Effectively, you will take the lunar energy and allow it to fill whichever items you have chosen as the vessel for the energy. In particular, when you use the Full or New Moons, you will be harnessing the optimum time, which will purify and energize your items, allowing you to repel any negativity they have absorbed. By purging the negative energy, you allow for the positive energy to enter.

What Is Positive Charging?

Everything has a charge—either positive, neutral, or negative. This is the energy that is encompassed within the item, vibrating it endlessly. This energy interacts with other objects, influencing them. The items around you will pick up energy everywhere you go, absorbing it, but some of this energy is negative and harmful. This is where positive charging comes in.

When you charge your object, you will focus your own energy and intention on allowing the negativity, that has been absorbed thus far, to be discharged, releasing it back into the universe. This then leaves your own object cleaned out, which then makes space for the positive energy that you will welcome in. When you choose to charge an object of your own with the Moon, allowing the item to absorb the energy of the Moon, you go through a simple process.

Charging Your Object

Regardless of whether you are attempting to embrace the energy from a New or Full Moon, you will go through the same steps to charging. You will want to make sure you have all of your tools—Water, a candle, a bowl, salt, and whatever you will be cleansing and charging.

Start by taking your bowl and filling it up with Water. Then, sprinkle salt across the top. Preferably, you should choose a natural sea salt, which is less processed than typical table salt. The salt is used for its ability to soak up and break down negative energy.

With your bowl prepared, place it outside just after Sunset. This should be during a Full or New Moon for the best end result; though really, just the act of purifying your object at another period of time will still have some sort of effect. The bowl should be positioned so the Moonlight will shine on the Water. In the event of a New Moon, you should ensure that it is sitting out to absorb the lunar energy being emanated.

Now, light your candle. You can also add a sage burn into this stage if you wish to cleanse your immediate vicinity.

Pick up the items that will be cleansed. For some, this is a crystal, piece of jewelry, or clothing, but you can purify and charge anything, large or small. If it is too large, it can be left on the ground, preferably in the moonlight. Hold up the smaller items in your hands, so they are bathed in the Moonlight and relax into a meditative state. Doing so involves you allowing yourself to focus on exactly that moment, as you breathe.

One of the easiest ways to enter a meditative state, if you do not yet know, is through taking deep inhales and exhales. Try taking a deep, long inhale for five seconds through your nose and holding it for a moment, before exhaling for another five seconds. During this process, allow your body to relax and focus on your breaths and your current state.

Once you are sufficiently relaxed and you feel like your mind is clear, take one last deep breath and lower your items back down to you. Then, exhale, blowing lightly over all of the items that you are attempting to purify. As you exhale, make sure that you keep your thoughts pleasant, positive, and relaxed. As you blow, you are dusting them off, so to speak, allowing you to blow away the negative energies that may have become affixed to them.

Now, close your eyes for a moment. Imagine the energy and how it flows all around you. You can feel this as you breathe, feeling the energy enter your lungs, expand, and fill your body with life. Now, imagine how that energy flows into the items that you are cleansing. Imagine the rays of the Moon, absorbing into the surface of the items. As you do this, you need to maintain focus. You can do this with some sort of affirmation or prayer, or literally just speak what you wish to attract. For example, you may say something along the lines of:

The energies of the Earth, the Moon, and the Universe, please bathe [object name here] in your positive energy, cleansing it from negativity.

Make sure that you always include a whisper of gratitude as well, thanking the universe for the energy that it sends toward you.

Place the items within the Water, if they can tolerate this or are small enough to fit. If they cannot sit in Water without being damaged, you can try leaving them next to the bowl, or even burying the item as well in order to get some stable energy of the Earth along with that of the Moon.

As you are setting down your item, now is the time to state your intention. If all this is for you is a cleanse and recharge, you can ask for that. If it is something more involved, make sure you specify that as well. However, for a beginner, you will probably start small. Perhaps try saying something along the lines of: "I request that any negative energy within my object be purged and that positive energy be allowed to flow within it."

Ideally, the items should sit out overnight, if possible. If you cannot leave the items outside for some reason, you can instead leave them in a window to allow them to still absorb some of the Moon's energy.

The next morning, if all you wished to do was cleanse your item, it is done. However, if you wish to set an intention as well, continue on. You will sit outside with your items. Sit in the lotus position if you can, and set up a candle, lighting it in front of you. Take each item you are purifying and hold them in your hand, one at a time. Keeping the item in your dominant hand with your other hand underneath, set your intention once more. Using your voice is the most effective way to really form that intention. For example, if you are purifying a piece of jewelry to bring you calmness, you declare that now; if you are asking that a certain item give you strength during moments of weaknesses, voice that request as well.

With the item in hand, take a deep breath and focus on the vibrations of the item, imagining that both the object's energy and your own are interacting and merging together, and then switch the hand in which the object rests, placing your dominant hand underneath the non-dominant hand. It should be done. Any time you need the item or object, try to feel those same vibrations once more.

Pregnancy: Birth Rate and The Full Moon

If the Full Moon is able to influence everything from the atmosphere to the flow of Blood within your body, thanks to the influence it has over gravity. It also relates to ovulation and menstruation as well, with sexual desires and ovulation both peaking right around the Full Moon. However, if you have ever gone into a labor and delivery unit at a hospital, you may have heard that there is a noticeable increase in women in labor around the Full Moon.

The idea is that the gravity created by the Moon impacts the human body. Because you are made of roughly 80 percent Water, it makes sense that the Moon would also influence childbirth, especially considering the fact that babies grow in a highly Water-based environment. While the amniotic fluid is not entirely Water, it is primarily comprised of Water, along with the baby's urine, hormones, and other antibodies that all mix together. The Full Moon, then, creates a gravitational pull, it is believed, and that pull leads to more births during the Full Moon period.

Now, many people deny this—they say the evidence and data are too slim to necessarily be confirmed as statistically significant. Many people will deem it as little more than the lunar effect—the idea that the Moon is capable of influencing far more than it actually does. It is believed that cognitive bias is responsible for this idea—basically, people think it is true, though it is not. However, is this really so far-fetched to believe? If the Moon has such a strong pull on Blood, it seems likely that there is some real relationship between the two. After all, people no longer consider the Moon to be linked with the weather either, though the gravitational pull of the Moon is undeniable—it is present in the tides, in the Earth, in the air itself, and even in the center of the world.

The Full Moon and Creativity

Creativity is difficult to manage-when you are creative, you are trying to make something out of nothing. This is no easy feat—so much thought goes into creating anything at all, getting the details just right. It becomes easy for your mind to cloud, especially with stress, worry, and even just thoughts in general.

However, you can tap into the Full Moon, using that relationship between yourself and the Moon to help you tap into creativity. By letting go of all of the negativity, the cloudiness of your thoughts, and your reservations, you can release them, freeing your mind and allowing for those creative juices to flow as they should be.

Releasing your reservations is quite simple—you can unlock your creativity with a simple ritual. This ritual of letting go during the Full Moon involves a handful of steps, and you can do it with relative ease.

Start first by identifying the energy that the Full Moon is emanating—remember, this can change with the signs and the month associated with that particular Moon. With the energy identified, it is time to create an intention.

Your intention is your hope for the ritual you are getting ready to complete. You should make sure that your intention is something that you know will work for you. In this case, it may be letting go of the stressors that are holding you back, and holding your creative mind hostage.

Next, make sure you spend time reflecting—do you know what you want? Why do you want that creativity? How will it help you? You want to make sure your agree, and that you can make sure that you know what you are hoping to achieve. In doing so, you can ensure that you understand your intentions and that you are aligning your goals with the life you are living.

Now, release your intention into the world—speak it out loud if you can. This is where you state exactly what you are hoping to achieve: Perhaps something like, "I wish for clarity and focus," or whatever else it is that you need to banish any of the negativity, that is preventing you from unlocking your creative potential. Allow any negative, clouding feelings, thoughts, and energy to release from you in any way possible. Dance, shake, draw, paint, sing, or do anything else necessary to eliminate the negativity.

You can follow this up with a Tarot reading if you are interested, allowing yourself to further connect with your own energy and intentions, or you can skip this step altogether and move on. With the negative energies expelled under the light of the Full Moon, you should find that your creative processes are free to flow once again relatively unrestricted. Now, release that creativity into the world, making it into a better place for everyone.

Ways to Tap into Your Intuition

Intuition is a tour's ability to understand, recognize, and acknowledge guidance. For some, it comes from the gut. It is that initial reaction when you have a certain feeling toward a specific event or person. This sense of knowing, this tiny voice in the back of your mind, is regularly quashed by logic, reasoning, and even doubts. However, that part of your mind that is capable of understanding and reading the world around you are so important to listen to. You should always trust your intuition. Despite the fact that most people choose not to, it is good for you to go through the process of doing so. When you try to develop your own intuition, there are several steps you should go through, and each will make you that much more open and primed to listen to the energies of the universe around you, heeding their warnings.

Living in the Present

Perhaps the most basic method of trusting your intuition is through living in the present. When you do this, you do not let the past weigh on your current feelings, and you do not worry about the future. Instead, you focus on the here and now—what you can directly and easily influence around you. In doing so, you are able to hear your intuition, unencumbered by doubts, fears, anxiety, or anything else.

Ignore the Ego

Oftentimes, the intuition that is felt is not rational—it is the energy of the universe guiding you. However, the ego is usually distracting you from that energy, whispering doubt in your ears through discussing all of the reasons why you should not trust your gut reaction, especially if it does not seem to make sense at that moment. Nevertheless, allowing yourself to live intuitively, even when illogical, can be crucial to really listen to the guidance around you.

Do not be Afraid to Ask

Sometimes, the best way to get the intuitive response you need is to ask questions. Stop and ask for the guidance that you want. Just as you would not hesitate to go ask a mentor, teacher, or friend for help, you should not hesitate to ask the universe for the answers you need.

Meditation

Meditation effectively allows you to clear your mind altogether—when you meditate, you are focusing on the moment. You are making it a point to listen to your body right then, understanding your current feelings as truly as you can. You are also able to listen to the world around you, allowing you to tap into that intuition.

Making and Using Moon Water

You have already been introduced to the concept of Moon Water—when you are purifying and charging your objects, you are utilizing Moon Water. All you have to do to create Moon Water is left purified Water out overnight, allowing it to bathe in the Full Moon's light. The next morning, your Moon Water is ready. Make sure that you save it for use during times that there is no Full Moon readily available—place it into a bottle with a label on it. Of course, you can always try using the colors of your container to create the intention that you wish to imbue to your Water, or you can choose to add a crystal to your Water as you create it. Of course, however, you should always check to ensure that any crystal you use is safe in Water.

CHAPTER 13:

The Phases of the Moon

Living by the Moon helps make your life more efficient. As a magic practitioner, when you time your rituals and spells with the phases of the Moon, it can feel like swimming with the current. It makes things go smoothly. They get an added oomph in their power as well. Working your life along with the cycle of the Moon can help you to feel more energetic and healthier, and it can aid in helping you give up your old habits. The key is to make sure that you work with nature. Moon rituals are a sacred and ancient practice that has roots in Egypt, India, Babylonia, and China were worshiping the Moon was part of their culture. They understood that the phases of the Moon influenced the decline or growth of their plants, humans, and animals. Basking up the Moonlight was viewed as something sacred and needed as part of each cycle. In current times, the Moon ritual carries a similar sacredness and brings about a primal practice into the world. These rituals are things that we need in our life, especially when life is Full of despair, challenges, and heartbreak. The most beautiful part about rituals is that they give you a chance to be quiet. They ask you to set intentions and to connect with the environment. You will find rituals in the next sections of this chapter.

First Phase: New Moon

The new Moon is a fresh start for everybody. This is the time where you do not see the Moon at all and the sky look black, except for the stars of course. Magic tends to be quite literal, and when the Moon is not in the sky, this can be the best time to work on the shadow self or acknowledge your dark sides that are normally hidden away from people. This is also a good time for starting new things and new beginnings.

For example, maybe you have a bit of a manipulative streak and you often try to ignore this part of you even if you are called out. Are there any good ways that you could use this skill, like getting ahead in your career without hurting other people? Maybe you could also use your skills to read other people so that you can encourage them to communicate more so that you do not control them. This is the time of the cycle to exploring your shadow side and find positive ways to use them. Additionally, since the new Moon is the beginning of the phase, it is a great time to set intentions and goals for the cycle. How would like you next month to look? Is there a toxic person that you would like to cut ties with? The new Moon is the perfect time to encourage new beginnings, especially when they have to do with love. Guess what beginnings require? Letting go of the past. If you want to let go of bad energy within your love life in order to attract your soul mate, then the new Moon can help you

A good idea for your magic during this time is to try some bath magic. Your bathtub is basically a gigantic cauldron. Water and salt are very cleansing, so run you a bath and fill it up with some bath salts or sea salt. You can even try using some witchy bath bombs if you want to. Really set the mood by lighting a few candles. Take a relaxing bath and start picturing all of your past pains and hurts being washed away by the Water and then draining away as you drain out the Water. Sure, you can make detailed and intricate spells, but they do not always have to be. They can be just simple and natural as taking a nice bath.

Second Phase: Waxing Moon

Some people like to break waxing and waning phases down into three parts. The first section of the waxing Moon is the waxing crescent. This is where the Moon looks like a smile. This part continues until the first quarter with the Moon is half full. Then, it becomes a waxing gibbous where the Moon looks fatter before it becomes full. The waxing crescent period can help to bring things out. This is a great time for constructive magic. This is a great time for magic on yourself that pertains to new beginnings, like making future plans or projects. If you want to bring new energies into your life, like patience, and a positive attitude, this is a great time for these types of goals. People who are artistic or creative love this time of the Moon's phase for spell work. This time brings more passion and inspiration into your work.

During the first quarter, the Moon's energy is connected to the attraction. This is a great time for the magic that draws things into you. This is a great time for meditations and spells that are meant to bring things into your life like success, protection, and money. This is also a great time to attract people like clients, lovers, and friends. If you are trying to find something that you have lost, or are trying to buy a house, this is a great time to perform spells for success with these things.

A great idea for magic during the entire waxing phase is to write out a letter of intent that states what you would like to get from your career. This could mean a raise or a change in your position, or it could be a complete change in careers. Evidence has proven that writing down things and journaling is a great emotional process, and help you to go after the things that you want. If you are looking to make more money, get a green candle; if you cannot find one, a plain white one will work just as well.

To keep things different, carve your name into the candle along with different money symbols to represent your desires. Read the letter you have written out loud with intention and meditate on it. Visualize yourself getting whatever it is that you want because you deserve it. Then you should like the candle and allow it to burn out. This transmits your desires out into the Universe.

Third Phase: Full Moon

The Full Moon can be a crazy time. Some wild things seem to happen during this phase of the Moon. Emotions are often elevated during this time, and everything tends to be intense. This intensity can be harnessed and used for pretty much any spell. A lot of people like to charge the crystals during this phase of the Moon by putting them either outside or in a windowsill to be exposed to the Moonlight. You can also create a Full Moon by placing a cup of Water under the light of the Full Moon. You can also place a letter of intention underneath the cup of Water. Allow the Water to be charged by the Moon and then you can drink it.

You can do pretty much do any type of magic under the Full Moon and gain extra power, but this is also a time where your psychic abilities are stronger. You should trust your instincts during this time, even if your emotions are running crazy. One of the easiest ways to use the Full Moon energy is to meditate under the light of the Full Moon for clarity.

Some great magic to practice during this phase is sex magic and use the power of orgasm to manifest what you want. Open up your shades and a window to allow the light of the Moonshine. You can do sex magic by yourself or with your partner. As you orgasm, visualize your intention, whatever it may be. Sex and the Full Moon are a recipe for success.

Fourth Phase: Waning Moon

The waning period of the Moon is a time where the Moon is growing smaller, heading back to the new Moon. The waning phase is a great time for banishing work or to cut cords with people. However, banishing a person from your life completely may not have to always be done. One of the more powerful banishing methods are casting spells to get rid of feelings for a person that you know is not good for you, self-doubt, or insecurity. Spells tend to work better than banishing spells include those that work on changing yourself. Get rid of those thoughts that tell you that you do not deserve anything better, because you do deserve better. Get rid of unfair treatment at your job. Get rid of unwanted negativities that are keeping you from getting the things you deserve.

Like that waxing phase, the waning phase is made up of three parts: the waning gibbous, the third quarter, and the waxing crescent. They look the same as the waxing phase, just in reverse.

Minor banishings are a great thing to do during the waning gibbous. This would be the time to clean your home, garden, office, and other personal spaces so that things do not end up building up. You can cleanse personal objects during this time too. Doing this regularly is a good idea. If you need some sort of closure, or you want to end something, this is a good time to perform spells for just that. This is a good time for introspection.

The third quarter is when you should deal with obstacles that could be standing in your way of reaching your goals. Whenever you are trying to work towards something, there will be roadblocks. This

Moon phase will provide you with appropriate energies to deal with these. Temptations are something that you can deal with during this time as well. This time can also help you through transitions.

The waning crescent is a good time to clear your home and life of stress, chaos, negativity, strife, and so much more. This is a suitable time for stronger banishing spells than any other time during the waning phase. This is the time to get rid of anything that has really been concerning, annoying, or frustrating you.

Some other great spells that you may want to perform during this entire phase could include writing your insecurities and fears down. There are some people who will take these things to a crossroads to get rid of it. You do not have to do it this way though. You can simply burn it and then bury the ashes.

When it comes to aligning your spell work up with the Moon phases, do not over think it. While you may think that the closest Moon phase does not work for the spell you need to do, think again. You may not want to wait three weeks for the best phase, so see if there is a time to work around it. Also, this is not an exact science. You and your intention are the most important things in your magic practice, so focus on that and do your best.

CHAPTER 14:

Tools for Moon Magic

Every witch needs their tools in order to perform a few rituals. They are very simple or can be very elaborate. It usually depends on the witch and their practice. For many of us, a few items to represent the Elements and a good stock of candles is enough, while for others, having the full set of Wiccan altar tools is preferred. There is such a unique variety of tools out there and you may already have a lot of what you need in your home. The key is to find things that you like that will only ever be used for your magical purposes.

You want items that you can help you to manifest your goals and purposes and that will not end up back in the hands of everyone else in your household or find their way into the regular rotation of cooking spoons and other useful items. The best choice is to keep your magical tools separate from all of your other tools, and have a space where you keep them safe and protected.

For many witches, the altar is the place to store the craftwork materials and this can be a good choice if you have space for it. If not, do not worry. You can simply keep your tools in a special cabinet or drawer, so you know where they are at all times. You will develop a special relationship with your magical tools and so you will want to make sure they are well cared for and stored in a place that feels right to you.

If you are already a practicing witch or Wiccan and you already have a lot of these tools, you may still find helpful information within these sections that will help you enjoy your magical implements even more!

Pentacle

This is a disc that has a magical symbol or sigil inscribed or engraved on it. This, most commonly, is a pentagram inside a circle. More specifically a pentacle even though other symbols could be used such as a triquetra. This disc is symbolic of the Earth element. It is used to represent the Earth during evocation to energize whatever is placed on top of it, and used as a symbol to bless the item.

The pentacle is simply a disk. It is a flat, round piece of material, often made out of metal or wood that is usually decorated with a symbol. The most commonly used symbol on the pentagram is the pentacle, a five-pointed star that represents the five Elements. The pentacle itself is the symbol for the Earth element in your circle and it is what you would put in the north facing position.

A common use of this tool is to lay it flat and set other tools or ingredients on top of it for consecration and charging. The pentacle tool acts as a stimulus to help your other tools become more powerful and prepared for the spells and rituals ahead. It can also be propped up and kept on the altar as a symbol of your magical practice.

You will find many variations of what the pentacle looks like and is made out of. The pentacle is the most common symbol, and you can also find them with Celtic knots, runes, and other sacred symbols important to your magic work.

A great way to use this tool with your Moon magic is to set it out under the Full Moon, or the days leading up to the Full Moon and let it charge in the light. You can then use the charged pentacle to consecrate other tools on your altar and empower them with both the symbol on the pentacle and the energy of the Moon.

You can do the same thing in other Moon phases as well and as needed. The pentacle is an excellent resource to help you charge other magical tools and it receives the Moon's energy well. You will find it very handy in any magic you perform and the Moon's energy is the perfect way to enhance its powers.

Sword

The sword is often called an athame in magical practices and is a simple blade, like a dagger, that is used for symbolic cutting of cords and ties, as well as literal cutting of items used in your magic work. The power of the blade is part of the energy of the east and the air element, and it will help you to perform sacred rites and rituals that require a specific action.

The act of 'cutting' is a very powerful way to invoke certain energies, or to let go of specific things. Being associated with the mind and the thoughts we have this tool is intended to bring sharp focus to your magic explorations. There is nothing sinister about this blade, and you will not need it to perform any ritual sacrifices or to draw Blood.

The sword or blade is a symbolic tool that will help you influence your magic in a very direct manner. When you are applying it to any Moon Magic you are practicing, you will find that it will be at its greatest power when it has been charged by Moonlight. It has also been a useful tool for banishing unwanted energies or drawing lines of protection and so using this tool for Waning Moon rituals and spells is a very popular choice.

The power of the sword to connect you to the authority of this airy magic is well balanced with the Moon's energy and her feminine force. The blade is a very Masculine tool, while the pentacle has a more feminine 'Earth Mother' energy. The feminine Moon will bring an important balance to your blade so that it is in harmony with the nature of your craftwork.

Chalice

A goblet or chalice stands for the element Water. Most Wiccans do not think of this as a tool but rather a symbol of the Goddess. The chalice has many similarities to the Holy Grail, but it has been used for witchcraft. Instead of representing the Blood of Christ, it symbolized the Goddess' womb. It is normally used to hold wine-light

The chalice is a cup that represents the element of Water and is placed to the west in a majority of spells and rituals. Your chalice is the fullness of your emotional bounty and when it is Full or overflowing you feel like you are as Full as the Moon in her peak. This cup is a wonderful Moon tool because of the connection of the Moon to Water. Water is governed by the Moon's energy and your work with Water in your magical spells can be very focused through the Moon's vibrations.

The Water that you use in your rituals is often utilized as an offering or as a way to conduct energy through your spiritual intentions. You can even use it as an offering to the Spirit to 'drink' from, or you can sip the Moon-bathed Water from your chalice in a ritual. A lot of witches will also use the chalice as a symbolic idea of asking for their cups to be filled, calling on the Moon to pull the tides of Waters in life, to Full up your chalice when the time is right.

This tool is useful as a literal vessel to contain Watery energy or liquids, or as a symbol of what needs to be filled in your life. You can use this tool with any Moon spell because of how linked the

Moon and Water are. The chalice supports the elemental Waters and brings more of the energy of the Moon to your altar or ritual table. These traditional Wiccan tools are very wonderful to have on hand for a specific experience and you will only need them if it is a part of your particular choice of practice. They are not a requirement to practice witchcraft and you may find that you want a simpler set of tools to represent the Elements and directions in another way.

Soil, Salt, and Herbs

The placement of your circle involves where you are setting each element. If you need a compass, you can determine what part of your house faces north and build your altar in an area where you can demonstrate a circle. You already know that the north-facing position of your circle is the Earth and so this is where you would place your soil, salt, and herbs. For those who are less traditional and are not wanting to use a pentacle in their rituals, a simple collection of Earthly materials will help you have what you need to invoke the energy and power of the Earth. You can bring soil in from your very own garden after it has been under the Moonlight, or from a sacred place you have traveled to that is only used when you are casting magic. You only need to place it in some kind of dish or container to hold it in a place where you can work with it.

Salt is another popular choice for Earth energy. Not only is salt Earthly, but it is also very purifying and cleansing and can be used often for cleansing your ritual tools or to act as a tool of protection while you are casting spells. Salt will work well with other Elements, too, such as Water. When Water and salt are mixed they create the elemental ocean which is governed by the Moon. Herbs can be another popular choice as they are a rich abundance of what grows from the Earth and her soils. Herbs are also often used for their magical properties and qualities, and so you may have a specific herb that you want to bring to the circle for whatever your current magical purposes are. For example, chickweed is an herb that brings love and romance into your life. It also is an herb that happens to be ruled by the Moon. You can use this herb in your circle or as part of a love spell under a Waxing Moon to help you attract love into your life. All herbs are associated with planetary energy and when you do some additional research into the wild world of herbals, you can find all of the exciting herbs that are connected to the energy of the Moon. Here is a list to get you started, so that you can play around with bringing them into your magic practices:

Cabbage

Chickweed

Clary

Cleavers

Iris

Moonwort

Privet

Poppy

Purslane

Saxifrage

Water Lily

Willow

And more!

The Earth element can be represented from the leaves and twigs around your yard, too. Using found materials that you collect from nature is one of the best ways to bring this elemental tool into your practice.

Smoke and Feathers

Next in the rotation of the circle is the elemental tool of Air. Air is not easy to represent as it is all around us, and is what we are breathing in but not seeing with our eyes. There are other ways to symbolically incorporate air into your rituals and spells. One favorite is to use smoke. Incense is always a popular choice and all incense, if you are getting the natural kinds, is made from a combination of woods, barks, plant materials, roots, and resins. Other forms of incense known as smudge sticks are bundles of dried herbs that are used to purify and cleanse an area or the tools you are using.

Either stick incense, smudge sticks, resins, or cones can be used to set curls of smoke into the eastern portion of your magic circle and all over your spells and rituals. The smoke that you bring to the energy of your rituals is another way you carry your message of magic into the cosmos. It can be a delicious smelling aroma that can even invoke visions and dream states to help you realize your goals.

Visions and dream states are part of the magic of the Moon, and so when you are using smoke in your Moon Magic practices, you may want to find the incenses that empower these abilities. Some of the following herbs are burned to transport you to your higher mind and clairvoyant senses: camphor, cinnamon, clove, mugwort, thyme, and wormwood. These are just a few to get you started and there is plenty to more to discover.

Smoke will help you engage with the dreamy quality of the Moon and seeing into your third eye. Another way to bring the elemental tool for air into your work is to use feathers. Feathers are from our avian friends who have spent so much of their time in flight high in the sky. Finding feathers on the ground and taking them home to your altar is an excellent way to bring the power of this element into your work.

Feathers can be decorative, or they can be collected into a wand to waft your smoking incense over your spells and rituals. Either of these elemental tools is perfect for the energy that they will bring to your Moon Magic.

Candle and Cauldron

When we use Fire magic, we are illuminating our spell work, just as the Moon illuminates our whole world. The Fire of the south is the placement of the candle or cauldron and both can be used, or they can be used separately.

The candle is a witch's greatest ally. In all of its make-up, the candle is actually the four Elements combined. The wick is the Earth that roots the candle and keeps it burning. The wax is the Water that can change from solid to liquid and eventually evaporate. The flame is the Fire, and while the air is only what it is surrounded by, the Fire would not burn without oxygen, just as we would not breathe without it. For any witch, a candle is a perfect tool in a pinch, when you need all of the Elements with you.

The candle will also come in a variety of colors and so when you are performing your Moon Magic rituals you may want to use a silver candle to bring more of your Moon energy into the candle flame.

The cauldron is a basic tool for the witch and has been used for centuries as a soup or cooking pot. Somehow, it became associated with witches brewing their potions, brews over the Fire, and is to this day only closely connected to witchcraft, despite being used by everyone who needed a pot to cook in.

Cauldrons come in all shapes and sizes and can be as small as a tennis ball and as big as a stockpot. Depending on what kind of magic you do, you will need to decide the best size for you if you are in the market for a cauldron. They are handy for burning herbs and incantations that are written on paper and can take up residence in the position of Fire, or simply be used in your rituals and spells wherever you are working.

The cauldron may not look it at first, but it is exactly what the Moon looks like when you fill it with Water and put it next to a candle flame or under the Full Moon. You can recreate the look of the Moon with a cauldron filled with liquid, and symbolically gaze into the face of the Moon by using this tool. It can be a lot of fun to have a little Moon in your circle of magic and as long as you are seeing at that, then that is what it becomes.

Firelight is an essential part of Wicca and witchcraft, and it certainly is a useful tool in your lunar spells. Consider whether you would prefer a cauldron, candle or both and add these wonderful items to your practice.

Using a new Moon candle when doing rituals under a new Moon can help set the right Moon for your ritual. The Sage Goddess candle is dark like the Moon and is scented with essential oil that smells great. It is great to use while meditating to so you can set your intentions for the new month. Use it the day before, the day of, and the day after the new Moon to get those intentions set in stone.

The candles you use on your altar can be any normal candle. You need to have candles of every color and lots of white ones. The size of the candles is important, too. Some spells and rituals require you to burn a candle on multiple days and then to allow them to burn out. The most important thing is to have candles of every color, shape, and size.

Bath Salts

Using Epsom salts will help you detox and clear all the excess energy out of your energy field. You can also use special Epsom salts that have essential oils and flowers in it.

Pendulum

Pendulums are great for divination. You can use them to ask which tarot deck you should use or any yes or no answer you might be looking for.

Black Moonstone

This dark crystal is great for new beginnings. You can use any shape or size, and it can be tumbled or rough. Carrying a tumbled stone in your pocket on the days that are leading up to the now Moon, can help keep you calm. Holding a larger piece in your hand while meditating or resting it on a body part can help keep you centered and grounded.

Labradorite

This is my favorite stone. It is great for working on new beginnings, creativity, transformation, and during the dark Moon. Holding one in your hand during meditation can help focus your intentions, and keep you focused. Keeping a stone in a prominent place, where you can see it daily, can help you remember the intentions you have set for yourself.

Eclipse Stone

This is also called a silver feldspar. It can help reveal things that have been hidden from you. It can help you see things like opportunities, creative ventures, or ideas. You can use this stone along with the Sage Goddess unearthed perfume.

Oracle Decks

The best part of any ritual is being able to connect to the Divine. You can do this in many ways; I like to use oracle decks. Doing a spread for every phase of the Moon is great. Write down and keep records of what you receive.

Grimoire

This can be as simple as a binder where you keep your ritual worksheets for all the Moon phases along with your card readings. It is your own Book of Shadows where you can record your Divine guidance.

Selenite crystal

Selenite is great to use during rituals. It can bring mental clarity. It absorbs negative energy and turns it into positive energy. It can be used to talk with your spirit guides and your higher self. Hold it over your third eye or heart to experience sensations of love and relief.

Wand

A wand stands for the element Air even though many traditions use it to symbolize Fire. It could be made from any material like rock, metal, or wood. Some wands can be set with crystals or gemstones. Some traditions conflate and confuse various staves and wands into one symbol. The wand can be used to summon specific spirits who are afraid of steel and iron.

Jewelry

In different Wicca traditions, jewelry showing pentacles or other symbols can be worn daily, or just during rituals. A Wiccan necklace if worm by all women inside a circle creates a Circle of Rebirth.

Besom

This is also known as a broom. This has been associated with witchcraft and witches. All the stories of witches flying on brooms came from the besom. It has been used in handfasting ceremonies for the couple to jump over. It can be used in fertility danced to represent the phallus.

Boline

This is a knife with a white handle. It might have a curved blade representative of a crescent Moon. It can be used for more uses than the athame. It can be used to cut ritual cords, to inscribe symbols or sigils on candles, or to cut or harvest herbs. Where the Boline serves on the physical plane, the athame works on the astral plane.

CHAPTER 15:

Moon Magic

From the beginning of human civilization, the Moon has had an important role in practices and myths in cultures all around the world. For millions of years, the Moon has served as a light source and a way to measure time. Just like the Sun, the Moon has been linked to many goddesses and gods in various cultures. Being used in both magic and myths, this heavenly body has been linked to many issues with our very existence like afterlife, rebirth, death, mystery, fertility, passion and love. The Moon is still prevalent in paganism, witchcraft, and Wiccan practices. Normally, Wiccan covens hold rituals on the Full Moon so they can honor the Goddess during the Esbats. This practice can be done alone, too.

The Power of the Moon

Every scientist in the world knows that the Earth has an energy all its own, that is different from what it gets from the Sun. The Moon gives off an energy that is very distinct but subtle at the same time. Different from the Sun's Masculine energy, the energy from the Moon is very feminine. This is the Goddess' energy.

It has been described as magnetic energy that makes total sense if you have ever felt 'pulled' by the Moon in one way or another.

Very sensitive people can feel an actual tug in the bodies during a new or Full Moon. Other people might feel more aware of things around them.

Herbal Magic

Plant magic is nothing new, it can be traced back to the ancient Egyptian times. It has been and is still being used for many purposes including love spells, protection spells, self-empowerment, and healing. Every plant comes with its magic, and when combined with a spell, add a healthy dose of power.

Regardless of how experienced the person doing the casting is, you will get the desired results because the plants are laced with such powerful magical properties. Because plant magic works so well and so quickly, it is one of the most popular forms of magic used today.

Spell Casting

To get the most out of a spell you are casting, while you are performing a ritual, sprinkle the herbs you are using onto the flame of the candle.

You can also take advantage of the magical properties in herbs by leaving them around your home to get rid of negative energy, invite happiness, provide protection, health, and peaceful energy.

Back in the day, witches would carry a charm bag full of a variety of herbs to attract what they want. If you want to get the most powerful herbs, it is best to collect them at night, especially when there is a Full Moon.

Due to the stigma attached to casting spells, witches used to give plants code names, such as 'tongue of dog,' and 'eye of newt.' Witches would amuse themselves as people who came across their recipes would go out looking for these seemingly nonexistent ingredients.

Candle Magic

Many people often say that candle magic is the oldest form of magic in the history of humans. It does not matter if this is true; indeed, the Fire has always been sacred to the pagan ancestors that supplicated and honored their gods with candles, torches, flaming wheels, and balefires. Since the Fire was the only source of light other than the Moon and Sun until the early 1900s, it is easy to see why Fire is a symbol of power throughout history.

The reverence for Fire has continued for a long time even after modern lighting caught on. Most religions today still use candles, whether in formal services or when lighting a votive for certain intentions.

Candle magic is the easiest way to cast spells, and because of this, it does not take many ceremonial or ritual tools. Anybody who has a candle could cast a spell. Remember back to when you had a birthday party. You always made a wish before you blew out your candles. This is the idea behind candle magic. Rather than just hoping that your wish comes true, you will be declaring your intent. Nobody remembers where that tradition originated from, and they will not be able to remember who came up with the notion of using candles for magic.

Practicing Moon Magic

Practicing Moon Magic is easy once you understand what the phases mean and how they relate to your life and the world around you. You have read about the phases, the Elements, and the Wheel of the Year and you can see the story of birth, death, and rebirth that happens with every Moon cycle and season. This concept of birth-death-rebirth is one of the major concepts behind the study of Wicca and the worship of nature. It makes sense that we would celebrate this natural rhythm with the phases of the Moon.

The practice of Moon Magic is a lot like any other Wiccan ritual or craftwork. It can bring enhanced powers to your magic and manifestation, or it can be the centerpiece of your worship. Each phase of the Moon will help you determine how to practice magic with her energies. For Full, Dark, or New Moons, you may want to have a ceremonial Esbat, to celebrate the time of the Moon's powers and the great shifts and transformations involved.

Other rituals will be about harnessing the power of the Moon for your specific spells and craftwork. The time of the Moon has a great impact on your manifestations and so if you are wanting to gain and attract something in your life, you will need the power of the waxing Moon. If you are releasing and letting go of things, you will want the waning energy of the Moon phase.

The principles of Moon Magic are all about working with the monthly rhythms of the Moon and coordinating all of your personal rituals and spells around these specific moments of energy. You can find so many different forms of magic when you practice in accordance with the Moon.

Moon Baths

A lovely way to enjoy the energy of the Moon, Moon baths are a simple gesture to the self and to the worship of nature in which one sits under the Moon, in whatever phase she happens to be in and absorbs the powerful energy and feeling of her phases. Each time you Moon-bathe, you are honoring and acknowledging the presence of the Moon's power in your magic, and your own personal power as an important element in the cosmic weave of all things.

You can Moon bathe at any Moon phase, though most practitioners will choose the bright light and power of the Full Mother Moon and will leave the other Moons to have separate purposes. The best way to decide how to Moon bathe is to use your intuitive powers to guide your focus and intentions.

Moon Harvesting Time

Moon harvesting does not mean that you harvest the Moon, of course. It can be a powerful experience to gather your herbs, medicines, other wildcrafted and garden goods for your witch's cabinet. When you are exploring the realms of herb and plant magic, it is good to be familiar with how they like to be harvested. Some plants and flower feel happiest when you harvest their medicinal components at night, especially under the Moonlight. Talking to plants and getting their feedback is a whole other course of study, and to keep it simple you can learn how to enjoy a night harvest instead of a daytime harvest. Harvesting under the Moon adds a special power and benefit to the herbs, which you choose to use for your spells and craftwork. Perhaps you have planted your own herbal garden, or maybe you are wildcrafting from the surrounding area. Either way, it is a magical adventure to harvest your basic spell materials under a brilliant Moon.

Moon Planting

Moon planting, in general, is a very quiet and gentle time to put your new growth into the soil. The Sun is not blazing hot either and so it can be very pleasant for you and your own comfort. The Full Moon can be a special significance to your first garden shoots coming up. If you were to plant some seeds on a waxing Crescent Moon, you could expect to see some new little green shoots coming up by the Full Moon.

Clearing, Charging and Consecrating

The magical work that you do is all about harnessing and working with energy. That is essentially what magic is. The Law of Attraction is about drawing energy to you through various practices.

Much of what spell casting and ritual is all about is the attraction of positive forces or banishing of unwanted energies. Magic is energy and that is an important thing to know when you are thinking in terms of clearing, charging and consecrating as a magical practice.

Clearing is a method for releasing and cleansing unwanted, old, or stagnate energies from your ritual tools and instruments. This can mean an elaborate ritual or spell to release these energies, or it can also mean that you are just plopping something in a warm, salty bath for ten minutes. Clearing is a means of purifying your sacred objects and even the energy of yourself so that you can return it to its original energy.

Charging is a method for adding power and energy to your tools and ingredients for your spells and rituals. Imagine putting electricity into a lightbulb. The lightbulb coils light up and there is a new, bright energy glowing. In a similar fashion, various types of energy can charge the energy of your crystals, candles, herbs, tinctures and more for magical purposes. This can be something you do in a casual way or through a more elaborate process. The energy of the Moon is certainly one way to add power to your tools, and there are of course many other choices for charging as well.

Consecration is more of a ritual or a rite performed to make something sacred. It can be a much more elaborate ceremony, that might use a few more tools and a specific set of instructions while charging something, that can be as simple as setting all of your crystals out under a Full Moon overnight. Consecration will be a powerful ritual that leaves your energy empowered for some incredibly valuable manifestation and spell work.

These three methods are connected to the work of the Moon and all of them are considered a common and traditional practice of Wicca and witchcraft. You can begin to understand the power of the Moon when you feel your fully charged, pendant, talisman or amulet hanging around your neck in front of your heart, charged and consecrated with the energy of a Full Moon.

Fires and Candlelight

So much of witchcraft revolves around the Elements, and one of the most powerful ways to ignite the passion, energy and performance of a spell is with Fire. Fire is the creative life force that breathes life into your craft, and it is also the Fire that brings the light. The Moon is a notorious glowing light, and the sky is noticed because of either its Full Moon luminosity or its barely present crescent shape in the night sky. Either way, the Moon has always mesmerized us with her ethereal glow and has brought many a sailor home in the dark of night.

One of the best ways to honor Moon Magic is with a candle flame or a roaring Fire. You can see the power of light in the candle burning as it glows; so too is the power of the Moon. In many ways, the campfire is our beacon of light and hope for connection to the Moon's glow. She watches from high above and sees our tiny embers burning down on the Earth's surface.

Spells and Rituals

Spells and rituals are what witchcraft is all about. The act of creating sacred space and performing a specific dance of magic is what calls many people to this form of spirituality and worship. Witchcraft is a creative art and allows each practitioner to connect more deeply with their own powerful energy through the powerful energy of the natural world.

Your kinship with the Moon is a major part of how you practice magic, and it is through every spell and ritual that you will determine the timing of your craft.

Your personal Grimoire, or Book of Shadows, will hold every spell and ritual you are wishing to perform at certain times for certain reasons, and a majority of your spells and incantations will have a very specific timing written next to them—think, when do you perform the spell.

CHAPTER 16:

The Triple Goddess

In most Wiccan traditions, the Goddess will take on a threefold form that is called the Triple Goddess. She has three individual aspects that are known as the Crone, the Mother, and the Maiden.

You might see this symbol on headpieces or crowns of High Priestesses.

Even though a woman will go through these phases during her lifetime, every aspect of the Triple Goddess will have qualities that both female and male can relate to at some point in our lives.

This threefold Goddess can reflect all the complexities of the human psyche along with the cycles of death and life, that are experienced by everyone who lives on Earth.

There are other ways to connect and honor the mother, maiden, and crone. Here are other meanings to the Triple Goddess symbol:

- Connection to the Divine Feminine
- Connection to all women
- Goddesses: Hecate, Kore, Persephone, Demeter
- Cycles of life, birth, death, and rebirth, in the continuation of the Moon phases
- Realms and planes: heaven, underworld, and Earth

The Maiden

This aspect is in line with the new waxing phase of the Moon. It represents the youth of a woman's life. This is her time to grow as reflected by the waxing Moon as it travels toward fullness. In nature cycles, the Maiden is thought of as the season spring, Sunrise, and dawn.

The Maiden represents carefree erotic aura, excitement, new beginnings, the female principle, expansion, inception, enchantment, new life, fresh potential, and beauty. In humans, she is their independence, intelligence, naivety, self-confidence, youth, and innocence.

She also represents creativity, self-expression, discovery, and exploration. Wiccans might worship the Maiden as the Celtic goddesses Brigid and Rhiannon, the Nordic goddess, Freya, or the Greek goddesses, Artemis and Persephone, along with many others.

The Mother

During the Full Moon, the Maiden turns into the Mother and gives birth to the Earth's abundance. The season she represents is summer, which is the most fruitful time of year since the fields and forests are flourishing with young animals growing into maturity.

The time of day she represents is midday. Within the human realm, she stands for love, patience, power, self-care, stability, fulfillment, fertility, and ripeness, the fullness of life, adulthood, responsibility, and nurturing. She is the giver of life and she is associated with manifestation.

The Mother is thought of by many Wiccans as the most powerful aspect of the three. It was the Mother Goddess that inspired Gerald Gardner's vision of the divine female.

Some of the ancient Goddesses that represent the Mother at most Wiccan altars are Bad and Danu, the Celtic goddess; Ceres, the Roman goddess; Selene and Demeter, the Greek goddesses; and Ambika, the Hindu goddess.

The Crone

When the Moon wanes and the night get darker, the Crone comes into her power. Some early iterations called her 'the Hag.' She is representative of a woman's post-childbearing years. Her seasons are autumn and winter.

She is associated with the end of the growing season, night, and Sunset. She is the wise, elder part of the Goddess and she governs past lives, rebirth, death, endings, and aging along with guidance, prophecy, visions, fulfillment, culmination, compassion, repose, wisdom, and transformations.

She was feared for millions of years. She reminds us that death is a part of life just like the dark side of the Moon is before the new Moon. The Crone has been associated with the underworld and death like the Celtic goddesses, Cailleach Bear and Morrigan; the Russian goddess, Baba Yaga; and the Greek goddess, Hecate.

The Triple Goddess is a complex and diverse expression of the divine feminine. For anyone who worships her, she will give them consistent opportunities to grow and learn by connecting to her three aspects. It does not matter if you recognize her as an ancient goddess, or as a part of the Triple Goddess.

You could just choose to honor the Maiden, Mother or Crone archetype. You might make a conscious effort to line up your worship with the Moon phases for a deeper and more rewarding spiritual connection.

CHAPTER 17:

Moon Ritual and Spell Basics

There are, quite literally, millions of spells. That might actually be a low number, depending on how distinct each spell needs to be. Most involve herbs, crystals, or stones. The spells in this book do occasionally call for additional items. However, each additional item is just an extra that helps set the tone of a spell or more finely focus its energy. The spells and rituals can be performed without anything extra at all. But the one thing they cannot function without is the magic of the Moon.

Rituals are rites during which Wiccans honor the Moon, the Goddess, and Her energy. There are several different kinds of rituals for each phase of the Moon. This book focuses on one piece.

Spells, on the other hand, are meant to tap into the energy of the Moon and use it to enact the will of the magic use. It is possible to honor the Goddess and the Moon while doing this, of course. However, honoring the source of the energy is not the main intent of a spell.

The spells and rituals in this book are meant to be largely accessible to most people. They are written for solitary practitioners but can easily be adapted to fit groups of magic users, which are sometimes known as covens. The only steadfast requirement is that they must be performed during the appropriate phase of the Moon or lunar event. Otherwise they may not work or, if they do work, they may create unintended outcomes.

Preparing for the Ritual

Rituals and spell work require a lot of energy. Some people can channel or offer this energy with absolutely no concerns. They come out the other side of a rite feeling refreshed and blessed. Some people, on the other hand, come out feeling drained. It all depends on how a magic user relates to their own energy.

Regardless of which category a magic user falls into, they should expect to come out of a ritual needing food, water, and rest. Even people who find rites energizing may come across one that leaves them more exhausted than usual. It is always a good idea to have snacks and drinks waiting for everyone who participates in a rite.

Though some groups suggest alcohol, as it is a traditional celebratory drink, this is not required. Water is ideal, as many magic users find themselves parched after the exertion of a rite. Other good options are fruit juices, flavored waters, and teas. Artificial drinks are less popular, as they belong more to the mundane world and less to a world where humans connect deeply with nature.

Ideal snacks for post-ritual fuel include nuts, fruit slices, and cut vegetables. If the ritual is particularly important, such as for a holiday, personal celebration, or rare lunar occurrence, some

Wiccans prefer to have whole meals waiting. Whichever route a practitioner takes, he should keep in mind the idea of staying connected with the world around them. As the ritual is meant to honor the Divine, refreshments after the ritual should honor the practitioners. This means opting for healthier options and ensuring there is something for everyone, regardless of dietary restrictions.

Ritual Bathing

Not all practitioners perform ritual baths. The concept may be new even to experienced magic users. However, it is an ancient concept that spans multiple cultures and magical practices.

At the base level, a ritual bath is a way for magic users to get themselves into the right frame of mind. Even if they bathed only that morning, a ritual bath changes the tone of their energies. They leave behind the stress and pressures of their mundane day. In their stead, practitioners can accept the calm, purposeful energy they will need during a ritual.

Ritual baths also help magic users wash away any unwanted energy. Everyone picks up stray bits of energy throughout the day, some good and some bad. For the most part, that energy remains part of people until they next ground, center, or bathe. Magic users shake this energy off more readily because they know how to handle it. A ritual bath helps them clear out unwanted energy much more easily.

When most people bathe, they do it in a small tub of standing water. That water comes from pipes in their home, and is not rooted in a natural source that can cleanse the water as they bathe. Few people have access to a clean body of water in which to wash away errant energy. Ritual baths in a standard bathtub would remove energy from the practitioner, of course. But the energy would just stay in the water until the practitioner drained the tub. At that point, much of the energy would just reattach itself to the magic user.

Showers, on the other hand, wash all the unwanted energy down the drain. Rather than swirling around the person only to reattach, errant energy is swept away before it can find its way back to the magic user. It also helps that these showers wash away the dirt and grime of a day in the mundane world, leaving the magic user feeling refreshed for their ritual.

Ritual bathing does not stop at the shower itself. Many practitioners take it a step further by continuing their chant or mindful self-awareness while they apply lotions, fix their hair, and – in some cases – apply makeup. Most people continue this focus into the next step, which is putting on ritual clothing, also known as ritual garb.

Ritual Garb

Most ritual garb is based on the style and clothing of pre-Christian Britain and Ireland. This is slowly changing, however, as practitioners with more diverse heritages join the religion and more people create their own version of Neo-Wicca.

Before a Wiccan can design their own ritual garb, however, it is important that they understand the basic requirements for such clothing. These requirements, as well as the cultural roots of Wicca, have shaped what is now known as traditional Wiccan ritual garb.

The most important aspect of ritual clothing is that it is comfortable. It should not be too tight or cut poorly, and the material should be comfortable against the practitioner's skin. Uncomfortable ritual clothing will only serve to distract the magic user. At best, this will interrupt their ability to properly honor the being at the center of their ritual. At worst, this can cause a spell to lose power or go astray.

Ritual garb must also be safe. This means that while flowing robes are popular, sleeves should be relatively snug against the wrists and arms, so they do not dip into a candle flame accidentally. The hem of a robe should also be an inch or so above the ground, so that practitioners do not trip on it when moving around during a ritual.

Safety is just as important when selecting footwear for a ritual. If the ritual is held indoors or on soft grass inside the bounds of private property, magic users can go barefoot or opt for soft-bottom slippers. If the ritual is held outdoors, particularly on land that other people have used, hard-bottom shoes are recommended. Rituals performed in the woods almost always require boots or modern shoes to protect the feet of the wearer from rocks, sharps sticks, and any garbage other people might have left behind.

Creating a Circle

Once the practitioner is ready to begin their ritual, they must cast a protective circle. These are energetic barriers that protect a magic user from outside energy – and keep their own energy focused on the ritual – until they have completed their rite. They are raised at the beginning of any spell or ritual, then are released as the last act of the rite.

There are several ways to cast a protective circle. Some practitioners choose to etch a permanent circle into the floor where whey perform spells and rituals. Others prefer to use a large loop of string, that can be laid out before a rite and collected up afterward. Still others use material like salt or chalk to create a temporary and disposable circle. Others rely solely on visualization.

Each variation on the circle has its pros and cons. Most Wiccans choose the version that works best to suit their needs. They consider whether or not they can practice openly, how much space they have, where the practice, and how often they are likely to perform a rite. With these criteria in mind, they decide which circle marking technique best suits their needs, and they practice it until they are adept at raising their energy.

Protective circles should be large enough to encompass all magic users involved in a ritual/spell, a central altar, and any markers used to indicate the cardinal directions. Regardless of the material used to lay the circle – or if the circle is made using visualization alone – practitioners should walk the inner perimeter of their circle before raising its energy. This should be done in a clockwise direction, which is also known as Deosil. Walking in this direction puts the magic user more in tune with the energy of the Earth, as it is the same direction that the Sun travels through the sky each day.

Once the outline has been placed around all of these components, the person in charge of the ritual closes their eyes and visualizes the circle as a ring of energy. Then they imagine this circle becoming a sphere, closing the ritual in on all sides and protecting those within from harm.

No energy can pass back and forth across the barrier unless it is invited. A physical being can cross the circle. However, this may break the energetic barrier. For this reason, it is important that anyone participating in a spell or ritual should stay inside the circle from start to finish unless there is an emergency. In this case, if only one person needs to leave, the practitioner leading the ritual can create a door by which the person can leave. If everyone needs to leave, the leaders can drop the magical barrier, releasing all the energy at once.

Bugs and pets can also break the shield of a protective circle, but it is not as easy for them to do, since they carry less energy than a human. Still, if possible, practitioners should keep their pets in a separate area from their ritual space. This will prevent any unintentional breaks in the circle and allow the ritual or spell to be completed in peace.

Some practitioners use chants to focus their energy while they raise their circles. Each ritual in this book includes its own specialty chant for those who wish to use them. Spells, on the other hand, rarely require chants since the protective circle is often smaller, and contains lower energy levels. Magic users can raise circles in these instances much more easily, so no chants have been written for the included spells.

Calling the Quarters

As the Moon and Sun are important in Wicca, so are the four cardinal directions. North, south, east, and west are often referred to as the Four Quarters or the Four Watchtowers. They are called before every ritual or spell so that their energy can support whatever work the magic user wants to do. Then, at the end of the rite, the energy is released before the protective circle is lowered. Unlike most energy, the energy of the Watchtowers is neutral and so is not stopped by things like protective circles.

Not only do each of the directions have their own energies, but they have Elements that they alone relate to. North is the direction of Earth, the most stable of the Elements. It is strong, subdued, and sturdy. South, conversely, is Fire. It is bright and hot, energetic and chaotic. East represents Air, which is the softest of the Elements. It easily changes direction, carries only that which is light as a feather, and brings breath to every lung, though it is the most intangible of the Elements. Finally, there is west, the watchtower of Water. Water, too, can change direction. But it usually takes more time, particularly deep Water. Water changes and shapes things gradually and can carry just about anything if respected.

Each element connects to the phases of the Moon and the faces of the Triple Goddess in its own way. Because of this, the incantations used to summon the Watchtowers tend to change from ritual to ritual depending on the phase of the Moon being honored. Spells are a little more lenient, since the Moon is aiding the spell rather than the focal point of it. As such, a general call to each Watchtower will suffice, regardless of the phase of the Moon.

Performing the Ritual

The majority of energy in a ritual or spell is used in the core performance. In rituals, it is used to when interacting with the energy of the being honored. When casting a spell, the energy it put into the spell itself, sort of like fuel being added to a car. It is the thing that makes the spell go.

Because each spell and ritual are a little bit different, the details will only be given in the subsections dedicated to each ritual or the selection of spells. Many of them follow a standard format, which is intentional. Having consistent formats for spells and rituals allows practitioners to learn the framework by heart. Once they do this, they can move within that framework without thinking, allowing them to devote more energy and attention to the ritual itself.

Practitioners new to magic are advised to follow the rituals as they are laid out in this book. Because these rituals were developed by an experienced magic user, they effectively utilize as much energy as possible. As practitioners gain more experience and confidence with their energy and their magic, they can change things as they see fit. If part of a ritual is not possible due to personal limitations, whether they be space or capability, small modifications are absolutely acceptable. Just be sure that the changes honor the flow and pace of the ritual.

Ending the Ritual

As energy is called into a protective circle at the beginning of a ritual, so it must be released at the end. This is usually done by thanking whatever entity is being honored – in this case, various phases of the Moon and their corresponding aspects of the Triple Goddess – and then bidding them farewell.

From there, the magic user moves to the Watchtowers. They release these energies in the reverse order they were summoned. If, for example, the practitioner summoned the energies of the Watchtowers in the order of north, east, south, and west, they would release the energies, starting with west and working backward.

This allows the practitioner to move in a counterclockwise direction, otherwise known as 'widdershins'. Though this direction is considered unlucky in some situations, it is simply a way to balance the energy of a ritual. It functions as a way to 'unwind' the energy that the practitioner 'wound up' by walking Deosil at the beginning of the ritual.

Cleaning Up

The Wiccan appreciate for balance and a sense of connection goes beyond the metaphysical and metaphorical. Wicca encourages both of these traits while also focusing on a sense of personal responsibility, all of which is particularly important for those who perform magical works. And this is why it is vital that all magic users clean up when they are done with a ritual.

Because each ritual is different, the cleanup will always look a little different. If a ritual call for a practitioner to put something on their altar, there is no reason to take the item down unless that is what the practitioner wants to do. Similarly, if a magic user drew a chalk circle on their floor and it is safe for them to leave it in place, they do not have to wipe it away when the ritual is over.

Many rituals involve things like flowers, herbs, and food. And though some practitioners enjoy leaving these things on their altar as offerings to the Goddess and the God, they can quickly sour. If someone chooses to leave offerings on their altar, they should check on those offerings a few times a day to make sure that no bugs or rot have set in. At that point, the Divine beings have taken all the energy they want or need from the offering. It is safe to dispose of it as any other plant waste.

Cleaning up after a ritual is especially important if it was held outdoors. Even dried plants can drop seeds that may or may not be invasive to the area. Animals may get into offerings of food that then make the animals sick. It goes without saying that no member of a religion focused on nature worship should be comfortable littering.

If the practitioner is wearing ritual garb, now is the time to take it off. They should do so slowly and with focused intent. As they do this, they should also feel for any differences in the energy of the garment from when it was put on. If there are vast differences or if the garment feels heavy or dirty, it may need to be laundered and cleansed before it is worn again. Cleansing is usually a simple affair in which Wiccans leave items out in the light of a Full Moon, so that all unwanted energy can be washed away.

CHAPTER 18:

How to find your favorite spells

The scope of Wiccan practice is quite impressive when we look at all the various ways in which it is followed. Except, given all the choices, it might be more difficult these days for interested beginners to find their way forward.

The first thing to remember is that it will probably take a while before you find your comfort zone within the Craft.

The tradition within Wicca of studying for a year and a day before being eligible for initiation into a coven speaks to the depth of the learning process. (In fact, plenty of covens will tell you that you are not necessarily ready to make that leap after only a year and a day.)

So, take your time. In the meantime, here are some suggestions for how you might take your next steps.

Read

Research is the best thing you can do to gain an informed sense of the Craft, and where your path into it might be found.

You are already well on your way there if you are reading this book, and this is just the tip of the iceberg when it comes to print and online resources.

Look into the things that you do not understand. Pursue further anything that catches your interest. When you come across something that does not give you a good feeling—a belief, a practice, a particular author's take on things—take note of it, and see if you can sort out why it does not resonate with you. Understanding what you do not want helps you clarify what it is you are truly looking for.

Study the Traditions

One of the easiest ways to figure out which type of practice is best suited to you is through studying the main Wiccan traditions. Again, it can be a challenge to find specific, detailed information about rites and rituals, etc., due to the traditions many orthodox covens have about keeping their knowledge secret.

If approaching a traditional coven is not possible or just is not your cup of tea, look up the traditions online, read books about them, and notice how you feel about each of them when you learn what they are about, and see how they operate.

If you find that they are unappealing to you in some way, discard the notion of joining that specific tradition or worshiping that specific pantheon.

Again, the point of it all is having an informed opinion, and that is gained through researching Wicca and its different paths.

Finding the Right Circle or Coven

Finding the circles and covens that operate in your area can be pretty close to impossible if you have no clue where to look.

While covens not looking for new members are unlikely to advertise their existence, some circles and pagan groups use local media to announce meetings, ritual gatherings, **etc.** There are also online communities, forums, blogs, **etc.** that feature lists of covens and circles.

If you do find a directory of covens online, it will likely show what tradition the coven practices and how to contact a member of the High Priestess if they are looking for new members.

Resources for Solitary Witches

Solitary practitioners who are new to the craft and do not have the guidance of other witches in their daily lives have to work a bit harder to find information. In the age of the Internet, this is much less of a problem. There are now countless resources out there for solo witches seeking guidance with spellcasting, rituals, and any other aspect of the faith.

Online Articles, Blogs, Videos, etc.

The Internet has indeed made it possible for the Wiccan community to be global.

There is probably no aspect of any tradition that has not been discussed online, and the diversity of voices from all over the world on any number of topics is truly astonishing.

There are some great blogs out there, and online videos can be wonderful resources for those who want to get closer to hands-on experience with rituals, etc. It is amazing what a good session with a search engine can do.

If you are looking for a good starting point, I recommend the excellent Celtic Connection resource, found at Wicca.com.

Online Forums and Message Boards

Online message boards, forums, and chat rooms can be a wonderful place to network with other Wiccans both in covens and outside of them.

As mentioned above, these are excellent places to find out about covens and circles in your area, and places near your location where there are meet-ups. They also have great tips for ordering from online stores selling magical items and ritual tools, as well as general pleasant banter with like-minded folks.

CHAPTER 19:

Rhythms of the Moon

Lunar Energy and Magic

Mainstream culture tends to laugh off the notion of Moon-influenced feelings and behavior, but, as we saw in Part One, the Moon does have effects on people and animals. This tends to be most obvious during the days surrounding the Full Moon, whether we are noticing unusual behavior in our pets or children or feeling ourselves to be abnormally moody.

But, while you may already be aware that the 'Full Moon' effect is not a myth, you may not realize that all phases of the Moon's cycle influence us on some level, however subtle it may be for those who are not yet attuned to lunar energy.

Tracking the Moon

Before considering the relationship between the Moon and magic, however, it is important to identify the phases of the lunar cycle in more detail. After all, you cannot truly take advantage of the opportunities that lunar energies present if you do not know what's happening in the sky when you are casting your spells!

Light and Shadow

In the first framework, the Moon's cycle is tracked by its appearance in the sky.

It begins as a barely detectable sliver at the New Moon. Over the next few days, the sliver becomes larger and more defined, almost resembling the tip of a fingernail—this is called the Crescent Moon. From here, the Moon continues to grow—or 'wax'— on its way to becoming Full. At the mid-point between New and Full, we see the waxing Half Moon, with the illuminated half on the right and the shadowed half on the left.

As the circle begins to be filled out with light, it becomes 'gibbous,' a word used in astronomy to describe the bulging appearance of the Moon during the days just before and after it is completely Full. Finally, when the circle is completely lit, we are looking at the Full Moon.

In the days just after the Full point, the Moon is gibbous again, then continues to shrink—or 'wane'—further back to Half. This time, the light half is on the left, with the shadowed half on the right.

More and more of the Moon is covered in shadow as it wanes back to its Crescent point, and then completely disappears. This window of time before it is visible again is the Dark Moon. Once the sliver returns, the cycle begins again.

Measuring Time

The other way of tracking the cycle of the Moon is to divide it into four quarters, spread out over roughly 28 days. Each quarter lasts approximately seven days, adding up to create what we call the lunar month.

The first quarter begins at the New Moon and ends at the waxing Half. The second quarter runs from there until the Full Moon. The third quarter begins immediately after the Moon turns Full and lasts until the waning Half Moon, and the fourth quarter closes out the cycle through the Dark Moon, ending just as the Moon reemerges into New.

It is interesting to note that while the two systems are not technically in conflict with each other, in terms of covering the Full lunar cycle, there is something of an asymmetrical "glitch" when you try to align them. The ordered, even-numbered quarter system contains 4 units, which does not quite align with the five major marking points—New, Half, Full, Half, Dark—of the older, somewhat looser framework.

This is because the quarter system does not actually take the Dark Moon period into account. In reality, the Moon takes 29.5 days to complete its orbit, which is a number that is not divisible by four equally, so there is a slight lag during the Dark time between the fourth and first quarters.

Furthermore, the period of amplified energetic influence that the Full Moon exerts is much longer than the brief period of time when it is fully illuminated. In the Witching world, the Full Moon phase is actually considered to be five days long—from the two days before Full, when the Moon is still gibbous, until two days after, when the waning is just becoming visible.

Some people go even further, designating a Full week to the Full Moon. But for the purposes of working with lunar energies, it can be argued that the Full Moon phase begins and ends when you feel it beginning and ending. To some extent, the entire lunar cycle is a bit like that. Remember, it is ultimately about your personal intuitive perception—your sixth sense.

Nonetheless, the quarter system may be more appealing to some, as it can be easier to keep track of. In fact, many calendars note the beginning mark of each quarter. And it is particularly helpful when you do not have the opportunity to go looking at the Moon every single night. (In fact, depending on where it is in its orbit and your own sleep schedule, you may not be able to see it at night.)

The truth is, it really does not matter how you track the phases, as long as you are at least aware of when the New and Full Moons occur—these are, after all, the two most energetically powerful times of the cycle.

So, if you are new to paying close attention to the Moon, start by paying attention to these two points. As you get into the habit of tracking the Moon in this way, you will find yourself attuning to the more subtle, continuous rhythms of the various energies of the Moon's complete cycle. You will also get a better feel for timing your magic to align as closely as possible with each lunar phase.

Now that the Full cycle has been more specifically illuminated, let us delve into the magical implications for working in harmony with the rhythms of the Moon.

CHAPTER 20:

Creating a lunar Grimoire

The most treasured and most private tool of many Wiccans is their Grimoire. Also known as the Book of Shadows, the Grimoire is the place where you will keep all of your inspiring information, spells, poems, prayers, herbal recipes, correspondences, and ritual protocols. This is the diary of your journey into Wicca. For solitary practice, it is built page by page, and it is a record of the growth and development of your practice.

Your Grimoire is quite like a journal with a magical, spiritual focus. Here is where you will write down your favorite spells and incantations, herbal recipes you like to use, essential oils that smell best to you, dates and names of the Esbats and the Sabbats and the rituals you performed for each, and anything else that you can think of that will enhance your personal practice of your craft.

You are not required to keep a Book of Shadows, and there is no one to fault you if you do not. But it is an invaluable tool in your practice. You will keep all of your most important magic information in your Grimoire. Any information that you find yourself using often should be recorded in your Grimoire. If you write down your favorite spells in your Grimoire, then you can read them during spell casting, and there is no need to remember the entire spell. Also, you can certainly record spells that worked well and their results.

Whatever you decide to include in your Grimoire should be tailored to you and your needs. If you are the kind of person who likes to have large gatherings for the Sabbats, then you should include a larger section for the Sabbats. If you put a lot of belief in the power of dreams and what they mean in the waking world, then you would probably include a larger section to record and analyze your dreams. And not everything that you include in your Grimoire needs to be specifically Wiccan in nature. You might include a poem or the lyrics to a song that makes you feel particularly spiritual, happy, or sad.

While the contents of the book are left up to the owner of the book, there are certain things that should never be found in your Grimoire. Since Wicca is about purity and goodness, any spell that involves hexes, curses, or black magic should never make its way into your Grimoire. If you keep a personal journal in your Grimoire, try not to write anything that is hateful or dark. This might cause your regret or anger in the future. The Grimoire is not a place to keep a kid's sports schedules or your grocery list. Do not just shove useless bits of information in the Grimoire just because it is handy to do so. And never keep anything in the Grimoire that has no special meaning for you. This can mean removing things from time to time, and that is okay. You are not the same today as you were five years ago, and the things that were meaningful then are probably meaningless now.

And since this book is a personal Grimoire, it needs to remain personal. This book is made just for you. Other people should never write in your Grimoire. Other people should never even see your Grimoire. The Grimoire is the account of your personal journey and should not be shared. This is important to keep the book sacred. In ancient times, a Grimoire was burned upon the death of its owner.

By putting together your own personal lunar Grimoire, you will first need a book. There are many options available for the actual book part of the Grimoire. Some people like to use a composition book or a spiral notebook. Some people like a blank journal with a hardcover. Another option is the three-ring binder with notebook paper. The best option is starting with something simple and later creating a more formal option if you choose to. This might mean using a three-ring binder for every day but recording certain special things in a hardbound book.

For ease of use, the three-ring binder is the best option for the beginner Grimoire. It is convenient to use notebook paper and add or remove pages as you need to. You can add pages in between existing pages. You can lay the book flat on a counter or table to copy a recipe or perform a spell. You can remove a page from the binder and discard it or return it to the binder later. If you purchase a three-hole punch, then you are free to use any type of paper you like in your Grimoire. You might even want to use different varieties of paper. Add in tabbed dividers to separate the sections in your book. And you can use anything to write in your Grimoire, but some people like to have a special pen that is only used in their Grimoire.

Do not spend too much time deciding how you want your book to be organized. You will probably want to make separate sections for separate things, and you might even want to make a **Table of Contents**. But you might decide next week that you do not even like this version, and you find yourself scrapping it for another option. Begin with a basic layout and build on that. The first page will definitely have whatever Wiccan creed you are living your life by set down there. There are several different creeds that you can follow as a follower of Wicca. Probably the most popular is the Wiccan Rede. All of the ethics of Wicca are summed up in the Rede. The word 'rede' means counsel or advice, and the Wiccan Rede advises you to do whatever you want, as long as it brings no harm to anyone or anything else. It is the basis of the morality of Wicca.

The Seven Hermetic Principles are seven ancient tenets for mastering oneself. In the laws of Hermeticism, there are different dimensions of existence that overlap each other. There are three planes known as the Great Planes, and these are the spiritual plane, physical plane, and mental plane. These planes overlap and influence each other.

The Charge of the Goddess is a text of inspirational messages often used in Wicca. This is the promise of the Goddess to all who follow her that she will be available to guide and teach them. The Charge reminds us that the Goddess considers all acts of pleasure and love to be sacred to her. The Delphic Maxims are a set of one hundred forty-seven different sayings that were alleged to have been given by the Oracle of the Greek God Apollo at Delphi. The most famous of the quotes is probably 'Know Thyself,' which is just as important in the Wiccan world as it is in the larger world. Other quotes will caution you to control yourself, pursue honor, respect the Gods, seek wisdom, and wish for things to be possible. All of the tenets of the Delphic Maxims can, in some way, be used in the world of Wicca and the practice of magic.

There are many different sections that you might want to include in your lunar Grimoire, and here are just a few.

Put the rules you intend to live your life by on the first page. There are several sets of rules that can be followed in Wicca, and you should choose one set as your guide for your journey. When you put these rules at the beginning of your Grimoire, they are easy to refer to, absorb, explore, and meditate on whenever you need to.

Keep a calendar of the Sabbats and other Holy Days. Since the Sabbats are crucial to the passage of the Wiccan Year, they are always celebrated with some sort of ritual, especially when they fall on the days of the Full Moon. Other Holy Days might include the monthly Esbats, the Full Moon celebrations that all Wiccans observe in some way. You can also keep track of any particular days that you observe with special celebrations, days that are meaningful to you in particular. You can also record any personal days that are special to you, such as naming ceremonies, handfasting rituals, marriage, rites of adulthood, initiations, and birthday celebrations.

Keep track of special symbols and correspondences that you like to use. Here is where you will record the tables of correspondence that you develop or collect for any correspondence that you use. You can also list any runes, languages, signs, and symbols that you prefer to work with.

Record your favorite lunar spells and rituals. This section is definitely important, because this is where you will record the words and instructions for new spells that you are particularly fond of, and will work well for you.

Create a section for culinary and witchy recipes you like to use. Every rite of passage and every holy day has some sort of special menu associated with it. Maybe you will want to include recipes for foods that are special to your family or your heritage.

If you are the crafty, creative type, keep your instructions here. Witches often like to be creative and make their own herb mixtures, scented candles, essential oils, and scented soaps, especially to give to others as gifts. Some even like to make their own magic tools or to source them out from unique places.

List your most favorite songs, poems, and prayers. You will always find good material while reading in books, attending public rituals, or researching online. This is where you will record favorite prayers that you might say at bedtime, mealtime, sunset, or dawn.

Keep a written record of your dreams. Some people find significant meanings in their dreams. They like to write their dreams down as soon as they wake up so they may study it and look for some meaning in the dream. You would especially want to record dreams that are vivid or those that you have over and over. Record something about your day before you go to sleep so that you can compare it to your dream later to see if there is any correlation.

When you have set up your lunar Grimoire with the sections you want to use, then it is time to decorate your book in the way you want to decorate it. You do not need to decorate it to use it, but anything you do to make the book more personal will increase your use and enjoyment of the book.

Some people will decorate the first page of each section with pictures appropriate to that section. Show off your talents if you have artistic ability. If you do not, then use pictures printed from the computer, cut from magazines, or scrapbooking supplies. Remember that while it is not necessary to decorate your lunar Grimoire in order to use it, more effort put into your book will make it feel like your personal treasure. You will add a bit of your heart and soul to the book with every little decoration.

Your lunar Grimoire will need to be cleansed and consecrated before it can be used. Choose the method of cleansing that you are most comfortable with. You are cleansing the book so that it is pure for your use. The book picks up vibrations from every person, place, or thing that it had touched before it came to you.

Now, you will begin to use your lunar Grimoire. It is not necessary to write in it every day, but you should write not less often than the days on which you cast spells and any Holy Days and Sabbats that you observe. Sometime during your Wiccan journey, you might find that your book is too Full to accept another word. This happens sometimes. If it happens to you, simply retire this book to a place of honor and begin a new Grimoire. Before you set it aside, look through your Grimoire from beginning to end. It is a record of your journey up to the time of its retirement, and it will have some amazing stories to tell.

CHAPTER 21:

The Moon's Influence on the Wiccan Year

In Wicca, the Moon is highly revered. She is the force that guides Wiccans through their year and also through the Mysteries of Life. She is an important presence in the life of all Wiccans whether they practice with a coven or as solitaries. The energy from the Moon is more subtle than the energy from the Sun; it is more receptive and feminine in its traits. This is the Goddess at work. This is a magnetic power, and it makes sense to anyone who has ever felt that the Moon is pulling them in a certain direction. Those who are extra sensitive will feel a real physical tug on their bodies during a New Moon or Full Moon celebration. Other people will just be aware that there is more energy in the air than normal.

The energy that we receive from the Moon is perfect for working with the energy that comes from our own intuition, since both are magnetic in nature, feminine, and receptive to suggestion. This is also known as our sixth sense. When it comes to working magic, this is our most important form of perception. When we connect consciously with the energy of the Moon, we are opening a pathway or channel to allow that energy to make needed and desired changes in our lives. When this is done in purposeful harmony with the rhythmic energies of the Moon you will truly increase the magical power of your work. Each phase of the lunar cycle and each celebration based on the cycle of the Moon give you specific energies that you can harness and use for your own gains.

A cycle of waxing and waning is the relationship between the Moon and the magic that you do. You will work magic to increase when the Moon is growing in size. You work magic for decrease as the Moon is shrinking in size. So, if you are working an intention to bring something new into your life then you will work that spell during a waxing Moon phase. And if you want to banish a bad habit from your life then you will work that spell during the waning phase of the Moon. When the Moon is new you will create spells with new intentions for your next round of spell casting. And during the Full Moon you will harvest what you have sown and celebrate the rewards you have gained.

The celebration of the Full Moon is one of the important celebrations in the life of a Wiccan. Once every four weeks the night is illuminated by the light of the Full Moon, and Wiccans everywhere gather in their covens or practice alone at their altars or under the light from the sky and worship the Full Moon and the Goddess. These Full Moon celebrations are called Esbats, and they are the counterparts to the Sabbats. There are eight Sabbats that mark the passing of the Sun through the Wiccan year, which is marked by the Wheel of the Year. Sabbat celebrations focus on the God and the contribution that he makes to the cycles of life that are found on Earth.

It is important to understand the Wheel of the Year for two reasons. One it is the calendar of the life of the Wiccan. These are the important celebrations in Wicca. Many of them align with Christian celebrations and many of the celebratory Elements are the same. You will notice that the symbol for the Triple Goddess is in the center of the Wheel. This is because each one of the Triple Goddesses rules over a particular part of the year, even though the celebrations are to honor the Sun and the God.

The Maiden rules over Imbolc and Ostara. Imbolc is the celebration that prepares us for the arrival of Spring. This is when we clean our houses and ourselves of negativity, bad habits, clutter, and anything else that might keep us from enjoying the freedom that Spring will bring to us. Ostara, the Spring Equinox, celebrates the end of Winter and the beginning of warm weather and new life. Plants and animals begin to grow, and the Maiden is truly in her element.

The Mother is in her power during Beltane, Litha, and Lammas (also known as Lughnasadh). During Beltane marriages or hand fasting takes place, and the Mother is worshipped to help ensure a good season of growing for crops, livestock, and families. Litha is the Summer Solstice and marks the time when the days will begin to be shorter each day. We give thanks to the Mother for the bounty she is preparing for us during the harvest time of Lammas, when we celebrate the abundance that we have received from the season of growing.

The Crone begins to exert her influence at the celebration of Mabon, when the final harvest is made, and the Mother has done her work. This is the time of the beginning of the end of the year when the Crone is in charge of the season. She will rule over Samhain when dead ancestors are celebrated and the Yule which many Wiccans consider to be the end of one year and the beginning of the next. The Yule also celebrates the return of the light and is the last time the Crone is celebrated until the next fall, because soon the Maiden will make her appearance.

Full Moon celebrations held during the Sabbats would give worship the element of the Triple Goddess who is holding court during that time. A Full Moon celebration during Samhain would celebrate the Crone along with the Goddess because the Crone is the major influencer for that time of year. The Goddess is important to these celebrations because the God would not exist without her. The Wiccan belief is that the year begins at Yule, because that is when the Goddess gives birth to the God. During Spring and Summer, the God grows stronger so that in the Fall the God and the Goddess can unite, and she will become pregnant with the new God, who will be born at Yule. The old God will die on Samhain. Here is an easy chart so that you can plan for your Esbats, your Full Moon celebrations:

- Imbolc – The Promise of Spring – February 2nd
- Ostara – The Spring Equinox – March 13th-22nd
- Beltane – Mayday – May 1st
- Litha – The Summer Solstice – June 19th – 23rd
- Lammas – The First harvest – August 1st
- Mabon – The Autumn Equinox – September 21st -24th
- Samhain – All Hallow's Eve – October 31st - November 1st
- Yule – The Winter Solstice – December 20th -23rd

So, when an Esbat falls during the time of a Sabbat there is reason for even more celebration, and it is perfectly acceptable to have a ceremony during the day for the Sabbat and a separate one at night during the time of the Moon to celebrate the Esbat. The Goddess will always be at the center of your Esbat celebration, no matter what aspect she is in at the time. You can honor the aspect with her title of Maiden, Mother, or Crone, or you can use one of her many names such as Athena, Diana, and Hecate.

If you are working on a specific goal for your Full Moon celebration, then you might call on a particular Goddess to assist you. If you are working a spell to attract romantic love to you then you might call on the Goddess Aphrodite to assist you. Some covens and solitaries only honor one Goddess all year round; some have a specific Goddess that they always honor, and then they choose a particular Goddess with a particular intention. Some just honor the Goddess of their choice that day. The possibilities you can create are endless, and you should choose the method that you are most comfortable with since this is your celebration.

While the Sabbats all have a specific meaning and are celebrated with that meaning in mind, the Esbats have no specific meaning. When you celebrate an Esbat you have room to interpret and exhibit what it means to you personally. The only goal of the Esbat is for you to connect with the Moon and its power. You will connect with the Goddess in a manner that is meaningful to you. Hence, there really is no right or wrong way to hold an Esbat celebration. There are some guidelines for you to follow so that your celebration will be meaningful to you and you will reap the most benefit from your Esbat celebration.

First you will determine your goal and set your intention. Why are you performing this Esbat? Do you simply want to become more in tune with the Goddess and her power or do you have a specific intention that you want to cast out into the universe? Next you will need to decide on the time and the place that you will hold your celebration. Will you be at your altar or someplace outdoors? Will you begin when the Moon begins to peek over the horizon, or will you wait until the stroke of midnight?

Now that you have decided your intention and your location you will plan your ceremony. Write down the details of your celebration and your spell, so that you are fully prepared and leave out no details try to be as specific as possible. Gather all of the tools that you will need for your ritual or to cast your spell and have them handy in one place. Do not feel the need to gather a lot of things because the best tool you have at your disposal is the power in your mind. Then, perform the ritual or spell you have designed, and always listen to your own intuition. If what you are performing does not feel right, then do not complete it; always pay attention to your inner voice.

The Esbats in Wicca are much less rigid than the Sabbat celebrations. There is more room for improvisation. These are celebrations that you will decide how they should be celebrated. You can make them simple or highly complicated. They can be nothing more than lighting a candle on a hilltop while you meditate in the light cast by the Full Moon. They can be highly involved in rituals, where you cast a circle and call down a Goddess. Anything you might read about performing an Esbat celebration is nothing more than a suggestion. In the end, you are the designer of your own celebration.

CHAPTER 22:

Moon Signs

There are many reasons Wiccans track lunar cycles. And Moon signs are one of the most common. Moon signs, like the more well-known idea of birth signs, tell Wiccans which astrological house the Moon rests in. Some practitioners even go so far as to mind out what house the Moon was in at the time of their birth.

Like Sun signs, this information is believed to affect a person's behavior, fortune, and future.

While the Sun takes roughly thirty days to move from one sign to the next, the Moon takes only two. Like the Sun, it progresses from one house to the next in a predictable cycle. These houses – such as Libra, Virgo, or Taurus - all have their own correspondences, traits, and affiliations.

Because the Sun and Moon move through the astrological houses at different speeds, a person's Sun sign may be very different from their Moon sign. A fiery solar Aries may find that their Moon sign is the calm Pisces. Wiccans who believe in astrology find that Moon signs change exactly how someone presents in their solar sign.

Libras, for example, are often so preoccupied with balance that they forget to look at the bigger picture. A solar Libra with a Virgo Moon, however, is much more grounded since Virgo is an Earth sign. This combination allows the person to draw back more easily and remember that small details are not the only part of balance that matters.

Some practitioners also feel their magic is strongest when the Moon 'is in' their house. Someone born under a Gemini Moon, for example, might find that their Gemini nature is stronger.

At the same time, they will find that their energy flows more easily and their spells are more effective. This effect is even stronger when the Sun and Moon are both aligned to a practitioner's particular combination.

lunar Events

The Moon usually follows an orderly progression through the sky. Everyone – magical and mundane – can glance up and see the same reassuring globe glowing with light reflected from the Sun.

Every now and then, however, something changes. The lunar calendar does not quite sync up with the Gregorian Calendar or something causes the Moonlight to have an unusual color. Most people just shrug it off when these things happen.

But some people, Wiccans in particular, place great importance on these occurrences. Their exact reaction differs from event to event, however.

The Blue Moon

There are two kinds of Blue Moons. One of them happens when the air is so heavy with smoke or dust that the Moon visibly turns blue. This is most common after heavy forest fires or volcanic eruptions. So, it is not surprising that many cultures have fearsome lore surrounding a visibly Blue Moon.

Some cultures believed that sleeping under the light of a Blue Moon would drive a person insane. Others believed that falling ill during a Blue Moon meant a person would die in eight days.

Others believed that if any person died under a Blue Moon, three more members of their family would soon follow. However, not all myths around this type of Blue Moon were so dire.

Wives who saw a Blue Moon in the sky were told turn over their mattresses, as it would make them more fertile. Anyone with a coin in their pocket when a Blue moon rose in the sky was supposed to turn it over to increase their wealth. Similarly, picking flowers and berries under the light of a Blue moon called abundance into a person's life.

However, this is only one type of Blue Moon. Although there is a lot of lore surrounding it, visibly Blue Moons do not have much effect on Wiccan magic. The second type of Blue Moon, however, does. Even though it is visibly normal, the second Full Moon in any given month is also known as a blue Moon.

Lunar cycles are either twenty-seven or twenty-nine days long, depending on the metric. The Moon of Earth takes a little over twenty-seven days to make one Full orbit, but it takes twenty-nine days to make it through one Full cycle, from waxing Moon to Full Moon.

Because a lunar cycle is so close to the Full length of most Gregorian months, a Blue Moon only happens roughly once every two and a half years.

The rarity of a Blue Moon is enough that it usually makes headlines when it rolls around. But as interesting as it is to the mundane world, magical communities find it even more important.

Blue Moons are sort of a "super Moon." It takes the energies of the Full Moon and doubles them.

It is also the Moon of 'long shot chances.' If practitioners cast to a spell to reach an unlikely goal, they stand a better chance of success during the blue Moon. A blue Moon is, as the saying goes, rare. What better time is there to reach for the stars that would normally seem much too far away?

The violet Moon

Unlike the blue Moon, the violet Moon is not widely recognized in scientific or mundane circles, despite the fact that they are more or less polar opposites. While the Blue Moon is the second Full Moon in a Gregorian calendar month, Violent Moons are the second new Moon. This time frame means they are about as rare as blue Moons.

There is no visible form of a violet Moon, however. Any Moon that comes close to a violet color is usually referred to as a blue Moon with all the same lore. violet Moons also have fewer pop culture appearances, though they are the subject of a few songs that are very popular in Wiccan circles.

Just as the violet Moon is the exact opposite of a blue Moon in terms of the Moon's phase, it is also opposite in the energy that it brings. If the new Moon is a time for shadow work, then the violet Moon is the time when Wiccans can reach the deepest levels of introspection.

Should the practitioner need to banish something, the violet Moon holds the deepest void of any lunar event. And should a magic user want to tap into the potential that precedes any birth, the violet Moon may be the greatest source of potential energy they could hope to encounter.

The Blood Moon

While both the blue Moon and the violet Moon hold potential positive energy, the Blood Moon is usually seen as a purely negative event. There is a Christian prophecy placing the Blood Moon as part of an approaching Armageddon. But Wiccans take a slightly less drastic view of the phenomena.

A Blood Moon occurs when the Earth moves between the Moon and the Sun, placing the Moon into the Earth's shadow.

This usually leads to an eclipse. However, before the eclipse, the Moon takes on a deep reddish tint. It is easy to see why this occurrence can make even the most literal-minded person a little bit uncomfortable.

The Moon is supposed to reflect bright, cool light. By contrast, the light of a Blood Moon feels hot and uncomfortable, too much like the way anger feels hot under the skin.

Though Wiccans do not see a Blood Moon as part of an 'End of Times' prophecy, they still take a dim view of the event. Because many Wiccans track the movement of the Moon, they usually know when an eclipse is scheduled to take place.

Many Wiccans will work heavy layers of protective magic in the days and weeks leading up to the eclipse to protect them from a potential Blood Moon.

Even if Wiccans do not take magical precautions, they will take mundane steps to avoid the negative energy around the Blood Moon. They will become more introspective so as to avoid conflict.

Some will avoid going out as much as possible and others may avoid the light of a Blood Moon altogether.

Is it important to note that not all cultures view a Blood Moon as a bad omen. Some view them as reminders to let go of grudges or to strengthen ties within the community.

But Wicca is based on the lore and practices of Pre-Christian Britain and Ireland. Because of this, Wiccans tend to stick with the lore from those locations. And the lore than has survived to present day paint Blood Moons in a very negative light.

Blood on the Moon

Blood on the Moon is a random phenomenon, unlike a Blood Moon which has at least some regularity to it. When Blood appears on the Moon, it is because of smoke or particles in the air, much like a visible blue Moon.

Instead of turning the Moon a single, uniform shade, however, it does one of two things. It either creates a red ring around the Moon or brownish-red spots across the face of the Moon. Either version of Blood on the Moon is a bad sign. Wiccans believe that it is a sign of bad things to come.

Many Wiccans will ward themselves with protective spells that draw on energies other than those of the Moon.

Some will stock up on protective stones such as quartz, which cleanses energy, and hematite, which ground someone and reflects negative energy back to its source.

The Harvest Moon

Unlike the other lunar events in this chapter, the Harvest Moon happens every year, without fail. It does not rely on an eclipse or atmospheric conditions. Unlike most other lunar events, the Harvest Moon is closely tied to the motion of the Earth itself.

The Harvest Moon is the last Full Moon before the Autumnal Equinox. To fully understand the importance of the Harvest Moon, one must understand the importance of the equinox.

There are two equinoxes each year, one in September and one in May. For those in the northern hemisphere, the March equinox is known as the Vernal Equinox while the event in September is known as the Autumnal Equinox. The titles are reversed for those in the southern hemisphere.

During each Equinox, the visible center of the Sun is directly over the equator. At first glance, this information might not seem particularly important. However, these two days are the closest the Earth comes to having perfect balance between night and day. This makes both days particularly important for Wiccans.

Their search for balance and their connection to nature mean that the equinoxes are ideal days for specific rituals and spells.

In addition to the near-perfect balance between light and dark, the Autumnal Equinox has also long been associated with the largest fall harvest throughout Europe, Britain, and Ireland. Long before the Gregorian Calendar – or any single unified calendar for that matter – farmers knew that the change in weather and daylight meant that it was time to bring in the last of their summer crops.

The idea of harvest, combined with the equinox's sense of balance, create the specific energy that makes the Harvest Moon so important in the Wiccan faith.

The Full Moon is always a time of nurture and abundance. Those traits are magnified ten-fold when they coincide when the Autumnal Equinox and the fall harvest. As farmers bring in the crops that they have nurtured all summer – crops that will, in turn, nurture them through the winter – in from the fields, Wiccans can cast spells to call forward safety and abundance during the cold months to come.

It is one of the last summer-like lunar events before deep autumn sets in as well. Many if the autumn holidays are meant to remember the dead and honor nature as much of it dies or goes dormant in preparation for winter.

The Harvest Moon is one final hurrah for life and the ecstatic energy of summer before the tone of the energy of the world shifts into a more subdued, sustainable frequency.

Eclipses

Eclipses stand separate from other lunar events, because they are just as dependent on the Sun and the Earth as they are on the Moon. Both lunar and solar eclipses are laden with magical lore.

Both affect magic in their own unique ways. Further complicating matters, there are several schools of thought on how each type of eclipse affects magic users.

Each magic user might have to stay attuned to their personal energies during eclipses to see how the events affect them personally.

The Lunar Eclipse

There are several types of lunar eclipses. They range from partial to total and, for some, depend on how exactly they are obscured.

Some eclipses are total, meaning the Earth passes between the Sun and the Moon, blocking the Moon's access to sunlight. Others occur when the Moon falls – partially or entirely – into the Earth's shadow although the Earth itself is not in the way of the sunlight.

Lunar eclipse lore does not readily distinguish between the different types of eclipses. This might be why there are so many different ways eclipses are said to affect magic users.

Practitioners should track eclipses as they come and go to see how they are affected by each one. They can then track these affects in their journal or Book of Shadows, which is also known as a Grimoire.

Because the timing of an eclipse can varies depending on where a person lives, magic users should try and get their eclipse information from a space-monitoring organization, just to ensure the accuracy of their data.

There is no hard and fast rule to determine how an eclipse will affect someone. However, there are a few very specific pieces of lore that surround the events and how they alter magical energy.

The two most common schools of thought are either that the energy of the Moon is blotted out entirely, or that it is much more potent than it is at any other time.

Those who feel that lunar eclipses blot out the energy of the Moon point to the fact that the Moon is no longer shining in the sky.

These practitioners feel that, without the light of the Moon, their lunar spells simply have no power.

Some people balk at this claim because the Moonlight is reflected from the Sun and, as such, should not be seen as the only mark of lunar power. But that is a deep-seated argument in the Wiccan community that is not easily solved in one book.

Practitioners, who feel that the lunar eclipse boosts the Moon's energy, find support for their belief in the way the Earth, sun, and Moon are in alignment.

Pop culture likes to make jokes when the planets align. But there is really power to be had when different energies line up and point to the same goal. In the event of an eclipse, some magic users find that the Moon's energy intertwines with that of the Earth and the Sun.

During the brief duration of the eclipse, this energy can fuel incredibly powerful spells and affect massive change.

Among those who find the Moon's power increased during eclipses are those who feel that an eclipse creates an entire lunar cycle in one short span. As the Moon moves either behind the Earth or into its shadow, it begins to wane.

Then, when the sunlight is completely blocked, the Moon is in its new or dark phase. Finally, the Moon waxes as it moves back into the Sun's light, until it is once again full.

Running through an entire lunar phase in the course of one day generates a huge amount of energy, or some magic users believe.

Sort of like winding up an antique engine or spinning a top so fast it become a blur. This shortened 'super phase' spins up a ton of energy that magic users can then siphon into powerful spells.

Even those who feel an increase in energy during this time should be careful, however. Energy generated during the eclipse is likely to be explosive and hot, unlike the cooler, more gentle energy most Moon magic relies on.

Spells cast with eclipse energy are not going to manifest patiently.

They will burst into action and the change they bring will be swift and, often, massive. Practitioners should be prepared to act quickly, lest the sudden changes overwhelm them.

The solar eclipse

Despite their name, solar eclipses are just as dependent on the Moon as they are the Sun. Unlike lunar eclipses, however, they do not directly involve the Earth. This changes the way the eclipse affects magical energy, though only slightly.

As with the lunar eclipse, there are some who feel that magical energy is essentially paused during a solar eclipse. Energy drawn from the Earth, the spirits, and the Divine is still available, of course.

But celestial energy is locked down while the Moon blocks the Sun from Earth's view. Unlike lunar eclipses, however, this is not simply a case of one heavenly body blocking the light of another.

In the case of solar eclipses, the Moon passes between the Earth and the Sun. This blocked out nearly all of the Sun's light, creating a darkened sky in sickly shades of brown and red. And that is if the sky does not darken completely.

But as the Moon blocks the Sun from the sky, it too goes dark, it is backlit but a thin corona of Sun, since it cannot block the Sun's light entirely. But it is unable to shine from Earth's point of view.

All the energy of the Sun and Moon are trapped between the two, until the Moon moves out of the Sun's path.

And, just as with lunar eclipses, there are people who find that solar eclipses have the complete opposite effect.

For some, this is due to the fact that solar eclipses can only happen during new Moons and, as such, the Moon and Sun are the same astrological house or zodiac sign.

The energy of that sign or house is then increased. This, in turn, expands the energy and power of people born in the same house or under that same sign, whether it is their Sun or Moon sign.

Another school of thought is that equinoxes are a sign of rapid change. The Moon covers the Sun entirely, effectively swallowing it whole. But, before too long, the Sun re-emerges, triumphant and unharmed.

This makes the energy of the solar eclipse especially well-suited for spells that want to enact quick change. Or, of course, spells intended to help someone come through a difficult situation unharmed.

A fourth and final group of magic users find that solar eclipses provide all the energy of a one-day cycle and a Full seasonal cycle in the span of just a few minutes.

Thanks to the eclipse, the Sun goes from a bright high-noon energy level through its normal daily waning to the dark of night, only to rise again, as the Moon moves out from in front of it.

This high speed 'rising' and 'setting' can also represent the Sun's movement through the sky during the seasons of the year. And thus, an eclipse provides the energy of not only a whole day in just a few minutes, but the energy of an entire season as well.

All of this energy is ideal for enacting sudden change or powering a powerful spell.

CHAPTER 23:

Moon magic Spells

Waxing Moon Spells
Money Spell Bottle

Materials:

5 Old pennies

5 Dimes

5 Quarters

5 Dried corn kernels

5 Sesame seeds

5 Cinnamon sticks

5 Allspice

5 cloves

5 Pecans

Directions:

You have to put all ingredients in a tall and thin bottle and seal it. Shake it for five minutes as you recite your spell. You can create your own spell to gain money or follow a ready-made spell from your coven or from a reliable source on the Internet. Then, you have to put the bottle on a table inside your home. Whenever you are at home, you must place your wallet, checkbook, or purse near your money spell bottle.

Get a Job Spell

Materials:

Green candle

Paper clip

Banknote

Directions:

Get the candle and light it. Make sure that you hold both sides of your banknote near the flame. Then, you have to attach the banknote to a picture of you. Blow out the candle as you put your banknote, and picture into your wallet or purse. Take it with you during your job interview. Good luck will then follow you and you will increase your chances of passing the interview, getting the job, and earning good money.

Waxing Moon Vitality

You will need the following tools and items:

1-2 yellow or orange taper/spell candles

A cauldron or Fire safe dish

A kindling or charcoal disk

Dried citrus peel

Dried ginger root

Dried chamomile

Dried rose petals

A piece of citrine

This spell is for your vitality and health. If you have been feeling lackluster, and you need the energy of the Moon and some aromatic herbs to help you out of your rut, then this is a great spell for you. It can go along with any other health plan or routine you are trying to work on or stay motivated with, or it can simply give you a lift when you are feeling low. This spell will be most helpful around the Waxing Gibbous Moon.

Set up your cauldron and get your kindling or charcoal burning.

From the Fire, light the wicks of your candles and let them burn on your altar, or in your workspace near the cauldron.

Place the piece of citrine near the candles and the cauldron flame and witness the firelight flicker in the reflection of the crystal. The energy of Fire will enhance the power of the citrine.

When the Fire has died down a little in the cauldron and the embers are glowing, begin to sprinkle your dried herbs in the pot to let them smoke.

Enjoy the aromas as you add a few pinches at a time and picture your health renewing. Spend time reflecting on how you feel when you are in your best health.

Pick up the citrine and hold it against your heart and say the following words, or something similar:

"Wild Moon, nearly Full,

I am drained and need your love.

Hold me in your bright embrace.

Let me feel your growing grace.

I will feel my power gain,

As I feel the Fire's flame,

As I smell the smoke of power,

My vitality grows every hour.

Shed on me your big, bright light,

Gaining fullness every night.

Drawing power from growing Moon,

I am Full again, and soon!

So, mote it be!"

Let the herbs continue to smoke until they are all gone. Appreciate the glowing embers while you relax with the citrine and the candles burning.

Go to bed early and get plenty of sleep.

Wear the citrine on your person the next day, in your pocket or as a necklace.

Feel your vitality grow!

All of these waxing spells are perfect to help you enhance and attract things in your life. You can add to these simple spells or build new ones out of these structures. Moving into the next chapter, it is all about the Full Moon.

A Spell for Positive Mental Health

When your mind and heart are strong and ready, then you will be able to accomplish anything. To cast this spell, you will need to assemble one red candle, an essential oil of your choice, and a sharp object to carve the candle with. The color red was chosen for the candle in this spell, because red is the color of strength and courage. However, if a different color candle speaks to you more strongly than the red one does then use that color. Also, the essential oil must be personally pleasing; do not just grab the first oil you see. Remember, this spell is about bringing strength to you. Use the oil you chose to anoint your candle. Hopefully the oil you chose will be one that alleviates harmful thoughts or depression. Use the sharp object to carve the words 'happy' and 'joy' into the sides of the candle. Now, set the candle into a candle holder and light it. Close your eyes and imagine the flame lighting your soul, warming it, while you repeat this verse three times:

"Farewell despair and anger

I will now be well and strong

I will feel joy and light

I will be happy

So, may it be"

Allow the candle to continue to burn. Stare at the flame and imagine the smoke carrying away all of the negative thoughts and feelings of pain and despair that are weighing you down. Your unhappiness will diminish as the candle melts away.

Hair Growth Spell

Many hair growth spells require that you use a homemade salve on your hair. That can be a problem for some hair textures, however. This spell is written to be safe for all hair textures and focuses mainly on visualization.

You will be doing a little bit of drawing, particularly in setting up a 'model head', to depict your ideal hair length. But you do not have to get particularly detailed. Just a 'U' shape for the head and a few lines for the shoulders will do. Your mental visualization is more important than the drawn image.

This spell also calls for a drawstring pouch. If you choose to reuse the pouch from previous spells in this book, please be sure you cleanse it first.

Any tools that are used in a spell – pens, candles, lighters, and incense sticks included – should always be cleansed between uses. It does not matter if the next use is magical on mundane. If you did not deliberately charge the item to carry out the spell, cleanse it before you use it again. You will need:

A sheet of paper

A pencil

A drawstring pouch

A surface on which to draw

A handheld mirror

Cast your circle and call on the energy of the waxing Moon. You can use any of the previous incantations in this book or write your own. Simply tailor it to fit the energies and Goddess aspect of the waxing Moon.

Once you have called the Maiden and her waxing Moon energy into your circle, settle yourself either at a table on your knees. Set aside your paper and your pencil and pick up the handheld mirror.

The first step of this spell is to acknowledge yourself with a kind smile. Spells to change your appearance do not mean that your current appearance is negative, and it is important to reaffirm that.

With your smile in place, turn your attention to your hair. Take in its current length and find something to appreciate about it.

You may like the color or the texture. Perhaps you like the way it currently frames your face or how easy it is to care for. All things grow best when they are treated positively, and your hair is no different.

Now envision this positive aspect of your hair growing as you visualize your hair reaching the desired length. If you appreciate that your hair is easy to care for, imagine that it stays healthy as it grows longer. Should you appreciate the texture of your hair, imagine your longer hair with the same texture. Try to maintain your smile as you conjure this mental image.

Hold the visualization in your mind and set the mirror aside. Pick up your pencil and trace out a basic shape to represent your head and shoulders. You can make it as simple or complex as you like.

If you do not feel comfortable drawing, you can print a simple head and shoulders outline from the Internet and use that.

Now draw in the hair you currently have. Again, this does not have to be very realistic. The imagine in your mind will carry the energy for this spell. Your physical drawing is just a way to carry that energy from the mental to the physical realm.

Pause for a moment and close your eyes. Focus on the mental image of your ideal hair length. With the refreshed image at the front of your thoughts, open your eyes and add hair to your drawing.

Draw until the hair on your drawing more or less matches the hair in your image. When this is done, set down your pencil and place your dominant hand flat on the page.

Close your eyes and visualize an aura of energy around the image in your head. When the image is entirely surrounded in your energy, channel it from your mind and into your hand, where you will push it into the paper. As you do this, touch your hair with your free hand and say this incantation:

"Maiden Goddess

Growing high above

I seek to grow in you

As you grow that which you love

My hair is my own

And I wish to see it grow

Nurtured by the energy

Of the waxing Moon's glow"

Finish channeling your mental image into your drawing as the incantation draws to a close. Open your eyes, pick up the paper, and fold it until it will fit in the drawstring pouch. Once you have released the energy from your circle and cleaned up the spell, put this pouch under your pillow.

Be sure and hold the pouch whenever you are preparing to handle your hair. This could be before a shower, when you are about to comb or brush it, or when you plan on styling it.

Part of the power in this spell is that the pouch acts as a physical reminder to take the best possible care of your hair. It is a spell that relies on real world action, as much as it relies on Divine power.

You can also take this pouch with you if you go to get your hair cut or trimmed. If you feel comfortable, you can show your drawing to the stylist, so they know the goal you have in mind.

This will help them guide you in the direction of appropriate products and care tips for your hair.

Mix a Bath Spell for a Ritual Happiness Bath

Since Water is one of the four Elements, it is the perfect medium for spiritual and physical cleansing. When you take the time to enjoy a cleansing bath, you are spending important time on yourself and your development. Taking a bath will also give you the much-needed time to relax and recover from the stresses of the world.

This bath ritual requires very few ingredients. Choose one colored pillar-shaped candle to work on this spell. You have some freedom in choosing the color of the candle. A yellow candle will promote happiness, joy, hope, and self-esteem. An orange-colored candle is perfect for promoting joy and success. A blue candle is the choice for peace, tranquility, and calmness. After you have chosen the candle color to promote the emotion you want to achieve, mix together one cup of rose petals, one cup of jasmine flowers, and one cup of unscented bath salts with five drops of rose, lavender, or jasmine essential oil. Stir this together well, and let it run in the bathwater as it fills the tub. Bring a few container candles into the bathroom to help in lighting the room. Do not light the spell candle until you are in the bathwater. Sit down in the warm Water and relax for a few minutes as the cares of the day seep away. Then light the spell candle, and say this verse:

"Where Water run and river flow

Goddess, I implore you here

Harmful thoughts, I now let go

I will be calm and have no fear"

Stand the spell candle on the side of your bathtub and lay back in the Water. Close your eyes and let the Water cover you with its warmth. Stay in the tub, as long as the Water feels comfortable. When you feel that you have relaxed enough, let the Water drain out and let yourself air dry. Leave the spell candle burning until the other candles are put out, and then blow out the spell candle.

A Spell to Banish Jealousy

The time of the waxing Moon is a great time to banish things from your life like bad moods, jealousy, mean thoughts, etc. Whenever you perform a banishment ritual, you should be in a good frame of mind. You will need to make a conscious decision to banish something from your life, and never do it when you are in a fit of rage, or directly after an argument with someone as these would have disastrous results.

To perform this banishing spell, you will need one glass jar with a lid, three fresh cloves of garlic, one tablespoon each of dried thyme, mint, and rosemary, and some apple cider vinegar. Put these items on your altar and put the herbs into the jar. Cover the herbs with the apple cider vinegar and tightly close the lid. Nothing must be able to get in or out. Gently shake the jar while imagining the jealousy and its source that you want to banish from your life. Continue gently shaking the jar while you contemplate removing this negative emotion from your life. When you feel that the contents of the jar are filled with your energy, place it back on your altar, and let it sit there until the next waxing Moon phase next month. Then, take it somewhere far from where you live and work, and throw it away with the trash.

Cast a Spell to Banish Feelings of Jealousy

The phase of the waxing Moon is the perfect time for you to banish unwanted things from your life, like mean thoughts, jealousy, and bad moods. You will perform a much stronger banishment spell if you are in a good mood when you cast the spell. Banishing something from your life should only be done when you have made a conscious thought to do so, and never when you are in a bad or angry mood. Doing this spell directly after an argument could have horrible results.

In order to cast this banishing spell, you will need some apple cider vinegar, one tablespoon of dried rosemary, one tablespoon of dried mint, one tablespoon of dried thyme, three fresh cloves of garlic, and one glass jar with a well-fitting lid. Take all of these items to your altar and drop the herbs into the glass jar.

Pour in just enough of the apple cider vinegar to cover the herbs in the jar and close the lid tightly. Now, gently shake the jar while you think about the emotion that you want to be removed from your life. Continue gently shaking the jar while you imagine how good it will feel when you are free of this emotion.

When you feel that you have filled the jar with your emotions, set the jar on the altar and leave it there undisturbed, until one month has passed and the next waxing Moon has arrived. Then, take the glass jar as far from your home as possible and throw it in the trash can.

WANING MOON SPELLS

Tea Cleansing Spell

Materials:

Herbs

Water

Direction:

You have to put your favorite herbs in a cauldron or pot of Water and then simmer for half an hour. Allow the wonderful aroma to fill your entire house. If possible, you must walk around your house carrying the cauldron or pot. This can help you spread the aroma around the house much better. You can also use the brew with a clean cloth to wipe or clean any part of your home that you want to be cleansed.

A Spell to Remove Obstacles to Good Sleep

Everyone has problems sleeping now and then but this spell will return you to good deep sleep. It will also help to assist to heal and rejuvenate your spirit, which will help you to renew your inner strength and combat illnesses.

You will need to have ready a blank piece of paper, one piece of smoky quartz, and two or three sprigs of dried or fresh lavender. Smoky quartz is the best choice of stones for this spell because it is known in many cultures as the dream stone. Also, its powers of detoxification will help you get ready to fall asleep quickly. Make sure the bedroom has been prepared with clean linens on the bed and fresh air. The room lighting should be dim, and the bedroom should be quiet. Sit in the bed comfortably and hold the piece of smoky quartz in your hand. Focus on the beauty of the stone and its inherent energy while you clear your mind of all thoughts. When you finally feel calm and grounded then close your eyes and hold the stone in your dominant hand and repeat this verse three times:

"The Moon is up, and I hold it

It will guard my dreams tonight."

Then take the stone with the lavender and fold the piece of paper around them. Slide this under your pillow and lie down and prepare for good sleep.

Broom Purification Spell

Materials:

Branch

Semi-precious stone or coin

Colored flowers

Directions:

Ideally, you should get a fresh branch for this spell. You can break off a branch from any tree before dawn. Make sure that you do not forget to thank the tree after breaking off one of its branches. You can leave a semi-precious stone or coin at its base as a token.

Next, you have to gather some colored flowers and tie it to the branch to make a broom. You have to sweep the floor of your home using this makeshift broom, as you imagine the flowers absorbing all the negativity from the rooms in your house. When you are done, you can leave this broom at the crossroads before the Sun rises.

Cast a Spell to Help You to Lose Weight

Casting this spell will make your metabolism work faster, and that alone will help you to lose weight. The results will not happen immediately, but it will work well over longer periods of time. Let us be honest here, no one ever became obese overnight. The pounds crept up on you gradually, and you need to remove them gradually for better long-term effects.

You will need to collect a small bag or pouch that is made of cloth, preferably some cloth in red or orange, one teaspoon of freshly ground ginger, one teaspoon of freshly ground cinnamon, one teaspoon of freshly ground cayenne pepper, and a red chime candle. For it to be effective, this spell should be done for seven days in a row, beginning on the first night after the Full Moon. Set all of the ingredients on your altar and then light the red candle. Imagine that the heat from the flame of the candle is slowly warming your insides while you stare intently into the flame of the candle. Watch the wax as it drips, and imagine the excess weight in you dripping off in the same way. Keep this image firmly set in your mind as you repeat the following verse three times:

"Awaken inside me this helpful Fire

Burn off all of the weight I no longer desire

The dancing flame will nourish and feed

And make my metabolism hasten with speed"

Now, drop all of the spices into the cloth bag. If you have done this spell once, the spices should be in the bag and should stay there. Hold the bag and move it in a circle around the flame of the candle in a clockwise manner, three times, while you imagine the bag absorbing the heat from the flame of the candle. Blow out the candle. Keep the pouch of spices somewhere on your body during the time when you are trying to lose weight. If you can keep it somewhere close to your midsection, then that is even better. Now, before each meal you eat, hold the pouch in your left hand for a few minutes, and imagine yourself pulling heat from the bag through your arm and into your stomach, in order to increase your digestive processes.

Self-Purification Spell

Materials:

White candle

Green candle

Black candle

Directions:

The white candle represents positive energy while the green candle represents healing. On the other hand, the black candle represents negative energy.

To cast this spell, you have to light the white candle and chant your spell for cleansing your body from negative energies. Next, you have to light the black candle and repeat the same spell. Finally, you have to light the green candle as you chant your spell of asking the Elements of the Earth, Wind, Fire, Spirit, and Water to help heal your body from negative energies. When you are done, you can relax yourself for fifteen minutes before you do chores or work for the rest of the day.

Negative Energy Cleansing Spell

Material:

Lemon

Directions:

Put yourself in a meditative position, ideally sitting down. You have to hold the lemon on top of your head and imagine black smoke escaping from your body through your head. Imagine this smoke being absorbed by the lemon. You can chant or recite a spell as you do this. You can recite a spell to help your body become pure. You have to recite your spell seven times. Then, you have to burn the lemon and throw it out.

Banishing Bad Habits Spell

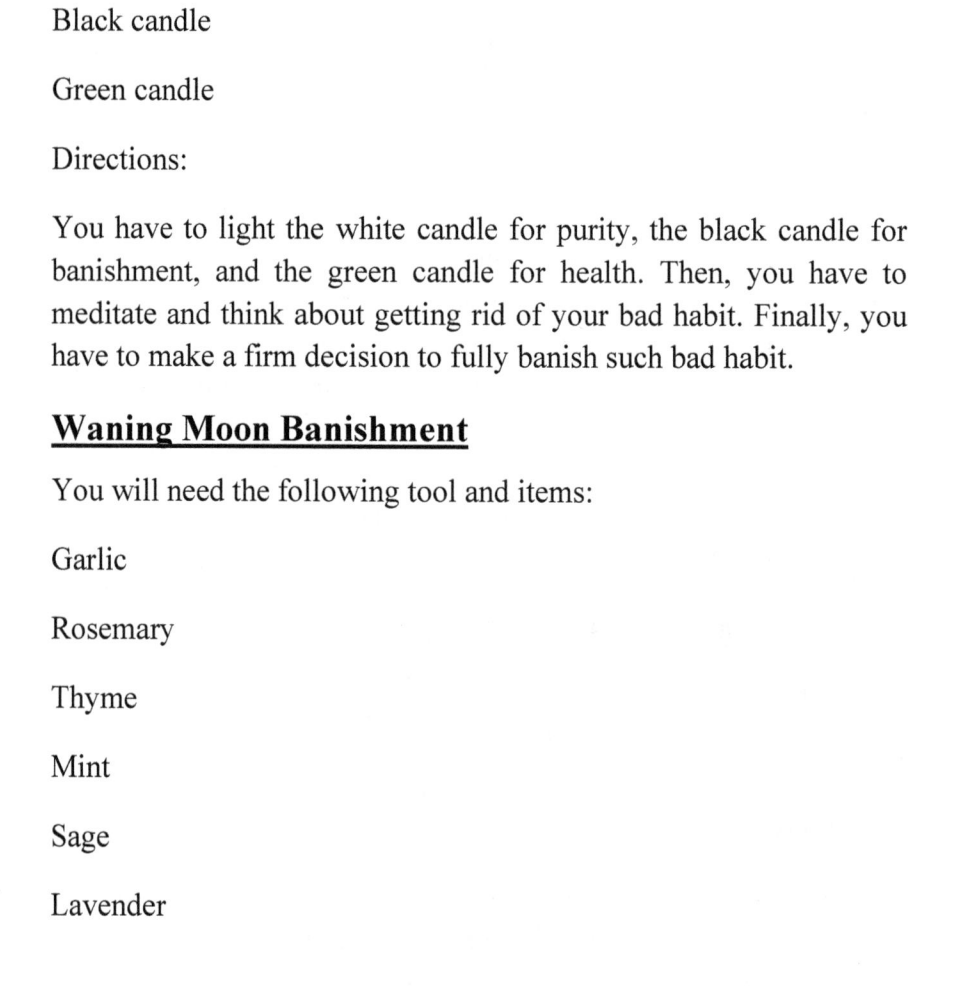

Materials:

White candle

Black candle

Green candle

Directions:

You have to light the white candle for purity, the black candle for banishment, and the green candle for health. Then, you have to meditate and think about getting rid of your bad habit. Finally, you have to make a firm decision to fully banish such bad habit.

Waning Moon Banishment

You will need the following tool and items:

Garlic

Rosemary

Thyme

Mint

Sage

Lavender

Apple cider vinegar

Glass jar, with an airtight lid

This spell is a concoction based on the "Four-Thieves Vinegar," that came for the old story of a pack of thieves who would steal from people's homes during the plague. This vinegar was made to ward off thieves and banish unwanted energies but was also not so bad for disinfecting at a time of major sickness.

The vinegar is used to sprinkle around your doorway, or any entrances to your home to banish unwanted energies or visitors. You can also use it in other banishment spells as a potent elixir, to ward of dark energies or unwanted people in your life.

Use fresh herbs for your elixir. Cut them and put them in the jar and use as many as you like of each. Use your intuition.

Cover the herbs with the apple cider vinegar and put the lid on the jar. At some point, you may decide to strain the herbs and put the liquid in a corked bottle. Either way works.

Allow the herbs to sit in the vinegar for about four weeks, so that they can infuse the liquid with their powers. Shake once a day over the course of the four weeks.

Use the liquid to sprinkle around the house, or as an addition to your homemade cleaning agents. You can use it to mop your floors or wipe down windowsills. Any portal of energy would be a good place to rub this vinegar.

The best time to make it is during a waning Moon, ideally around a Waning Crescent Moon.

If you need immediate banishment, follow these simple steps: place chopped garlic cloves under your doormat, and smudge the entrances and exits with white sage.

If it is specific energy or a person you wish to banish from your life, use loving words to invite them to leave, such as:

"With all my heart and loving might,

I banish [insert energy or person] from my sight.

I ask that they do no more harm

And stay away, causing no alarm.

I wish them well as they go,

As I will harm none, as above so below."

When in a pinch, a few words, some garlic cloves, and a bit of white sage are all you need to banish unwanted energy.

The last step for any banishing ritual or spell is to pay your respects to the energies you are saying goodbye to. Sometimes this simple act can be all it takes to help them move on. A simple, "Thank you for your lessons, you may now go," is all you have to say. Respect and gratitude, while harming none, is a large part of the Wiccan creed and the way of the witch.

NEW MOON SPELLS

New Moon Ritual for a Job

Keep some type of talisman with you as you are doing this ritual. This could be a ring, a Moon pendant, or a crystal. After the ritual, make sure that you keep your object with you for the next thirty days and allow it to remind you of how amazing you feel as you stick to your healthy new habits.

You will need:

Talisman

Green candle

Paper

Pen

Green envelope

Before starting your rituals, take a salt bath so that you can relax and take this time to get ready for your ritual. You can also add in some herbs that correspond with your intent and spell. Next, save the space you are using for your ritual with some sage to prepare.

You want your space to feel relaxed, safe, and private. This ritual can be done by a solitary witch or with an entire coven. It can be done inside or outside, just make sure it is someplace that is private and safe.

Turn off any sources of distraction and noise and if you can, keep your pets out so that you do not get distracted.

You can play some soft music if you want, and then make sure you are comfortable. Gather the things you need and begin.

Light your candle and then take the pen and paper, and write down a list of everything that you would like your job to be. Please be sure be specific as possible. Write down the title, the company, how your office will look, and anything else that is important to you.

Flip the paper over, and then on the other side write down ten things that you would bring to the job. Once you have finished writing, seal the paper inside of a green envelope, and then leave the letter and candle in place that you see every day.

On the next Full Moon, light the candle again and then burn the letter and envelope. This does not mean that it is going to take the entire lunar cycle to manifest your job opportunity, it can take more or less time, it is simply complete the cycle of coming up with your intentions for the job on the two most powerful lunar cycle days.

New Moon Love

This spell is all about love. If you are already with someone and you want to reignite the passion in your relationship, or if you want to call a new love into your life, this spell is a perfect opening for you.

You will need the following tools and items:

3 Taper/spell candles (pink or red or both)

Cinnamon or rose incense

A small pot

Some soil

Wildflower seeds

Fresh Water in a cauldron, chalice, or another dish (charge with New Moon energy prior to beginning your spell)

Rose petals

A small piece of paper

A writing tool

This spell should take place at an altar or workspace. You can cast your circle of protection first and work inside of the circle. You can work outside under the Moon, or indoors. It is up to you to decide.

Set the candles in a triangle on your altar or workspace. Make the point of the triangle farthest from where you are sitting.

Light the incense and let it burn. You can waft it over your workspace and around your body for added benefit.

Set the small clay pot in the center of the triangle of candles. The pot only needs to be about 4" in diameter, but you can decide based on how big your space is. Be sure it has a drainage hole and a dish underneath to catch Water.

One by one, light the candles, starting with the two closest to you and lighting the point of the triangle last. As you light the candles, say the following words, or something similar:

"I call upon thee, Maiden Moon,

To bless my magic with your youth."

Once the candles are lit, on the piece of paper write the following words, or something similar (there are two versions-one for those already in a relationship, and one for those asking for new love):

Example 1:

"Maiden Moon, I am asking you

To reignite my love and soon.

With new beginning, hope, and joy,

I ask for my current love to employ,

More passion, feeling, love and charm,

Through every winter, rain, and storm.

I ask thee for thy growing grace,

To help my old love find new place.

For all you are and all you do,

Thank you for all, to this New Moon.

And so, it is!"

Example 2:

"Maiden Moon, I am asking you,

To bring new love by the next Full Moon.

With new beginning, hope, and joy,

I ask for a new love to enjoy.

I ask for passion, faith, and trust,

For romance, heart, and a dash of lust.

I ask thee for thy growing grace,

To help my new love find my place.

For all you are and all you do,

Thank you for all, to this New Moon.

So, mote it be!"

Fold the paper as small as you can and place it in the pot. Cover it with the soil. Almost to the top of the pot.

Sprinkle the wildflower seeds on top of the soil. You may want to wet the soil first with your sacred Water. Sprinkle some more soil on top of the seeds and make sure they are loosely covered. Do not pack them down too tightly.

While watering the whole pot, speak the following words, or something similar:

"With Water of the New Moon's grace,

I feed the soil and take this place,

To grow these seeds of love so true,

I will watch them grow under the lover's Moon.

And so, it is."

With the seeds Watered, you can let the pot sit on the altar or workspace. Ideally, you will want to let it sit there until the candles fully burn down.

If you are not able to allow time for that, give at least thirty minutes of candlelight to the pot of seeds, to imbue them with the magic of Fire.

Once your candle time is done, move the pot to a location, in front of a window, or in a sacred space outside. (In colder weather it will need to stay indoors).

After finding the right spot where the seeds can get some sunlight, sprinkle the rose petals all around the pot, making a wreath around the base.

Allow the petals to remain around the pot for the remainder of the spell time (until the flower stems are shooting up).

This spell will grow over time with the Waxing Moon. Keep your spell alive by lighting a candle next to the pot at night, or lighting some incense next to it. You can also make it such that the pot gets the Moonlight shining on it every night.

Let love bloom!

Tea Cleansing Spell

Materials:

Herbs

Water

Direction:

You have to put your favorite herbs in a cauldron or pot of Water and then simmer for half an hour. Allow the wonderful aroma to fill your entire house. If possible, you must walk around your house carrying the cauldron or pot. This can help you spread the aroma around the house much better. You can also use the brew with a clean cloth to wipe or clean any part of your home that you want to be cleansed.

Broom Purification Spell

Materials:

Branch

Semi-precious stone or coin

Colored flowers

Directions:

Ideally, you should get a fresh branch for this spell. You can break off a branch from any tree before dawn. Make sure that you do not forget to thank the tree after breaking off one of its branches. You can leave a semi-precious stone or coin at its base as a token.

Next, you have to gather some colored flowers and tie it to the branch to make a broom. You have to sweep the floor of your home using this makeshift broom, as you imagine the flowers absorbing all the negativity from the rooms in your house. When you are done, you can leave this broom at the crossroads before the Sun rises.

New Moon Ritual to Release a Past Love

You need:

A picture of your ex

Matches

Fireproof dish

Before starting your rituals, take a salt bath, so that you can relax and take this time to get ready for your ritual. You can also add in some herbs that correspond with your intent and spell. Next, save the space you are using for your ritual with some sage to prepare.

You want your space to feel relaxed, safe, and private. This ritual can be done by a solitary witch or with an entire coven. It can be done inside or outside, just make sure it is someplace that is private and safe.

Turn off any sources of distraction and noise and if you can, keep your pets out so that you do not get distracted.

You can play some soft music if you want, and then make sure you are comfortable. Gather the things you need and begin.

Once you are ready to begin, take the photo of your ex. The point of this ritual is to provide you a new beginning from that person, so keep that in mind. Take your matches and set the bottom of the picture on Fire and then sit in your fireproof dish. As you watch the photo burn up, picture the end of the relationship and how all of the emotions that you are feeling right now will change just like the picture is turning to ash. After the picture is completely burned up and you can touch the ash without getting burned, take it outside and bury it in the earth, so that your old relationship can be used to help something else grow.

Self-Purification Spell

Materials:

White candle

Green candle

Black candle

Directions:

The white candle represents positive energy while the green candle represents healing. On the other hand, the black candle represents negative energy.

To cast this spell, you have to light the white candle and chant your spell for cleansing your body from negative energies. Next, you have to light the black candle and repeat the same spell. Finally, you have to light the green candle as you chant your spell of asking the Elements of the Earth, Wind, Fire, Spirit, and Water to help heal your body from negative energies. When you are done, you can relax yourself for fifteen minutes before you do chores, or work for the rest of the day.

Cast a Spell to Open Up Your Spiritual Pathways for Spell Work

You will not be successful when you try to work a spell for a particular intention if your spiritual pathways are blocked. It also will not work well if you feel that you are stuck forever in a particular situation because your emotions and your spirit feel sluggish or uncooperative.

You will need to gather together two cups of filtered Water, one white chime candle, one clear quartz crystal, and one cone of cinnamon-scented incense. Use the pattern of the Elements on your altar to set all of these things in their proper place. You will put incense in the east to represent air, the candle you will place in the south to represent Fire, the crystal will go in the north to represent Earth, and the bowl of Water you will place in the west to represent Water. Now, you will light the incense in order to bring the air into your circle. You will rub your hands together for a few moments until they start to feel warm and then pick up the crystal and hold it in your dominant hand for a few moments. This process will transfer some of your energy to the crystal, and it will help you to make your spell stronger. Now, you will light the white candle and use it to bring the element of Fire into your circle. Next, you will dip your fingertips into the Water to complete the casting of the circle with the element of Water. Then, you need to repeat the following verse:

"I call to thee for power and might

All the Elements of the Universal light

Open all paths and doors for me

Help as you can, so may it be"

Spend a few minutes meditating while you stare at the bright light of the candle. Imagine a clear open road stretching long before you, a clear path for your upcoming journey. After you let the candle burn completely, throw the remains away while you continuously give thanks to the candle for its assistance to you. Keep the crystal on your person or near you at all times. Then anytime you begin to feel stuck again, just hold the crystal in your hand and visualize the free, open pathway.

New Moon Ritual for Romance

You need:

3 red candles

A rose quartz

A small Pot

Dirt to fill the pot

Seeds of choice

A piece of paper

A pen

A red envelope

Before starting your rituals, take a salt bath so that you can relax. Take this time to get ready for your ritual. You can also add in some herbs that correspond with your intent and spell. Next, save the space you are using for your ritual with some sage to prepare.

You want your space to feel relaxed, safe, and private. This ritual can be done by a solitary witch or with an entire coven. It can be done inside or outside, just make sure it is someplace that is private and safe.

Turn off any sources of distraction and noise and if you can, keep your pets out so that you do not get distracted.

You can play some soft music if you want, and then make sure you are comfortable. Gather the things you need and begin.

Start by lighting your three red candles. Add some dirt into the pot and place the seeds in it. Add the rest of the dirt into the pot, and then place the quartz in the pot. If the quartz is too bit, sit it next to the pot.

Take your pen and paper and write down everything that you want from your romantic partner. Make sure that you are as specific as possible, especially about how they make you feel, their attributes, and possibly their name. Flip the paper over, and then write down a list of qualities that you will bless them with. Once you are done, place the paper into a red envelope and seal it up.

Keep this envelope in your pillow, and sleep on it until the seeds that you planted have grown enough to be replanted outside. Burn the letter and then bury the ashes with your plant.

Every time that you walk past your plant, or when you make sure the envelope is tucked into your pillow, remind yourself about everything that you hope to get and give with this new romantic relationship.

Cast a Spell Designed to Attract Success and Abundance to You

You will need to be filled with gratitude, joy, and faith—the key ingredients of success—if you ever hope to bring these qualities into your life. This spell is designed to bring you success in any area that you set your intention to, and your success will bring you abundance. You will need to bring together some sea salt, one small flat white plate, seven fresh or dried petals from a red rose, and one white chime candle. Lay the plate on top of your altar, and make a circle out of the sea salt on the white plate. Gently lay the seven rose petals on the top of the circle of the sea salt. Put the white candle down in the center of the ring of sea salt and then light it. Imagine all of the doors in your life at once opening up for you and all of your pathways becoming clear for you. Repeat out loud the following chant: "From today forward, only good luck and positive energy will flow to me." Empty your mind and focus your thoughts on all of the new opportunities that will be open to you. Blow out the candle and keep it safe. Repeat the spell daily for the next six days. On the seventh day, allow the candle to finish burning until the candle is completely gone.

Self-Purification Spell

Materials:

A white candle

A green candle

A black candle

Directions:

The white candle represents positive energy while the green candle represents healing. On the other hand, the black candle represents negative energy.

To cast this spell, you have to light the white candle and chant your spell for cleansing your body from negative energies. Next, you have to light the black candle and repeat the same spell. Finally, you have to light the green candle as you chant your spell of asking the Elements of the Earth, wind, Fire, spirit, and Water to help heal your body from negative energies.

When you are done, you can relax yourself for fifteen minutes before you do chores or work for the rest of the day.

FULL MOON SPELLS

Tea Cleansing Spell

Materials:

Herbs

Water

Direction:

You have to put your favorite herbs in a cauldron or pot of Water, and then simmer for half an hour. Allow the wonderful aroma to fill your entire house. If possible, you must walk around your house carrying the cauldron or pot. This can help you spread the aroma around the house much better. You can also use the brew with a clean cloth to wipe or clean any part of your home that you want to be cleansed.

Self-Purification Spell

Materials:

White candle

Green candle

Black candle

Directions:

The white candle represents positive energy while the green candle represents healing. On the other hand, the black candle represents negative energy.

To cast this spell, you have to light the white candle and chant your spell for cleansing your body from negative energies. Next, you have to light the black candle and repeat the same spell. Finally, you have to light the green candle as you chant your spell of asking the Elements of the Earth, wind, Fire, spirit, and Water to help heal your body from negative energies. When you are done, you can relax yourself for fifteen minutes before you do chores, or work for the rest of the day.

Full Moon Journal Ritual

A big reason why people tend to be more emotional during the Full Moon is that it brings to light many unconscious feelings. This can also include relationships and habits that are not aligned with our highest good. If we do not make sure that we face and process these things, we can end up finding ourselves feeling overwhelmed, confused, and hypersensitive.

One of the best things that we can decide to do during this time is to express these repressed feelings in a healthy and safe way. This ritual will help to bring all of your darkest feelings out into the light by writing them down.

You can do this outside in the Moonlight or inside, it does not matter. Take a pen and paper and start writing down all of your feelings. Do you notice if there are any insights or surprises? Are there are feelings in certain areas that you are suppressing or ignoring? Have you been compromising your boundaries and truth? Do you want to release everything that is not serving you?

You do not need to start trying to figure out the answers at this point. What is important is that you ask yourself some hard questions. You will learn how to awaken your intuition more as you continue to work with the Moon, which will help to guide you in the things that you do.

For now, once you feel as if you have released everything that you need to on that piece of paper, burn it. Place it in a fireproof dish and light it on Fire. Before you burn it, you can choose to write a statement at the end like, "I release everything that is no longer serving me for total transmutation, healing, and purification for my highest good."

As you watch the paper burn, wash the ashes away or give them back to Mother Earth, and feel the light of the Moon wash away your dark areas.

Cast a Love Spell to Bring Love to You

This spell will carry even more power if it is cast on a Friday night during a Full Moon celebration. Keep thinking of love making its way to you while you cast this spell. You will need some jasmine essential oil, one pink spell candle, a plain piece of paper, and a pen or pencil. First, you will anoint the candle with the jasmine essential oil. Write a letter to your love partner with the pen and the paper to boost the love in your relationship. Keep thinking of the future while you write it. Tell your love partner how happy you are in the relationship and all of the things that you love about them. Write anything you feel the need to do. Place the letter on a tabletop or your altar, and put the candle on top of it. Say out loud the following words as you light the candle:

"I call on the energies of the universe to draw my love to me

As this flame represents my deep burning desire."

Think about how much your love means to you and your world. When you have finished meditating, fold up the piece of paper, and let some wax dribble onto it in order to seal the paper folded shut. When the candle has burned all the way down, bury the remnants of the candle and put the letter someplace that you can consider it to be safe. Now, go out and make romantic gestures to your partner to help hasten the good effects of the spell.

A Husk of Harvest Spell for Wealth

You will cast this spell during the months of harvest during the Full Moon, because this will make it doubly powerful. This spell is deceptively easy to cast. Get together one Full leaf of a dried corn husk, a one-dollar bill, a piece of green ribbon or yarn, and some patchouli essential oil. You will not be able to use the one-dollar bill again after this spell. Gently flatten the corn husk with the tips of your fingers, and rub over it with some of the patchouli oil along the inside of the husk. While you are rubbing the oil on the husk, repeat the following words:

"Let the power of this harvested corn

Bring to me money from dusk to morn

Now that my success will be born

With harvest wealth and financial health"

On the top of the husk from the corn, lay the one-dollar bill and roll the two items together into a tight, tiny tube. Use the green ribbon to tie this tube, so it will remain rolled. Leave just enough ribbon, so you are able to hang the tube over the main door that leads to your house. Make sure it is hung above the door high enough, so that the door opening and closing will not hit it. Now, wait a little bit and watch the wealth come to you.

Full Moon Divination Bath

This bath ritual builds on the previous ritual. You can certainly use them separately if you do not have time for both. One of the main ingredients is the Moon Water that you charged by the Fire. You will want to have that available even when you are not doing a Full Moon Ritual.

You will need the following tools and items:

Full Moon charged Water (however, as much you want to charge, 4 cups/1 gallon is ideal)

As many candles as you want in your bath space

A white sage smudge stick

This is a very simple ritual and it has more to do with the meditation than the tools. If you want to add a different kind of incense or make a magical bath tea, you can certainly enhance the experience with some additional herbs, or even put crystals into your bathwater.

Draw a bath by candlelight, as hot as you would like it to be.

Smudge the bathroom and the bathwater with your white sage stick.

Lower yourself into the Water and make sure that you can reach your sacred Moon Water.

Relax in the bath for several minutes and reflect. Be sure that the water temperature is comfortable and keep in mind that you will be adding tepid Water from the Moon charging ritual.

When you are ready to perform the next step, sit upright in the bath and bring the Moon Water close to you, holding it in your hands above the bathwater.

While looking into the charged Water say the following or something similar:

"Water of Moon's reflected face,

I see myself in your place.

I ask for vision, intuition, and sight,

To see beyond with Full Moonlight.

Show me the door, let me through.

I am ready to see the Universe through you.

Open my eye to another dimension,

As I relax in your bath and release all of my tension.

And so, it is!"

Pour the Moon Water into the bath and set the vessel aside.

Lower yourself back into the bathwater and if you are comfortable doing so, lower your head into the Water so that your ears are under the Water's surface, but your face is still sticking out of the Water.

Relax in this place and hear the rhythm of your own heartbeat in the Water. Let your eyes close and wait for visions to come to you.

You may relax in the bath as long as you like and when you are ready to get out, be sure to keep the lights low in your home and avoid technology for the rest of the night because more visions and clairvoyant expressions may come to you.

Full Moon Smudging Ritual

This is a great ritual to do after an emotional spell, like the previous ritual. This is also great to do on its own. The only thing that you will need for this is a sage wand or bundle.

Smudging is a very powerful cleansing tool that was a common ritual for the Natives and other Earth-based religions during ceremonies. It is believed that sage helps to release negative, stagnant, and toxic energies and it can even get rid of spirits that are attached to the Earth.

Smudging during a Full Moon is a very powerful ritual, and if you have done the previous ritual where you released things, it can help to push those energies further out of your life.

To do this ritual, light one end of the sage bundle and fan out the flames so that it is only smoking. Keep a fireproof dish under the bundle to catch any ashes, and then begin to waft the smoke around your body. As you are doing this, set an intention. A good choice would be, "I release everything that is not serving my highest good."

Once you have finished smudging yourself, you can go through and smudge your home by wafting the sage smoke into all of the corners and spaces of every room in your house, or anywhere else you feel needs to be smudged. Trust what your intuition tells you on this, and you may end up smudging places you did not think needed to be or staying in one area longer than another.

Make sure you are completely safe as you are doing this, and keep your distance from fabrics, children, pets, and always make sure you have a dish underneath. Watch out for any falling ash, and put it out if it lands elsewhere than the dish.

Once you have finished this ritual, go through and open your windows to help the smoke leave the house and allow your new energy to come in. Additionally, you will get the Moonlight shining through as well. The sage can also be used to clear your spiritual objects as well.

Full Moon Magical Infusion

The Full Moonlight will amplify anything you do on this night, so it is the perfect time to infuse the Moon's energy into your spiritual tools, such as crystals, incense, and essential oils.

I suggest smudging these items with sage before you start this spell so that they are clear and pure before you let them absorb the Moon's energy. In order to charge them, you need to set an intention with each of the objects and they place them in a place where they can get as much Moonlight as possible during the night.

For example, if you have a crystal that you want to use for a certain reason, you can state what your intention is for that crystal, and then say, "I welcome the magic and light of the Full Moon to empower and bless this crystal, and open me to all its gifts for my highest good."

Pick up all of your objects the next morning. There are some crystals and spiritual tools that may end up reacting with the Sunlight. As you put the object that you charged back into its rightful space, thank them, and the Moon for all of its energy, and notice how there is now a shift with the item each time that you work with them.

Conclusion

If Moon magic is where you find your magical home, embrace it. Bolster your spells with images of the Moon, songs in Her honor, and representations of all the phases of the Moon. Call upon all aspects of the Goddess and learn to walk in the shadows that fall when it is the dark of the Moon.

You may also find that studying Moon magic leads you as much to astronomy as astrology. Do not fight this pull. Understanding the Moon and the celestial bodies that move around it will only serve to enhance your power. In your studies you will find that Moon magic intersects with other branches of celestial magic, such as star magic and Sun magic. Go where your studies leads you.

In Wicca, the Moon is highly revered. She is an important presence in the life of all Wiccans whether they practice with a coven or as solitaries. The energy from the Moon is more subtle than the energy from the Sun; it is more receptive and feminine in its traits. This is the Goddess at work. This is a magnetic power, and it makes sense to anyone who has ever felt that the Moon is pulling them in a certain direction. Those who are extra sensitive will feel a real physical tug on their bodies during a New Moon or Full Moon celebration. Other people will just be aware that there is more energy in the air than normal.

The energy that we receive from the Moon is perfect for working with the energy that comes from our own intuition, since both are magnetic in nature, feminine, and receptive to suggestion. This is also known as our sixth sense. When it comes to working magic, this is our most important form of perception.

You will work magic to increase when the Moon is growing in size. You work magic for decrease as the Moon is shrinking in size. So, if you are working an intention to bring something new into your life then you will work that spell during a waxing Moon phase. And if you want to banish a bad habit from your life then you will work that spell during the waning phase of the Moon. When the Moon is new you will create spells with new intentions for your next round of spell casting. During the Full Moon you will harvest what you have sown and celebrate the rewards you have gained.

You should have all of the tools and information that you need to begin practicing Moon magic in your normal everyday life. This book is meant to be read as an introductory guide to Moon magic for complete beginners, and even newcomers to Wicca in general.

If this is something that has resonated with you, it may be time to continue your research and begin gathering your tools that you will need to use.

Learn and grow within the Moonlight. She is always ready to guide you.

CPSIA information can be obtained
at www.ICGtesting.com
Printed in the USA
BVHW090829220221
600777BV00001B/9

9 781801 928458